perspectives
on
public
bureaucracy

WINTHROP PUBLISHERS, INC.
Cambridge, Massachusetts

perspectives
on
public
bureaucracy

a reader
on
organization

second edition

edited with introductions by
Fred A. Kramer
university of massachusetts, amherst

Library of Congress Cataloging in Publication Data

Kramer, Fred A   1941-   comp.
 Perspectives on public bureaucracy.

 Includes bibliographical references.
 1.   Public administration—Addresses, essays, lectures.
2.   Organization—Addresses, essays, lectures.
3.   Bureaucracy—Addresses, essays, lectures.   I.   Title.
JF1351.K7   1977   350′.0008   77-461
ISBN 0-87626-668-5

Copyright © 1977, 1973 by Winthrop Publishers, Inc.
    17 Dunster Street, Cambridge, Massachusetts 02138

Current printing (last number):   10   9   8   7   6   5   4   3   2   1 for Evelynne, who is still the one

contents

decision-making theory 127

the future: integrating rationality, humanism, and politics 175

preface

This selection of readings in organization theory has been chosen
to reflect the practical nature, problems, and behavior of public
administrators. Mason Haire has suggested that "all managerial
policies have a theory behind them," although the theory is generally
implicit.* Administrators tend to deal in practical, workable terms
to solve the problems that confront them. They often do not
recognize the theoretical foundation that governs most of their
behavior.

The theme that ties these diverse selections together is the concern
with change—change designed to make government bureaucracy
more responsive to changes in the organizational environment.
Different views of change lead to different management strategies,
different structural alignments, and different uses of decision-making
tools. No "one best way" of organizing all public bureaucracy is
assumed. Rather, the implicit argument of the selections is that
certain organizational forms and techniques will work in some
situations, whereas other situations will call for different adaptive
responses. This book is just an introduction to the problems of
creating a bureaucratic structure in the public sector that can be
both flexible and responsible.

All the selections have been chosen because they suggest, in my

*Haire, *Psychology in Management* (New York: McGraw-Hill, 1964), p. 19.

view, perspectives on bureaucratic behavior in public organizations.
If the student or practitioner has been exposed to the various
perspectives, he will be more able to understand the motives and
drives of the people with whom he works. Hopefully, such an
understanding will suggest means for coping with the situation at
hand and will reduce the frustration involved in trying to make an
impact on large-scale organizations that are locked into patterns of
behavior by inertia.

I have great respect for many of the early writings in organization
theory. Although many of the early observations may strike
sophisticated critics as being naive and simplistic, many practitioners
of public administration have been exposed to these views and have
internalized the values implicit in them. If an administrator is
wedded to the more traditional forms and practices of
administration, a person seeking to change his behavior must
have some grounding in the source of those practices.

A further word about the selections is in order. Several criteria
were used in choosing the articles for inclusion in this volume.
Principally, the selections were chosen because, in my experience
in federal and state government, they reflect the way bureaucrats
actually deal with organizational problems in public bureaucracies.
Some of the classic public administration pieces were included
because so many people feel free to criticize the respective authors
without having read their arguments. Furthermore, I sought to use
selections that were not readily accessible to students of public
administration in a convenient reprint form. There is one major
exception to this policy: the Lindblom article. Its concise argument
of what has become the pluralist position in political science
warrants its inclusion here.

This volume was undertaken at the suggestion of Jim Murray and
Paul O'Connell of Winthrop Publishers. It is an outgrowth of the
introductory public administration text that I have written for
Winthrop. Thanks go to several colleagues whose kind words or
actions concerning the first edition led to and encouraged this
revision. Among them are Frederic Bergerson, Patrick Cowles,
John Dempsey, Eric Einhorn, George Frederickson, Thomas Lynch,
Lewis Mainzer, Richard Stillman, Kenneth Warren, and Deil
Wright.

My sincerest gratitude goes to the authors of these selections; and
to my students at the University of Massachusetts and Virginia State
College, who read them.

perspectives
on
public
bureaucracy

mechanistic
monocratic
organization

It may strike the reader as odd that a collection of readings devoted to change in public bureaucracies would begin with two selections usually identified as stressing stability. Change that is forced upon public organizations through technological or political factors does not affect all bureaucratic units to the same extent. Even in times of violent change some elements of government will still be operating on a "business as usual" basis. Max Weber's development of an "ideal type" bureaucracy and Luther Gulick's account of the "principles of administration" influence the attitudes of many administrators toward change in public bureaucracies.

Although Weber did not coin the term *bureaucracy*,[1] his name is intimately associated with the concept because he sought to neutralize the pejorative connotation of the term through the development of an antiseptic, "ideal type" model. An ideal type is a methodological construct that attempts to conceptualize a pure or idealized form of the phenomena about which one wants to generalize. Although one can conceive of various characteristics that would describe the idealized picture of a phenomenon—say, bureaucracy—he would not find all of those characteristics, in their pure form, present in any particular bureaucratic structure he might study. An ideal type corresponds to a pole at one end of a continuum; reality lies along the continuum, but not at the pole position that represents the idealized form. Whereas ideal types are

1

not subject to proof or disproof by empirical verification, they do provide standards against which specific cases can be compared. Therefore, the pure bureaucratic structure described by Weber does not occur in the real world, but is a grouping of the characteristics that Weber thought contributed to a hypothetically rational and effective organization.

Although Weber's most lasting contribution in social science is the stress he placed on bureaucracy, he was more generally concerned with the state and the sources of its legitimation or authority. Weber's view of authority involved three ideal type relationships: traditional; charismatic; and legal-rational.[2] Traditional authority claimed legitimacy on the basis of the sanctity of the powers of control that had been handed down from the past and that have presumably always existed. Persons exercising authority in a traditional system do so according to traditionally transmitted rules. In the ideal type traditional authority system postulated by Weber, change is inhibited by precedent. Those exercising authority are afraid to stretch the traditional ways of doing things because the ensuing change might undercut their own sources of legitimacy. One of the attributes of traditional authority, however, is that there is an area of control open to the whims of the people who occupy places of authority in the system. This creates intensely personal relations between the rulers and the ruled. Caprice is an accepted form of dealing with people who resort to the traditional authorities to resolve conflicts. If the traditional ruler oversteps even these loose traditional bounds of arbitrariness, he personally may be deposed but a successor would be chosen by traditional means and the system of authority would continue.

Charismatic authority is intensely personal, too, but the sources of that authority are quite different. The charismatic individual has authority by virtue of innate personal qualities through which he is able to inspire devotion from his followers. The position a charismatic leader occupies in society is not sanctified by traditional criteria. The charismatic person is not bound by the traditional rules and is capable of sparking revolutionary changes. Charismatic authority does not accept any system of rules for organizing society. There is no law, no hierarchy, no formalism except the basic demand of devotion to the charismatic figure. His followers are duty-bound to help him in his effort to accomplish his mission. They follow not because of rules but because of personal devotion. The leader intervenes whenever and wherever he feels like it, unbound by tradition or law. This makes charismatic authority anathema to regularized routines.

Weber claimed that before the industrial revolution, the traditional and charismatic authorities were responsible for just about all of the orientation for action. The early modern period brought in the need to establish social organization on a stable basis, but a stable basis that would still be open to change. The legal-rational system of authority, to Weber, was such a system. The intensely personal nature of authority in the change-oriented charismatic situation and the whimsical use of personal power in the change-negating traditional system gave way to a more impersonal kind of authority based on rules. Such rules could be rationally changed to cope with changes in the environment in a systematic, more highly predictable way than could be accounted for by either of the other ideal types of authority. The quintessence of legal-rational authority was to be found in the ideal type bureaucracy.

In reading Weber's view of bureaucracy, the student should ask himself the following questions: What functions does the hierarchy perform? Is Weber describing an efficient machine? Under what conditions might his bureaucracy work best? What is the role of the individual in the organization? How do bureaucracies cope with change? Is an ideal type construct helpful in understanding the way bureaucrats behave?

Whereas Weber's seminal work in bureaucracy has long been respected, Gulick's "Notes on the Theory of Organization" has not had so venerable a history. Academic public administrators know the work primarily because of Herbert Simon's trenchant criticism of Gulick's principles of public administration as being merely proverbs.[3] "Look before you leap," and "He who hesitates is lost" are two proverbs that purport to give guidance under similar conditions. Which does one follow? Similarly, Simon viewed most of the principles of public administration as being antithetical and therefore not useful as guides to organizational behavior. Simon was looking for concepts upon which to build a science of administrative behavior, and he felt that the proverbs did not provide an adequate basis for science.

Practitioners with little administrative background, however, have often found the principles useful. To the novice administrator of a model cities program, for example, almost any criteria for organizing his responsibilities is appreciated. The simplicity of the Gulick formulations lend themselves readily to use. The common sense embodied in the principles does provide, as even Simon admitted, "criteria for describing and diagnosing administrative situations."[4] Gulick's formulation of the principles, when taken as codified common sense rather than rigorous theory, gives the administrator a ready-made, albeit rough, framework that can be used to sort out his values. The sorting out of values, when combined with a study of the conditions under which various principles may be applicable, can be of great use. Much of the empirical organization research has focused on the consequences of formal organizational forms under varying environmental conditions.[5]

Some of the principles have fared far better than others. POSDCORB, an acronym for Planning, Organizing, Staffing, Directing, Co-ordinating, Reporting, and Budgeting, is an example of Gulick's thought that is widely accepted today by practitioners and even some academics. After years of wandering in the wilderness, POSDCORB has been heralded as an extremely useful summary statement of what administrators do, with the recommendation that an *E*, for Evaluation, be added to the formulation. Such a suggestion came from a distinguished academician who ended his guest editorial in the *Public Administration Review,* the leading journal in the field, with the plea: "Let's give evaluation its due—let's put an E in POSDECORB."[6]

Although many of the principles appear to have validity, the student should apply his analytic powers to them. Are they really proverbs? What might be alternative principles that seem equally valid but have different consequences if acted upon? Does Gulick qualify his remarks so that the modern reader would not regard them as principles? Do the principles adequately reflect reality? Are these principles consistent with views of public bureaucracy in a democratic society? What is the role of professionals in the organization? Can politics be divorced from administration? How does Gulick propose to deal with change? Gulick has been criticized as being overly mechanistic. Is he?

NOTES

1. Martin Albrow attributes the term to Vincent de Gournay, a French physiocrat who first used "bureaucracy" to describe Prussian government

in 1745. See Albrow, *Bureaucracy* (New York: Frederick A. Praeger, Inc., 1970), p. 3.

2. See Max Weber, *The Theory of Social and Economic Organization,* Talcott Parsons, tr. (New York: The Free Press, 1947), pp. 341–42, 358–63.

3. Herbert A. Simon, *Administrative Behavior: A Study of Decision-Making Processes in Administrative Organizations* (New York: The Macmillan Company, 1957), pp. 20–44.

4. *Ibid.,* p. 36.

5. For an example of such research see John J. Morse and Jay W. Lorsch, "Beyond Theory Y," *Harvard Business Review* 48, no. 3 (May/June 1970): 61–68.

6. Orville F. Poland, "Why Does Public Administration Ignore Evaluation," *Public Administration Review* 31, no. 2 (March/April 1971): 202.

bureaucracy

max weber

CHARACTERISTICS OF BUREAUCRACY

Modern officialdom functions in the following specific manner:

I. There is the principle of fixed and official jurisdictional areas, which are generally ordered by rules, that is, by laws or administrative regulations.

1. The regular activities required for the purposes of the bureaucratically governed structure are distributed in a fixed way as official duties.

2. The authority to give the commands required for the discharge of these duties is distributed in a stable way and is strictly delimited by rules concerning the coercive means, physical, sacerdotal, or otherwise, which may be placed at the disposal of officials.

3. Methodical provision is made for the regular and continuous fulfilment of these duties and for the execution of the corresponding rights; only persons who have the generally regulated qualifications to serve are employed.

In public and lawful government these three elements constitute "bureaucratic authority." In private economic domination, they constitute bureaucratic "management." Bureaucracy, thus understood, is

From Max Weber: Essays in Sociology, *edited and translated by H. H. Gerth and C. Wright Mills. Copyright 1946 by Oxford University Press, Inc. Reprinted by permission. Footnotes deleted.*

fully developed in political and ecclesiastical communities only in the modern state, and, in the private economy, only in the most advanced institutions of capitalism. Permanent and public office authority, with fixed jurisdiction, is not the historical rule but rather the exception. This is so even in large political structures such as those of the ancient Orient, the Germanic and Mongolian empires of conquest, or of many feudal structures of state. In all these cases, the ruler executes the most important measures through personal trustees, table-companions, or court-servants. Their commissions and authority are not precisely delimited and are temporarily called into being for each case.

II. The principles of office hierarchy and of levels of graded authority mean a firmly ordered system of super- and subordination in which there is a supervision of the lower offices by the higher ones. Such a system offers the governed the possibility of appealing the decision of a lower office to its higher authority, in a definitely regulated manner. With the full development of the bureaucratic type, the office hierarchy is monocratically organized. The principle of hierarchical office authority is found in all bureaucratic structures: in state and ecclesiastical structures as well as in large party organizations and private enterprises. It does not matter for the character of bureaucracy whether its authority is called "private" or "public."

When the principle of jurisdictional "competency" is fully carried through, hierarchical subordination—at least in public office—does not mean that the "higher" authority is simply authorized to take over the business of the "lower." Indeed, the opposite is the rule. Once established and having fulfilled its task, an office tends to continue in existence and be held by another incumbent.

III. The management of the modern office is based upon written documents ("the files"), which are preserved in their original or draught form. There is, therefore, a staff of subaltern officials and scribes of all sorts. The body of officials actively engaged in a "public" office, along with the respective apparatus of material implements and the files, make up a "bureau." In private enterprise, "the bureau" is often called "the office."

In principle, the modern organization of the civil service separates the bureau from the private domicile of the official, and, in general, bureaucracy segregates official activity as something distinct from the sphere of private life. Public monies and equipment are divorced from the private property of the official. This condition is everywhere the product of a long development. Nowadays, it is found in public as well as in private enterprises; in the latter, the principle extends even to the leading entrepreneur. In principle, the executive office is separated from the household, business from private correspondence, and business assets from private fortunes. The more consistently the modern type of business management has been carried through the more are these separations the case. The beginnings of this process are to be found as early as the Middle Ages.

It is the peculiarity of the modern entrepreneur that he conducts himself as the "first official" of his enterprise, in the very same way in which the ruler of a specifically modern bureaucratic state spoke of himself as "the first servant" of the state. The idea that the bureau activities of the state are intrinsically different in character from the management of private economic offices is a continental European notion and, by way of contrast, is totally foreign to the American way.

IV. Office management, at least all specialized office management —and such management is distinctly modern—usually presupposes thorough and expert training. This increasingly holds for the modern executive and employee of private enterprises, in the same manner as it holds for the state official.

V. When the office is fully developed, official activity demands the full working capacity of the official, irrespective of the fact that his obligatory time in the bureau may be firmly delimited. In the normal case, this is only the product of a long development, in the public as well as in the private office. Formerly, in all cases, the normal state of affairs was reversed: official business was discharged as a secondary activity.

VI. The management of the office follows general rules, which are more or less stable, more or less exhaustive, and which can be learned. Knowledge of these rules represents a special technical learning which the officials possess. It involves jurisprudence, or administrative or business management.

The reduction of modern office management to rules is deeply embedded in its very nature. The theory of modern public administration, for instance, assumes that the authority to order certain matters by decree—which has been legally granted to public authorities—does not entitle the bureau to regulate the matter by commands given for each case, but only to regulate the matter abstractly. This stands in extreme contrast to the regulation of all relationships through individual privileges and bestowals of favor, which is absolutely dominant in patrimonialism, at least in so far as such relationships are not fixed by sacred tradition.

THE POSITION OF THE OFFICIAL

All this results in the following for the internal and external position of the official:

I. Office holding is a "vocation." This is shown, first, in the requirement of a firmly prescribed course of training, which demands the entire capacity for work for a long period of time, and in the generally prescribed and special examinations which are prerequisites of employment. Furthermore, the position of the official is in the nature of a duty. This determines the internal structure of his relations, in the following manner: Legally and actually, office holding is not considered a source to be exploited for rents or emoluments, as was normally the case during the Middle Ages and frequently up to the threshold of recent times. Nor is office holding considered a usual exchange of services for equivalents, as is the case with free labor contracts. Entrance into an office, including one in the private economy, is considered an acceptance of a specific obligation of faithful management in return for a secure existence. It is decisive for the specific nature of modern loyalty to an office that, in the pure type, it does not establish a relationship to a *person,* like the vassal's or disciple's faith in feudal or in patrimonial relations of authority. Modern loyalty is devoted to impersonal and functional purposes. Behind the functional purposes, of course, "ideas of culture-values" usually stand. These are *ersatz* for the earthly or supra-mundane personal master: ideas such as "state," "church," "community," "party," or "enterprise" are thought of as being realized in a community; they provide an ideological halo for the master.

The political official—at least in the fully developed modern state —is not considered the personal servant of a ruler. Today, the bishop, the priest, and the preacher are in fact no longer, as in early Christian times, holders of purely personal charisma. The supra-mundane and sacred values which they offer are given to everybody who seems to be worthy of them and who asks for them. In former times, such leaders acted upon the personal command of their master; in principle, they were responsible only to him. Nowadays, in spite of the partial survival of the old theory, such religious leaders are officials in the service of a functional purpose, which in the present-day "church" has become routinized and, in turn, ideologically hallowed.

II. The personal position of the official is patterned in the following way:

1. Whether he is in a private office or a public bureau, the modern official always strives and usually enjoys a distinct *social esteem* as compared with the governed. His social position is guaranteed by the prescriptive rules of rank order and, for the political official, by special definitions of the criminal code against "insults of officials" and "contempt" of state and church authorities.

The actual social position of the official is normally highest where, as in old civilized countries, the following conditions prevail: a strong demand for administration by trained experts; a strong and stable social differentiation, where the official predominantly derives from socially and economically privileged strata because of the social distribution of power; or where the costliness of the required training and status conventions are binding upon him. The possession of educational certificates . . . are [*sic*] usually linked with qualification for office. Naturally, such certificates or patents enhance the "status element" in the social position of the official. For the rest this status factor in individual cases is explicitly and impassively acknowledged; for example, in the prescription that the acceptance or rejection of an aspirant to an official career depends upon the consent ("election") of the members of the official body. This is the case in the German army with the officer corps. Similar phenomena, which promote this guild-like closure of officialdom, are typically found in patrimonial and, particularly, in prebendal officialdoms of the past. The desire to resurrect such phenomena in changed forms is by no means infrequent among modern bureaucrats. For instance, they have played a role among the demands of the quite proletarian and expert officials (the *tretyj* element) during the Russian revolution.

Usually the social esteem of the officials as such is especially low where the demand for expert administration and the dominance of status conventions are weak. This is especially the case in the United States; it is often the case in new settlements by virtue of their wide fields for profit-making and the great instability of their social stratification.

2. The pure type of bureaucratic official is *appointed* by a

superior authority. An official elected by the governed is not a purely bureaucratic figure. Of course, the formal existence of an election does not by itself mean that no appointment hides behind the election—in the state, especially, appointment by party chiefs. Whether or not this is the case does not depend upon legal statutes but upon the way in which the party mechanism functions. Once firmly organized, the parties can turn a formally free election into the mere acclamation of a candidate designated by the party chief. As a rule, however, a formally free election is turned into a fight, conducted according to definite rules, for votes in favor of one of two designated candidates.

In all circumstances, the designation of officials by means of an election among the governed modifies the strictness of hierarchical subordination. In principle, an official who is so elected has an autonomous position opposite the superordinate official. The elected official does not derive his position "from above" but "from below," or at least not from a superior authority of the official hierarchy but from powerful party men ("bosses"), who also determine his further career. The career of the elected official is not, or at least not primarily, dependent upon his chief in the administration. The official who is not elected but appointed by a chief normally functions more exactly, from a technical point of view, because, all other circumstances being equal, it is more likely that purely functional points of consideration and qualities will determine his selection and career. As laymen, the governed can become acquainted with the extent to which a candidate is expertly qualified for office only in terms of experience, and hence only after his service. . . .

3. Normally, the position of the official is held for life, at least in public bureaucracies; and this is increasingly the case for all similar structures. As a factual rule, *tenure for life* is presupposed, even where the giving of notice or periodic reappointment occurs. In contrast to the worker in a private enterprise, the official normally holds tenure. Legal or actual life-tenure, however, is not recognized as the official's right to the possession of office, as was the case with many structures of authority in the past. Where legal guarantees against arbitrary dismissal or transfer are developed, they merely serve to guarantee a strictly objective discharge of specific office duties free from all personal considerations. In Germany, this is the case for all juridical and, increasingly, for all administrative officials.

Within the bureaucracy, therefore, the measure of "independence," legally guaranteed by tenure, is not always a source of increased status for the official whose position is thus secured. Indeed, often the reverse holds, especially in old cultures and communities that are highly differentiated. In such communities, the stricter the subordination under the arbitrary rule of the master, the more it guarantees the maintenance of the conventional seigneurial style of living for the official. Because of the very absence of these legal guarantees of tenure, the conventional esteem for the official may rise in the same way as, during the Middle Ages, the esteem of the nobility of office rose at the expense of esteem for the freemen, and as the king's judge surpassed that of the people's judge. In Germany, the military officer or the administrative official can be removed from office at any time, or at least far more readily than the "independent judge," who never pays with loss of his office for even the grossest offense against the "code of honor" or against social conventions of the salon. For this very reason, if other things are equal, in the eyes of the master stratum the judge is considered less qualified for social intercourse than are officers and administrative officials, whose greater dependence on the master is a greater guarantee of their conformity with status conventions. Of course, the average official strives for a civil-service law, which would materially secure his old age and provide increased guarantees against his arbitrary removal from office. This striving, however, has its limits. A very strong development of the "right to the office" naturally makes it more difficult to staff them with regard to technical efficiency, for such a development decreases the career-opportunities of ambitious candidates for office. This makes for the fact that officials, on the whole, do not feel their dependency upon those at the top. This lack of a feeling of dependency, however, rests primarily upon the inclination to depend upon one's equals rather than upon the socially inferior and governed strata. The present conservative movement among the Badenia clergy, occasioned by the anxiety of a presumably threatening separation of church and state, has been expressly determined by the desire not to be turned "from a master into a servant of the parish."

4. The official receives the regular *pecuniary* compensation of a normally fixed *salary* and the old age security provided by a pension. The salary is not measured like a wage in terms of work done, but according to "status," that is, according to the kind of function (the "rank") and, in addition, possibly, according to the length of service.

The relatively great security of the official's income, as well as the rewards of social esteem, make the office a sought-after position, especially in countries which no longer provide opportunities for colonial profits. In such countries, this situation permits relatively low salaries for officials.

5. The official is set for a "*career*" within the hierarchical order of the public service. He moves from the lower, less important, and lower paid to the higher positions. The average official naturally desires a mechanical fixing of the conditions of promotion: if not of the offices, at least of the salary levels. He wants these conditions fixed in terms of "seniority," or possibly according to grades achieved in a developed system of expert examinations. Here and there, such examinations actually form a character *indelebilis* of the official and have lifelong effects on his career. To this is joined the desire to qualify the right to office and the increasing tendency toward status group closure and economic security. All of this makes for a tendency to consider the offices as "prebends" of those who are qualified by educational certificates. The necessity of taking general personal and intellectual qualifications into consideration, irrespective of the often subaltern character of the educational certificate, has led to a condition in which the highest political offices, especially the positions of "ministers," are principally filled without reference to such certificates. . . .

TECHNICAL ADVANTAGES OF BUREAUCRATIC ORGANIZATION

The decisive reason for the advance of bureaucratic organization has always been its purely technical superiority over any other form of organization. The fully developed bureaucratic mechanism compares with other organizations exactly as does the machine with the non-mechanical modes of production.

Precision, speed, unambiguity, knowledge of the files, continuity, discretion, unity, strict subordination, reduction of friction and of material and personal costs—these are raised to the optimum point in the strictly bureaucratic administration, and especially in its monocratic form. As compared with all collegiate, honorific, and avocational forms of administration, trained bureaucracy is superior on all these points. And as far as complicated tasks are concerned, paid bureaucratic work is not only more precise but, in the last analysis, it is often cheaper than even formally unremunerated honorific service.

Honorific arrangements make administrative work an avocation and, for this reason alone, honorific service normally functions more slowly; being less bound to schemata and being more formless. Hence it is less precise and less unified than bureaucratic work because it is less dependent upon superiors and because the establishment and exploitation of the apparatus of subordinate officials and filing services are almost unavoidably less economical. Honorific service is less continuous than bureaucratic and frequently quite expensive. This is especially the case if one thinks not only of the money costs to the public treasury—costs which bureaucratic administration, in comparison with administration by notables, usually substantially increases—but also of the frequent economic losses of the governed caused by delays and lack of precision. The possibility of administration by notables normally and permanently exists only where official management can be satisfactorily discharged as an avocation. With the qualitative increase of tasks the administration has to face, administration by notables reaches its limits—today, even in England. Work organized by collegiate bodies causes friction and delay and requires compromises between colliding interests and views. The administration, therefore, runs less precisely and is more independent of superiors; hence, it is less unified and slower. All advances of the Prussian administrative organization have been and will in the future be advances of the bureaucratic, and especially of the monocratic, principle.

Today, it is primarily the capitalist market economy which demands that the official business of the administration be discharged precisely, unambiguously, continuously, and with as much speed as possible. Normally, the very large, modern capitalist enterprises are themselves unequalled models of strict bureaucratic organization. Business management throughout rests on increasing precision, steadiness, and, above all, the speed of operations. This, in turn, is determined by the peculiar nature of the modern means of communication, including, among other things, the news service of the press. The extraordinary increase in the speed by which public announcements, as well as economic and political facts, are transmitted exerts a steady and sharp pressure in the direction of speeding up the tempo of administrative reaction towards various situations. The optimum of such reaction time is normally attained only by a strictly bureaucratic organization.

Bureaucratization offers above all the optimum possibility for carrying through the principle of specializing administrative functions according to purely objective considerations. Individual performances are allocated to functionaries who have specialized training and who by constant practice learn more and more. The "objective" discharge of business primarily means a discharge of business according to *calculable rules* and "without regard for persons."

"Without regard for persons" is also the watchword of the "market" and, in general, of all pursuits of naked economic interests. A consistent execution of bureaucratic domination means the leveling of status "honor." Hence, if the principle of the free-market is not at the same time restricted, it means the universal domination of the "class situation." That this consequence of bureaucratic domination has not set in everywhere, parallel to the extent of bureaucratization, is due to the differences among possible principles by which polities may meet their demands.

The second element mentioned, "calculable rules," also is of paramount importance for modern bureaucracy. The peculiarity of modern culture, and specifically of its technical and economic basis, demands this very "calculability" of results. When fully developed, bureaucracy also stands, in a specific sense, under the principle of *sine ira ac studio* [without wrath or affection]. Its specific nature, which is welcomed by capitalism, develops the more perfectly the more the bureaucracy is "dehumanized," the more completely it succeeds in eliminating from official business love, hatred, and all purely personal, irrational, and emotional elements which escape calculation. This is the specific nature of bureaucracy and it is appraised as its special virtue.

The more complicated and specialized modern culture becomes, the more its external supporting apparatus demands the personally detached and strictly "objective" *expert,* in lieu of the master of older social structures, who was moved by personal sympathy and favor, by grace and gratitude. Bureaucracy offers the attitudes demanded by the external apparatus of modern culture in the most favorable combination. As a rule, only bureaucracy has established the foundation for the administration of a rational law conceptually systematized on the basis of such enactments as the latter Roman imperial period first created with a high degree of technical perfection. During the Middle Ages, this law was received along with the bureaucratization of legal administration, that is to say, with the displacement of the old trial procedure which was bound to tradition or to irrational presuppositions, by the rationally trained and specialized expert. . . .

THE PERMANENT CHARACTER OF THE BUREAUCRATIC MACHINE

Once it is fully established, bureaucracy is among those social structures which are the hardest to destroy. Bureaucracy is *the* means of carrying "community action" over into rationally ordered "societal action." Therefore, as an instrument of "societalizing" relations of power, bureaucracy has been and is a power instrument of the first order—for the one who controls the bureaucratic apparatus.

Under otherwise equal conditions, a "societal action," which is methodically ordered and led, is superior to every resistance of "mass" or even of "communal action." And where the bureaucratization of administration has been completely carried through, a form of power relation is established that is practically unshatterable.

The individual bureaucrat cannot squirm out of the apparatus in which he is harnessed. In contrast to the honorific or avocational "notable," the professional bureaucrat is chained to his activity by his entire material and ideal existence. In the great majority of cases, he is only a single cog in an ever-moving mechanism which prescribes to him an essentially fixed route of march. The official is entrusted with specialized tasks and normally the mechanism cannot be put into motion or arrested by him, but only from the very top. The individual bureaucrat is thus forged to the community of all the functionaries who are integrated into the mechanism. They have a common interest in seeing that the mechanism continues its functions and that the societally exercised authority carries on.

The ruled, for their part, cannot dispense with or replace the bureaucratic apparatus of authority once it exists. For this bureaucracy rests upon expert training, a functional specialization of work, and an attitude set for habitual and virtuoso-like mastery of single yet methodically integrated functions. If the official stops working, or if his work is forcefully interrupted, chaos results, and it is difficult to improvise replacements from among the governed who are fit to master such chaos. This holds for public administration as well as for private economic management. More and more the material fate of the masses depends upon the steady and correct functioning of the increasingly bureaucratic organizations of private capitalism. The idea of eliminating these organizations becomes more and more utopian.

The discipline of officialdom refers to the attitude-set of the official for precise obedience within his *habitual* activity, in public as well as in private organizations. This discipline increasingly becomes the basis of all order, however great the practical importance of administration on the basis of the filed documents may be. The naive idea of Bakuninism of destroying the basis of "acquired rights" and "domination" by destroying public documents overlooks the settled orientation of *man* for keeping to the habitual rules and regulations that continue to exist independently of the documents. Every reorganization of beaten or dissolved troops, as well as the restoration of administrative orders destroyed by revolt, panic, or other catastrophes, is realized by appealing to the trained orientation of obedient compliance to such orders. Such compliance has been conditioned into the officials, on the one hand, and, on the other hand, into the governed. If such an appeal is successful it brings, as it were, the disturbed mechanism into gear again.

The objective indispensability of the once-existing apparatus, with its peculiar, "impersonal" character, means that the mechanism —in contrast to feudal orders based upon personal piety—is easily made to work for anybody who knows how to gain control over it. A rationally ordered system of officials continues to function smoothly after the enemy has occupied the area; he merely needs to change the top officials. This body of officials continues to operate because it is to the vital interest of everyone concerned, including above all the enemy. . . .

THE POWER POSITION OF BUREAUCRACY

Everywhere the modern state is undergoing bureaucratization. But whether the *power* of bureaucracy within the polity is universally increasing must here remain an open question.

The fact that bureaucratic organization is technically the most highly developed means of power in the hands of the man who controls it does not determine the weight that bureaucracy as such is capable of having in a particular social structure. The ever-increasing "indispensability" of the officialdom, swollen to millions, is no more decisive for this question than is the view of some representatives of the proletarian movement that the economic indispensability of the proletarians is decisive for the measure of their social and political power position. If "indispensability" were decisive, then where slave labor prevailed and where freemen usually abhor work as a dishonor, the "indispensable" slaves ought to have held the positions of power, for they were at least as indispensable as officials and proletarians are today. Whether the power of bureaucracy as such increases cannot be decided *a priori* from such reasons. The drawing in of economic interest groups or other non-official experts, or the drawing in of non-expert lay representatives, the establishment of local, inter-local, or central parliamentary or other representative bodies, or of occupational associations—these *seem* to run directly against the bureaucratic tendency. How far this appearance is the truth must be discussed in another chapter rather than in this purely formal and typological discussion. In general, only the following can be said here:

Under normal conditions, the power position of a fully developed bureaucracy is always overtowering. The "political master" finds himself in the position of the "dilettante" who stands opposite the "expert," facing the trained official who stands within the management of administration. This holds whether the "master" whom the bureaucracy serves is a "people," equipped with the weapons of "legislative initiative," the "referendum," and the right to remove officials, or a parliament, elected on a more aristocratic or more "democratic" basis and equipped with the right to vote a lack of confidence, or with the actual authority to vote it. It holds whether the master is an aristocratic, collegiate body, legally or actually based on self-recruitment, or whether he is a popularly elected president, a hereditary and "absolute" or a "constitutional" monarch.

Every bureaucracy seeks to increase the superiority of the professionally informed by keeping their knowledge and intentions secret. Bureaucratic administration always tends to be an administration of "secret sessions": in so far as it can, it hides its knowledge and action from criticism. Prussian church authorities now threaten to use disciplinary measures against pastors who make reprimands or other admonitory measures in any way accessible to third parties. They do this because the pastor, in making such criticism available, is "guilty" of facilitating a possible criticism of the church authorities. The treasury officials of the Persian shah have made a secret doctrine of their budgetary art and even use secret script. The official statistics of Prussia, in general, make public only what cannot do any harm to the intentions of the power-wielding bureaucracy. The tendency toward secrecy in certain administrative fields follows their material nature: everywhere that the power interests of the domination structure toward *the outside* are at stake, whether it is an economic competitor of a private enterprise, or a foreign, potentially hostile polity, we find secrecy. If it is to be successful, the management of diplomacy can only be publicly controlled to a very limited extent. The military administration must insist on the concealment of its most important measures; with the increasing significance of purely technical aspects, this is all the more the case. Political parties do not proceed differently, in spite of all the ostensible publicity of Catholic congresses and party conventions. With the increasing bureaucratization of party organizations, this secrecy will prevail even more. Commercial policy, in Germany for instance, brings about a concealment of production statistics. Every fighting posture of a social structure toward the outside tends to buttress the position of the group in power.

The pure interest of the bureaucracy in power, however, is efficacious far beyond those areas where purely functional interests make for secrecy. The concept of the "official secret" is the specific invention of bureaucracy, and nothing is so fanatically defended by the bureaucracy as this attitude, which cannot be substantially justified beyond these specifically qualified areas. In facing a parliament, the bureaucracy, out of a sure power instinct, fights every attempt of the parliament to gain knowledge by means of its own experts or from interest groups. The so-called right of parliamentary investigation is one of the means by which parliament seeks such knowledge. Bureaucracy naturally welcomes a poorly informed and hence a powerless parliament—at least in so far as ignorance somehow agrees with the bureaucracy's interests. . . .

Only the expert knowledge of private economic interest groups in the field of "business" is superior to the expert knowledge of the bureaucracy. This is so because the exact knowledge of facts in their field is vital to the economic existence of businessmen. Errors in official statistics do not have direct economic consequences for the guilty official, but errors in the calculation of a capitalist enterprise are paid for by losses, perhaps by its existence. The "secret," as a means of power, is, after all, more safely hidden in the books of an enterpriser than it is in the files of public authorities. For this reason alone authorities are held within narrow barriers when they seek to influence economic life in the capitalist epoch. Very frequently the measures of the state in the field of capitalism take unforeseen and unintended courses, or they are made illusory by the superior expert knowledge of interest groups. . . .

notes on the theory of organization

luther h. gulick

Every large-scale or complicated enterprise requires many men to carry it forward. Wherever many men are thus working together the best results are secured when there is a division of work among these men. The theory of organization, therefore, has to do with the structure of co-ordination imposed upon the work-division units of an enterprise. Hence it is not possible to determine how an activity is to be organized without, at the same time, considering how the work in question is to be divided. Work division is the foundation of organization; indeed, the reason for organization.

1. THE DIVISION OF WORK

It is appropriate at the outset of this discussion to consider the reasons for and the effect of the division of work. It is sufficient for our purpose to note the following factors.

Why Divide Work?

Because men differ in nature, capacity and skill, and gain greatly in dexterity by specialization;

Papers on the Science of Administration, *edited by Luther H. Gulick and Lyndall Urwick. Copyright 1937 by the Institute of Public Administration, New York. Reprinted by permission. Footnotes have been abridged and renumbered.*

Because the same man cannot be at two places at the same time;

Because one man cannot do two things at the same time;

Because the range of knowledge and skill is so great that a man cannot within his life-span know more than a small fraction of it. In other words, it is a question of human nature, time, and space. . . .

The introduction of machinery accentuates the division of work. Even such a simple thing as a saw, a typewriter, or a transit requires increased specialization, and serves to divide workers into those who can and those who cannot use the particular instrument effectively. Division of work on the basis of the tools and machines used in work rests no doubt in part on aptitude, but primarily upon the development and maintenance of skill through continued manipulation. . . .

The nature of these subdivisions is essentially pragmatic, in spite of the fact that there is an element of logic underlying them. They are therefore subject to a gradual evolution with the advance of science, the invention of new machines, the progress of technology and the change of the social system. In the last analysis, however, they appear to be based upon differences in individual human beings. But it is not to be concluded that the apparent stability of "human nature," whatever that may be, limits the probable development of specialization. The situation is quite the reverse. As each field of knowledge and work is advanced, constituting a continually larger and more complicated nexus of related principles, practices and skills, any individual will be less and less able to encompass it and maintain intimate knowledge and facility over the entire area, and there will thus arise a more minute specialization because knowledge and skill advance while man stands still. Division of work and integrated organization are the bootstraps by which mankind lifts itself in the process of civilization.

The Limits of Division

There are three clear limitations beyond which the division of work cannot to advantage go. The first is practical and arises from the volume of work involved in man-hours. Nothing is gained by subdividing work if that further subdivision results in setting up a task which requires less than the full time of one man. . . .

The second limitation arises from technology and custom at a given time and place. In some areas nothing would be gained by separating undertaking from the custody and cleaning of churches, because by custom the sexton is the undertaker; in building construction it is extraordinarily difficult to re-divide certain aspects of electrical and plumbing work and to combine them in a more effective way, because of the jurisdictional conflicts of craft unions; and it is clearly impracticable to establish a division of cost accounting in a field in which no technique of costing has yet been developed.

This second limitation is obviously elastic. It may be changed by invention and by education. If this were not the fact, we should face a static division of labor. It should be noted, however, that a marked change has two dangers. It greatly restricts the labor market from which workers may be drawn and greatly lessens the opportunities open to those who are trained for the particular specialization.

The third limitation is that the subdivision of work must not pass beyond physical division into organic division. It might seem far more efficient to have the front half of the cow in the pasture grazing and the rear half in the barn being milked all of the time, but this organic division would fail. Similarly there is no gain from splitting a single movement or gesture like licking an envelope, or tearing apart a series of intimately and intricately related activities.

It may be said that there is in this an element of reasoning in a circle; that the test here applied as to whether an activity is organic or not is whether it is divisible or not—which is what we set out to define. This charge is true. It must be a pragmatic test. Does the division work out? Is something vital destroyed and lost? Does it bleed? . . .

2. THE CO-ORDINATION OF WORK

If subdivision of work is inescapable, co-ordination becomes mandatory. There is, however, no one way to co-ordination. Experience shows that it may be achieved in two primary ways. These are:

1.   By organization, that is, by interrelating the subdivisions of work by allotting them to men who are placed in a structure of authority, so that the work may be co-ordinated by orders of superiors to subordinates, reaching from the top to the bottom of the entire enterprise.

2.   By the dominance of an idea, that is, the development of intelligent singleness of purpose in the minds and wills of those who are working together as a group, so that each worker will of his own accord fit his task into the whole with skill and enthusiasm.

These two principles of co-ordination are not mutually exclusive, in fact, no enterprise is really effective without the extensive utilization of both.

Size and time are the great limiting factors in the development of co-ordination. In a small project, the problem is not difficult; the structure of authority is simple, and the central purpose is real to every worker. In a large complicated enterprise, the organization becomes involved, the lines of authority tangled, and there is danger that the workers will forget that there is any central purpose, and so devote their best energies only to their own individual advancement and advantage.

The interrelated elements of time and habit are extraordinarily important in co-ordination. Man is a creature of habit. When an enterprise is built up gradually from small beginnings the staff can be "broken in" step by step. And when difficulties develop, they can be ironed out, and the new method followed from that point on as a matter of habit, with the knowledge that that particular difficulty will not develop again. Routines may even be mastered by drill as they are in the army. When, however, a large new enterprise must be set up or altered overnight, then the real difficulties of co-ordination make their appearance. The factor of habit, which is thus an important foundation of co-ordination when time is available, becomes a serious handicap when time is not available, that is, when change rules. The question of co-ordination therefore must be approached with different emphasis in small and in large enterprises; in simple and in complex situations; in stable and in new or changing organizations.

Co-ordination Through Organization

Organization as a way of co-ordination requires the establishment of a system of authority whereby the central purpose or objective of an enterprise is translated into reality through the combined efforts of many specialists, each working in his own field at a particular time and place.

It is clear from long experience in human affairs that such a structure of authority requires not only many men at work in many places at selected times, but also a single directing executive authority.[1] The problem of organization thus becomes the problem of building up between the executive at the center and the subdivisions of work on the periphery an effective network of communication and control.

The following outline may serve further to define the problem:

I.   First Step: Define the job to be done, such as the furnishing of pure water to all of the people and industries within a given area at the lowest possible cost;

II.   Second Step: Provide a director to see that the objective is realized;

III.   Third Step: Determine the nature and number of individualized and specialized work units into which the job will have to be divided. As has been seen above, this subdivision depends partly upon the size of the job - (no ultimate subdivision can generally be so small as to require less than the full time of one worker) and upon the status of technological and social development at a given time;

IV.   Fourth Step: Establish and perfect the structure of authority between the director and the ultimate work subdivisions.

It is this fourth step which is the central concern of the theory of organization. It is the function of this organization (IV) to enable the director (II) to co-ordinate and energize all of the sub-divisions of work (III) so that the major objective (I) may be achieved efficiently.

The Span of Control

In this undertaking, we are confronted at the start by the inexorable limits of human nature. Just as the hand of man can span only a limited number of notes on the piano, so the mind and will of man can span but a limited number of immediate managerial contacts. . . . The limit of control is partly a matter of the limits of knowledge, but even more is it a matter of the limits of time and of energy. As a result the executive of any enterprise can personally direct only a few persons. He must depend upon these to direct others, and upon them in turn to direct still others, until the last man in the organization is reached.

This condition placed upon all human organization by the limits of the span of control obviously differs in different kinds of work and in organizations of different sizes. Where the work is of a routine, repetitive, measurable and homogeneous character, one man can perhaps direct several score workers. This is particularly true when the workers are all in a single room. Where the work is diversified, qualitative, and particularly when the workers are scattered, one man can supervise only a few. This diversification, dispersion, and non-measurability is of course most evident at the very top of any organization. It follows that the limitations imposed by the span of control are most evident at the top of an organization, directly under the executive himself.

But when we seek to determine how many immediate subordinates the director of an enterprise can effectively supervise, we enter a realm of experience which has not been brought under sufficient scientific study to furnish a final answer. . . .

It is not difficult to understand why there is . . . divergence of statement among authorities who are agreed on the fundamentals. It arises in part from the differences in the capacities and work habits of individual executives observed, and in part from the non-comparable character of the work covered. It would seem that insufficient attention has been devoted to three factors, first, the element of diversification of function; second, the element of time; and third, the element of space. A chief of public works can deal effectively with more direct subordinates than can the general of the army, because all of his immediate subordinates in the department of public works will be in the general field of engineering, while in the army there will be many different elements, such as communications, chemistry, aviation, ordnance, motorized service, engineering supply, transportation, etc., each with its own technology. The element of time is also of great significance as has been indicated above. In a stable organization the chief executive can deal with more immediate subordinates than in a new or changing organization. Similarly, space influences the span of control. An organization located in one building can be supervised through more immediate subordinates than can the same organization if scattered in several cities. When scattered there is not only need for more supervision, and therefore more supervisory personnel, but also for a fewer number of contacts with the chief executive because of the increased difficulty faced by the chief executive in learning sufficient details about a far-flung organization to do an intelligent job. The failure to attach sufficient importance to these variables has served to limit the scientific validity of the statements which have been made that one man can supervise but three, or five, or eight, or twelve immediate subordinates.

These considerations do not, however, dispose of the problem. They indicate rather the need for further research. But without further research we may conclude that the chief executive of an organization can deal with only a few immediate subordinates; that this number is determined not only by the nature of the work, but also by the nature of the executive; and that the number of immediate subordinates in a large, diversified and dispersed organization must be even less than in a homogeneous and unified organization to achieve the same measure of co-ordination.

One Master

From the earliest times it has been recognized that nothing but confusion arises under multiple command. "A man cannot serve two masters" was adduced as a theological argument because it was already accepted as a principle of human relation[s] in everyday life. In administration this is known as the principle of "unity of command."[2] The principle may be stated as follows: A workman subject to orders from several superiors will be confused, inefficient, and irresponsible; a workman subject to orders from but one superior may be methodical, efficient, and responsible. Unity of command thus refers to those who are commanded, not to those who issue the commands.[3]

The significance of this principle in the process of co-ordination and organization must not be lost sight of. In building a structure of co-ordination, it is often tempting to set up more than one boss for a man who is doing work which has more than one relationship. Even as great a philosopher of management as Taylor fell into this error in setting up separate foremen to deal with machinery, with materials, with speed, etc., each with the power of giving orders directly to the individual workman.[4] The rigid adherence to the principle of unity of command may have its absurdities; these are, however, unimportant in comparison with the certainty of confusion, inefficiency and irresponsibility which arise from the violation of the principle.

Technical Efficiency

. . .

It has been observed by authorities in many fields that the efficiency of a group working together is directly related to the homogeneity of the work they are performing, of the processes they are utilizing, and of the purposes which actuate them. From top to bottom, the group must be unified. It must work together.

It follows from this (1) that any organizational structure which brings together in a single unit work divisions which are non-homogeneous in work, in technology, or in purpose will encounter the danger of friction and inefficiency; and (2) that a unit based on a given specialization cannot be given technical direction by a layman.

In the realm of government it is not difficult to find many illustrations of the unsatisfactory results of non-homogeneous administrative combinations. It is generally agreed that agricultural development and education cannot be administered by the same men who enforce pest and disease control, because the success of the former rests upon friendly co-operation and trust of the farmers, while the latter engenders resentment and suspicion. Similarly, activities like drug control established in protection of the consumer do not find appropriate homes in departments dominated by the interests of the producer. In the larger cities and in states it has been found that hospitals cannot be so well administered by the health department directly as they can be when set up independently in a separate department, or at least in a bureau with extensive autonomy, and it is generally agreed that public welfare administration and police administration require separation, as do public health administration and welfare administration, though both of these combinations may be found in successful operation under special conditions. No one would think of combining water supply and public education, or tax administration and public recreation. In every one of these cases, it will be seen that there is some element either of work to be done, or of the technology used, or of the end sought which is non-homogeneous.

Another phase of the combination of incompatible functions in the same office may be found in the common American practice of appointing unqualified laymen and politicians to technical positions or to give technical direction to highly specialized services. As Dr. Frank J. Goodnow pointed out a generation ago, we are faced here by two heterogeneous functions, "politics" and "administration," the combination of which cannot be undertaken within the structure of the administration without producing inefficiency.

Caveamus Expertum

At this point a word of caution is necessary. The application of the principle of homogeneity has its pitfalls. Every highly trained technician, particularly in the learned professions, has a profound sense of omniscience and a great desire for complete independence in the service of society. When employed by government he knows how to render this service. He tends to be utterly oblivious of all other needs, because, after all, is not his particular technology the road to salvation? Any restraint applied to him is "limitation of freedom," and any criticism "springs from ignorance and jealousy." Every budget increase he secures is "in the public interest," while every increase secured elsewhere is "a sheer waste." His efforts and maneuvers to expand are "public education" and "civic organization," while similar efforts by others are "propaganda" and "politics."

Another trait of the expert is his tendency to assume knowledge and authority in fields in which he has no competence. In this particular, educators, lawyers, priests, admirals, doctors, scientists, engineers, accountants, merchants and bankers are all the same— having achieved technical competence or "success" in one field, they come to think this competence is a general quality detachable from the field and inherent in themselves. They step without embarrassment into other areas. They do not remember that the robes of authority of one kingdom confer no sovereignty in another; but that there they are merely a masquerade.

The expert knows his "stuff." Society needs him, and must have him more and more as man's technical knowledge becomes more and more extensive. But history shows us that the common man is a better judge of his own needs in the long run than any cult of experts. Kings and ruling classes, priests and prophets, soldiers and lawyers, when permitted to rule rather than serve mankind, have in the end done more to check the advance of human welfare than they have to advance it. The true place of the expert is, as A.E. [Buck] said so well, "on tap, not on top." The essential validity of democracy rests upon this philosophy, for democracy is a way of government in which the common man is the final judge of what is good for him.

Efficiency is one of the things that is good for him because it makes life richer and safer. That efficiency is to be secured more and more through the use of technical specialists. These specialists have no right to ask for, and must not be given freedom from supervisory control, but in establishing that control, a government which ignores the conditions of efficiency cannot expect to achieve efficiency.

3. ORGANIZATIONAL PATTERNS

Organization Up or Down?

One of the great sources of confusion in the discussion of the theory of organization is that some authorities work and think primarily from the top down, while others work and think from the bottom up. This is perfectly natural because some authorities are interested primarily in the executive and in the problems of central management, while others are interested primarily in individual services and activities. Those who work from the top down regard the organization as a system of subdividing the enterprise under the chief executive, while those who work from the bottom up, look upon organization as a system of combining the individual units of work into aggregates which are in turn subordinated to the chief executive. It may be argued that either approach leads to a consideration of the entire problem, so that it is of no great significance which way the organization is viewed. Certainly it makes this very important practical difference: those who work from the top down must guard themselves from the danger of sacrificing the effectiveness of the individual services in their zeal to achieve a model structure at the top, while those who start from the bottom, must guard themselves from the danger of thwarting co-ordination in their eagerness to develop effective individual services. . . .

Organizing the Executive

. . . What is the work of the chief executive? What does he do?
The answer is POSDCORB.

POSDCORB is, of course, a made-up word designed to call attention to the various functional elements of the work of a chief executive because "administration" and "management" have lost all specific content. POSDCORB is made up of the initials and stands for the following activities:

Planning, that is working out in broad outline the things that need to be done and the methods for doing them to accomplish the purpose set for the enterprise;

Organizing, that is the establishment of the formal structure of authority through which work subdivisions are arranged, defined and co-ordinated for the defined objective;

Staffing, that is the whole personnel function of bringing in and training the staff and maintaining favorable conditions of work;

Directing, that is the continuous task of making decisions and embodying them in specific and general orders and instructions and serving as the leader of the enterprise;

Co-ordinating, that is the all important duty of interrelating the various parts of the work;

Reporting, that is keeping those to whom the executive is responsible informed as to what is going on, which thus includes keeping himself and his subordinates informed through records, research and inspection;

Budgeting, with all that goes with budgeting in the form of fiscal planning, accounting and control.

This statement of the work of a chief executive is adapted from the functional analysis elaborated by Henri Fayol in his "Industrial and General Administration." It is believed that those who know administration intimately will find in this analysis a valid and helpful pattern, into which can be fitted each of the major activities and duties of any chief executive.

If these seven elements may be accepted as the major duties of the chief executive, it follows that they *may* be separately organized as subdivisions of the executive. The need for such subdivision depends entirely on the size and complexity of the enterprise. In the largest enterprises, particularly where the chief executive is as a matter of fact unable to do the work that is thrown upon him, it may be presumed that one or more parts of POSDCORB should be suborganized. . . .

Aggregating the Work Units

In building the organization from the bottom up we are confronted by the task of analyzing everything that has to be done and determining in what grouping it can be placed without violating the principle of homogeneity. This is not a simple matter, either practically or theoretically. It will be found that each worker in each position must be characterized by:

1. The major *purpose* he is serving, such as furnishing water, controlling crime, or conducting education;

2. The *process* he is using, such as engineering, medicine, carpentry, stenography, statistics, accounting;

3. The *persons or things* dealt with or served, such as immigrants, veterans, Indians, forests, mines, parks, orphans, farmers, automobiles, or the poor;

4. The *place* where he renders his service, such as Hawaii, Boston, Washington, the Dust Bowl, Alabama, or Central High School.

Where two men are doing exactly the same work in the same way for the same people at the same place, then the specifications of their jobs will be the same under 1, 2, 3, and 4. All such workers may be easily combined in a single aggregate and supervised together. Their work is homogeneous. But when any of the four items differ, then there must be a selection among the items to determine which shall be given precedence in determining what is and what is not homogeneous and therefore combinable.

A few illustrations may serve to point [out] the problem. Within the City of New York, what shall be done with the doctor who spends all of his time in the public schools examining and attending to children in the Bronx? Shall we (1) say that he is primarily working for the school system, and therefore place him under the department of education? (2) say that he is a medical man, and that we will have all physicians in the department of health? (3) say that he is working with children, and that he should therefore be in a youth administration? or (4) say that he is working in the Bronx and must therefore be attached to the Bronx borough president's office? Whichever answer we give will ignore one or the other of the four elements characterizing his work. The same problem arises with the lawyer serving the street construction gang on damage cases in Brooklyn, the engineer who is working for the department of health in Richmond, and the accountant examining vouchers and records in Queens for the district attorney. . . .

Organization by Major Purpose

Organization by major purpose, such as water supply, crime control, or education, serves to bring together in a single large department all of those who are at work endeavoring to render a particular service. Under such a policy, the department of education will contain not only teachers and school administrators, but also architects, engineers, chauffeurs, auto mechanics, electricians, carpenters, janitors, gardeners, nurses, doctors, lawyers, and accountants. Everything that has to do with the schools would be included, extending perhaps even to the control of traffic about school properties. Similarly the department of water supply would include not only engineers and maintenance gangs, but also planners, statisticians, lawyers, architects, accountants, meter readers, bacteriologists, and public health experts.

The advantages of this type of organization are three: first, it makes more certain the accomplishment of any given broad purpose or project by bringing the whole job under a single director with immediate control of all the experts, agencies and services which are required in the performance of the work. No one can interfere. The director does not have to wait for others, nor negotiate for their help and co-operation; nor appeal to the chief executive to untangle a conflict. He can devote all his energies to getting on with the job.

Second, from the standpoint of self-government, organization by purpose seems to conform best to the objectives of government as they are recognized and understood by the public. The public sees the end result, and cannot understand the methodology. It can therefore express its approval or disapproval with less confusion and more effectiveness regarding major purposes than it can regarding the processes.

Third, it apparently serves as the best basis for eliciting the energies and loyalties of the personnel and for giving a focus and central drive to the whole activity, because purpose is understandable by the entire personnel down to the last clerk and inspector.

The statement of these strong points of organization by major purpose points the way to its dangers. These are to be found, first, in the impossibility of cleanly dividing all of the work of any government into a few such major purposes which do not overlap extensively. For example, education overlaps immediately with health and with recreation, as does public works with law enforcement. The strong internal co-ordination and drive tends to precipitate extensive and serious external conflict and confusion, just as there is more danger of accident with a high powered motor car. This is apparent particularly in the development of a reasonable city plan, or in arriving at a consistent policy throughout the departments for the maintenance of properties, or in handling legal matters, or arranging similar work and salary conditions. The lawyers, engineers, accountants, doctors of different departments will all have their own ideas as to how similar matters are to be dealt with.

Second, there is danger that an organization erected on the basis of purpose will fail to make use of the most up-to-date technical devices and specialists because the dominance of purpose generally tends to obscure the element of process, and because there may not be enough work of a given technical sort to permit efficient subdivision.

Third, there is also danger in such an organization that subordinate parts of the work will be unduly suppressed or lost sight of because of the singleness of purpose, enthusiasm and drive of the head of the department. For example, medical work with children when established under the department of education as a division is likely to receive less encouragement than it would if independently established in the health department, because after all the department of education is primarily interested in schools and has its own great needs and problems.

Fourth, a department established on the basis of purpose falls easily into the habit of overcentralization, and thus fails to fit its service effectively to the people. Or if it does decentralize its services, as do the fire department, the police department, the health department and the department of education of New York City, the representatives of these departments in the field do not always make the best use of each other's assistance and co-operation, and when any difficulty does arise, it is such a long way to the top where co-ordination can be worked out, that it is easier to get along without it.

Fifth, an organization fully equipped from top to bottom with all of the direct and collateral services required for the accomplishment of its central purpose, without the need of any assistance from other departments, drifts very easily into an attitude and position of complete independence from all other activities and even from democratic control itself.

Organization by Major Process

Organization by major process, such as engineering, teaching, the law, or medicine, tends to bring together in a single department all of those who are at work making use of a given special skill or technology, or are members of a given profession. Under such a policy the department of law would comprise all of the lawyers and law clerks, including those who are devoting their time to school matters, or water supply suits, or drafting ordinances. The department of engineering and public works would have all the engineers, including those concerned with planning, design, construction, maintenance and other phases of engineering work, wherever that work was found. This would include the work in the parks, on the streets, in the schools, and in connection with water, sewer, waste and other services. The department of health would include all of the doctors, nurses, and bacteriologists, and would not only carry on the general public health work, but would do the medical and nursing work for the schools, the water department, the department of social welfare, etc., as has been outlined above.

In every one of these cases it will be observed that the basis of organization is the bringing together in a single office or department of all the workers who are using some particular kind of skill, knowledge, machinery, or profession. This principle of organization has the following advantages:

First, it guarantees the maximum utilization of up-to-date technical skill and by bringing together in a single office a large amount of each kind of work (technologically measured), makes it possible in each case to make use of the most effective divisions of work and specialization.

Second, it makes possible also the economies of the maximum use of labor saving machinery and mass production. These economies arise not from the total mass of the work to be performed, not from the fact that the work performed serves the same general purpose but from the fact that the work is performed with the same machine, with the same technique, with the same motions. For example, economy in printing comes from skill in typesetting, printing, and binding and the use of modern equipment. It makes no difference to the printer whether he is printing a pamphlet for the schools, a report for the police department, or a form for the comptroller. Unit costs, efficiency in the doing of the job, rest upon the process, not the purpose.[5]

Third, organization by process encourages co-ordination in all of the technical and skilled work of the enterprise, because all of those engaged in any field are brought together under the same supervision, instead of being scattered in several departments as is the case when organization is based upon some other principle.

Fourth, it furnishes an excellent approach to the development of central co-ordination and control when certain of the services such as budgeting, accounting, purchasing, and planning are set up on a process basis and used as instruments of integration even where other activities are set up on some other basis.

Fifth, organization by process is best adapted to the development of career service, and the stimulation of professional standards and pride. A career ladder can be erected very much more easily in a department which is from top to bottom engineers, or doctors, or statisticians, or clerks, than it can in a department which is partly engineers, partly doctors, partly statisticians, partly clerks. . . .

These are the major advantages of organization on the basis of process. There are, of course, offsetting difficulties. As in the case of any other principle of organization, it is impossible to aggregate all of the work of the government on such a basis alone. It is not difficult to do so for engineering and medicine and teaching, but it becomes impossible when we reach typing and clerical work. It cannot furnish a satisfactory basis for doing the whole job in any large or complicated enterprise.

In the second place, there is always the danger that organization by process will hinder the accomplishment of major purposes, because the process departments may be more interested in *how* things are done than in *what* is accomplished. For example, a housing department which must clear the slums, build new low cost tenements and manage them, and inspect existing housing and approve new building plans, may find it difficult to make rapid progress if it must draw its legal help from the corporation counsel, its architects from the department of engineering, its enforcement officers from the police department, and its plans from the planning commission, particularly if one or more of these departments regards public housing as a nuisance and passing fad. There are also accountants who think that the only reason for the running of a government is the keeping of the books!

Third, experience seems to indicate that a department built around a given profession or skill tends to show a greater degree of arrogance and unwillingness to accept democratic control. This is perhaps a natural outgrowth of the insolence of professionalism to which reference has already been made.

Fourth, organization by process is perhaps less favorable to the development of a separate administrative service, because it tends to bring rather narrow professional specialists to the top of each department, men who are thereby disqualified for transfer to administrative posts in other fields.

And finally, the necessity of effective co-ordination is greatly increased. Purpose departments must be co-ordinated so that they will not conflict but will work shoulder to shoulder. But whether they do, or do not, the individual major purposes will be accomplished to a considerable extent and a failure in any service is limited in its effect to that service. Process departments must be co-ordinated not only to prevent conflict, but also to guarantee positive co-operation. They work hand in hand. They must also time their work so that it will fit together, a factor of lesser significance in the purpose departments. A failure in one process affects the whole enterprise, and a failure to co-ordinate one process division may destroy the effectiveness of all of the work that is being done.

While organization by process thus puts great efficiency within our reach, this efficiency cannot be realized unless the compensating structure of co-ordination is developed.

Organization by Clientele or Matériel

Organization on the basis of the persons served or dealt with, or on the basis of the things dealt with, tends to bring together in a single department, regardless of the purpose of the service, or the techniques used, all of those who are working with a given group or a given set of things. Examples are the veterans' administration which deals with all of the problems of the veteran, be they in health, in hospitals, in insurance, in welfare, or in education; and the immigration bureau which deals with immigrants at all points, including legal, financial, and medical services. Departmentalization on the basis of *matériel* is more common in private business than in public. Department stores, for example, have separate departments for furniture, hardware, drugs, jewelry, shoes, etc., and have separate buyers and sales forces for each. In many communities the school is in reality such a service, as it concentrates most of the community services touching children in school, including medical inspection, corrective treatment, free lunches and recreation, and certain phases of juvenile crime. The Forest Service is another organization based on *matériel*—in this case, trees.

The great advantage of this type of organization is the simplification and co-ordination of the service of government in its contact with the consumer. He does not encounter first one and then other representative, each of whom does or demands something different or even something contradictory. . . .

A second advantage is found in the increasing skill which attends the handling over and over of the same material.

A third gain arises from the elimination of duplicate travel, particularly in dealing with widely separated or sparsely distributed work.

The disadvantages of an organization which brings together all of the contacts with a given individual or thing are:

First, it tends to sacrifice the efficiency of specialization, because it must after all perform several otherwise specialized functions through the same organization or even at times through the same agent. . . .

A second difficulty is found in the impossibility of applying the principle of division by persons served to all of the work of a government, without encountering extensive conflict and duplication. It is not difficult to pick out special groups like the aged, the youth, the criminal, the veteran, the real estate owner, etc., but when all is said and done there remains a great number of the ordinary citizens that does not fall into *any single* grouping. Each individual will appear in various groups at various times, and in the general group known as "the public" the rest of the time. And it is clearly impossible to organize a special department for the public, with all of the heterogeneous elements which this would entail from the standpoint of dissimilar technologies and conflicting objectives. It must be remembered also that even such departments as seem to be organized on the basis of persons served do not as a matter of fact cover all of the services rendered to or government contacts with a class of individuals. . . .

A third difficulty arises from the danger of dominance by favor-seeking pressure groups. Departments set up by clientele seldom escape political dominance by those groups, and are generally found to be special pleaders for those groups, at times in opposition to the general interest of society as a whole. This is in part due to the fact that the organization itself is often brought into being through the action of a pressure group and its demand for a special agency to serve it, but it is also continued through the efforts of the agency once established to marshal and maintain a group in its support. It follows that agencies so set up as to maintain or develop their own pressure backing are peculiarly difficult of democratic control and tend not to fit into a co-ordinated social policy.

Organization by Place

Organization on the basis of the place at which the service is performed brings together all of those who work in a limited area regardless of the service they are performing or of the techniques they represent. . . .

. . . [For example,] in some of the largest city police systems the city is divided into precincts, and most of the police activities within a given area are under the complete direction of a precinct officer through whom all communication to and from headquarters must go. . . .

. . . The real work of government is done out among the people in the various sections of the state or city. In the supervision of these forces it is often necessary to establish some form of regional organization, if for no other reason than to save the time of the supervisory officers who cannot be in two places at once. It is thus generally a question as to how high up in the organization geographical subdivision shall be introduced. Obviously this may be done at the very top, as the first division of the work under the chief executive of an enterprise, or it may be introduced far down the line after the major divisions have been set up by purpose, by process, or by clientele. The former may be termed *primary* geographical subdivision and the latter *secondary, tertiary,* or *subordinate* geographical subdivision. A department or major activity, like the Tennessee Valley Authority, which is set up on the basis of geographical boundaries is in fact a primary geographical subdivision of the government. . . .

The advantages of departmentalization on the basis of geographical areas, that is on the basis of superior geographical subdivision, are fairly obvious in practice. They consist first of the greater ease of co-ordination of services rendered and controls exercised within a given area; second, of the greater tendency to adapt the total program to the needs of the areas served, not alone because of the discretion resting within the divisions, but also because the needs and differences of the areas will be more vigorously represented at headquarters in the general consideration of broad policy; and third, of the greater ease with which co-operative relations may be established with subordinate governmental units, which are of necessity first of all geographically defined units. Decentralization of geographical divisions strengthens these tendencies, and serves, moreover, to reduce travel costs, short circuit adjustment problems, cut red tape, and speed up all joint activities and administrative decisions. It increases not only the awareness of the officials to local needs and to the interrelation of service and planning problems, but develops a new sensitivity to the process of democratic control through intimate association of the officials with the people served.

With decentralized subdivision a large amount of discretion must be delegated to the men in charge of field offices; in fact, they must be men of ability equal to if not superior to those who would be selected to head centralized departments of similar scope.

The difficulties of primary geographic subdivision are also not far to seek. They consist of the increased difficulty of maintaining a uniform nation-wide, state-wide, or city-wide policy; the danger of too narrow and short-sighted management; and the increased difficulty of making full use of technical services and the highest specialization because of the division of the work into limited blocks. Decentralization tends to enhance these difficulties by reason of physical isolation. It introduces other factors as well, such as higher costs for supervisory personnel, the general hesitancy of central administrative heads to delegate sufficient real power, the lesser prestige of localized officials, and the increased tendency of such a system to come under the control of localized logrolling pressure groups. Political parties under our system of representation are based upon geographical areas. An administrative system also set up by areas is peculiarly subject to spoliation by politicians as long as we have the spoils system.

Whenever the concept of geographic areas is introduced into the structure of organization, either as a primary or as a subordinate plan of division of work, there is always the further practical problem of delineating appropriate boundaries. This is particularly difficult when it is planned to deal with several activities widely differing in their nature and technology. There is always the danger that the tasks to be dealt with do not follow compact geographic boundaries and that the administrative separation introduced by the geographic division will complicate rather than simplify the work.

Line and Staff

. . . When the work of government is subjected to the dichotomy of "line" and "staff," there are included in staff all of those persons who devote their time exclusively to the knowing, thinking and planning functions, and in the line all of the remainder who are, thus, chiefly concerned with the doing functions. The overhead directing authority of the staff group, usually a board or committee, is the "general staff."

Obviously those in the line are also thinking and planning, and making suggestions to superior officers. They cannot operate otherwise. But this does not make them staff officers. Those also in the staff are *doing* something; they do not merely sit and twiddle their thumbs. But they do not organize others, they do not direct or appoint personnel, they do not issue commands, they do not take responsibility for the job. Everything they suggest is referred up, not down, and is carried out, if at all, on the responsibility and under the direction of a line officer.

The important point of confusion in considering line and staff has arisen in speaking of the budget director, the purchasing agent, the controller, the public relations secretary, as "staff" officers. On the basis of the definition it is clear that they are all line officers. They have important duties of direction and control. When administrative responsibility and power are added to any staff function, that function thereby becomes immediately and completely a line function. There is no middle ground.

The chief value of the line and staff classification is to point to the need (1) of developing an independent planning agency as an aid to the chief executive, and (2) of refusing to inject any element of administrative authority and control into such an agency.

The necessity for central purchase, for personnel administration, for budgeting and for fiscal control rests on other considerations and not on the philosophy of the general staff.

4. INTERRELATION OF SYSTEMS OF DEPARTMENTALIZATION

Students of administration have long sought a single principle of effective departmentalization just as alchemists sought the philosophers' stone. But they have sought in vain. There is apparently no one most effective system of departmentalism.

Each of the four basic systems of organization is intimately related with the other three, because in any enterprise all four elements are present in the doing of the work and are embodied in every individual workman. Each member of the enterprise is working for some major purpose, uses some process, deals with some persons, and serves or works at some place.

If an organization is erected about any one of these four characteristics of work, it becomes immediately necessary to recognize the other characteristics in constructing the secondary and tertiary divisions of the work. For example, a government which is first divided on the basis of place will, in each geographical department, find it necessary to divide by purpose, by process, by clientele, or even again by place; and one divided in the first instance by purpose, may well be divided next by process and then by place. While the first or primary division of any enterprise is of very great significance, it must none the less be said that there is no one most effective pattern for determining the priority and order for the introduction of these interdependent principles. It will depend in any case upon the results which are desired at a given time and place.

An organization is a living and dynamic entity. Each activity is born, has its periods of experimental development, of vigorous and stable activity, and, in some cases, of decline. A principle of organization appropriate at one stage may not be appropriate at all during a succeeding stage, particularly in view of the different elements of strength and of weakness which we have seen to exist in the various systems of departmentalization. In any government various parts of its work will always stand at different stages of their life cycle. It will therefore be found that not all of the activities of any government may be appropriately departmentalized neatly on the basis of a single universal plan. Time is an essential element in the formula.

Another variable is technological development. The invention of machines, the advance of applied science, the rise of new specializations and professions, changes in society and in the way men work and move in their private life must be continually reflected in the work of government, and therefore in the structure of government. Medieval governments made use of warriors, priests, artists, builders, and tax gatherers; they had no place for sanitary engineers, chemists, entomologists, pneumatic drill operators and typists. Before you organize a statistical division there must be statistical machinery and statistical science, but as soon as there are such machinery and science, any large organization which fails to recognize the fact in its organization may greatly lessen its utilization of the newly available tools and skills.

A further variable influencing the structure of any enterprise is its size, measured not so much by the amount of work done as by the number of men at work and their geographical dispersion. A drug store is an excellent illustration of the problem encountered. It must have a prescription department with a licensed pharmacist, no matter how small it is, because of the technological requirements involved. But it does not need to have a separate medicine and supply department, refreshment department, book department, toy department, sporting goods department, cigar department, and delivery department, each with a trained manager, buyer and sales force, unless it is a big store. In the small store, the pharmacist may even be the manager, the soda jerker, and the book dispenser. If the business is big enough, it may be desirable to have more than one store in order to reach the customers, thus introducing geographical subdivision. Similarly, in government the nature of the organization must be adapted not only to the technological requirements but also to the size of the undertaking and the dispersion of its work. . . .

Structure and Co-ordination

The major purpose of organization is co-ordination, as has been pointed out above. It should therefore be noted that each of the four principles of departmentalization plays a different rôle in co-ordination. In each case the highest degree of co-ordination takes place within the departments set up, and the greatest lack of co-ordination and danger of friction occurs between the departments, or at the points where they overlap.

If all of the departments are set up on the basis of purpose, then the task of the chief executive in the field of co-ordination will be to see that the major purposes are not in conflict and that the various processes which are used are consistent, and that the government as it touches classes of citizens or reaches areas of the community is appropriate, rational, and effective. He will not have to concern himself with co-ordination within the departments, as each department head will look after this.

If all of the departments are set up on the basis of process, the work methods will be well standardized on professional lines, and the chief executive will have to see that these are co-ordinated and timed to produce the results and render the services for which the government exists, and that the service rendered actually fits the needs of the persons or areas served.

If place be the basis of departmentalization, that is, if the services be decentralized, then the task of the chief executive is not to see that the activities are co-ordinated locally and fit the locality, but to see that each of these services makes use of the standard techniques and that the work in each area is part of a general program and policy.

If the work of the government be departmentalized in part on the basis of purpose, in part on the basis of process, in part on the basis of clientele, and in part on the basis of place, it will be seen that the problems of co-ordination and smooth operation are multiplied and that the task of the executive is increased. Moreover, the nature of his work is altered. In an organization in which all of the major divisions follow one philosophy, the executive himself must furnish the interdepartmental co-ordination and see that things do not fall between two stools. In an organization built on two or more bases of departmentalization, the executive may use, for example, the process departments as a routine means of co-ordinating the purpose departments. None the less the task of the executive is extraordinarily complicated. There is also great danger in such an organization that one department may fail to aid or actually proceed to obstruct another department. When departments cross each other at right angles, the danger of collision is far greater and far more serious than when their contacts are along parallel lines at their respective outer limits. . . .

The Means of Interdepartmental Co-ordination

In the discussion thus far it has been assumed that the normal method of interdepartmental co-ordination is hierarchical in its operation. That is, if trouble develops between a field representative (X) of one department and the field representative (A) of another department, that the solution will be found by carrying the matter up the line from inferior to superior until the complaint of Mr. X and the complaint of Mr. A finally reach their common superior, be he mayor, governor or President. In actual practice, there are also other means of interdepartmental co-ordination which must be regarded as part of the organization as such. Among these must be included planning boards and committees, interdepartmental committees, co-ordinators, and officially arranged regional meetings, etc. These are all organizational devices for bringing about the co-ordination of the work of government. Co-ordination of this type is essential. It greatly lessens the military stiffness and red tape of the strictly hierarchical structure. It greatly increases the consultative process in administration. It must be recognized, however, that it is to be used only to deal with abnormal situations and where matters of policy are involved, as in planning. The organization itself should be set up so that it can dispose of the routine work without such devices, because these devices are too dilatory, irresponsible and time-consuming for normal administration. Wherever an organization needs continual resort to special co-ordinating devices in the discharge of its regular work, this is proof that the organization is bad. These special agencies of co-ordination draw their sanction from the hierarchical structure and should receive the particular attention of the executive authority. They should not be set up and forgotten, ignored, or permitted to assume an independent status. . . .

In the devices of co-ordination, one must recognize also joint service contracts and coincident personnel appointments. Independent agencies may be pulled together in operation through such use of the same staff or service. There are many illustrations of the former, especially in engineering services. The county agent who is at the same time a county, a state, and a federal official is an example of the latter.

A great obstacle in the way of all of these plans of co-ordination is found in the danger of introducing confusion in direction through the violation of the principle of unity of command, and also in the difference in the level of authority of those who are brought together in any interdepartmental or intergovernmental co-ordinating arrangement. The representatives of the Department of Agriculture, for example, may have a large measure of responsibility and power, and may therefore be in a position to work out an adjustment of program through conference and to agree to a new line of conduct, but the representatives of the Army, coming from an entirely different kind of an organization, are sure to be in a position where they cannot make any adjustments without passing the decision back to headquarters.

5. CO-ORDINATION BY IDEAS

Any large and complicated enterprise would be incapable of effective operation if reliance for co-ordination were placed in organization alone. Organization . . . does not take the place of a dominant central idea as the foundation of action and self-co-ordination in the daily operation of all of the parts of the enterprise. Accordingly, the most difficult task of the chief executive is not command, it is leadership, that is, the development of the desire and will to work together for a purpose in the minds of those who are associated in any activity.

Human beings are compounded of cogitation and emotion and do not function well when treated as though they were merely cogs in motion. Their capacity for great and productive labor, creative co-operative work, and loyal self-sacrifice knows no limits provided the whole man, body-mind-and-spirit, is thrown into the program.

Implications

. . . The following specific elements . . . bear directly upon the problem of co-ordination:

1.   Personnel administration becomes of extraordinary significance, not merely from the standpoint of finding qualified appointees for the various positions, but even more from the standpoint of assisting in the selection of individuals and in the maintenance of conditions which will serve to create a foundation of loyalty and enthusiasm. . . .

2.   Even where the structure of the organization is arranged to produce co-ordination by authority, and certainly in those realms in which the structure as such is wanting, the effort should be made to develop the driving ideas by co-operative effort and compromise so that there may be an understanding of the program, a sense of participation in its formulation, and enthusiasm in its realization.

3.   Proper reporting on the results of the work of the departments and of the government as a whole to the public and to the controlling legislative body, and public appreciation of good service rendered by public employees is essential, not merely as a part of the process of democratic control, but also as a means to the development of service morale.

4.   As a matter of public policy the government should encourage the development of professional associations among the employees of the government, in recognition of the fact that such associations can assist powerfully in the development of standards and ideals. . . .

5.   A developing organization must be continually engaged in research bearing upon the major technical and policy problems encountered, and upon the efficiency of the processes of work. In both types of research, but particularly in the latter, members of the staff at every level should be led to participate in the inquiries and in the development of solutions.

6.   There is need for a national system of honor awards which may be conspicuously conferred upon men and women who render distinguished and faithful, though not necessarily highly advertised, public service.

7.   The structure of any organization must reflect not only the logic of the work to be done, but also the special aptitudes of the particular human beings who are brought together in the organization to carry through a particular project. It is the men and not the organization chart that do the work.

Dominant Ideals

The power of an idea to serve as the foundation of co-ordination is so great that one may observe many examples of co-ordination even in the absence of any single leader or of any framework of authority. The best illustration is perhaps a nation at war. Every element steps into line and swings into high gear "to help win the war." The co-ordination is enthusiastic and complete, within the limits of knowledge of course. In an old stable community, small enough for each person to know the other, even competing businesses generally work along together in harmony. The town board, the school board, the park commission, the overseer of the poor, though answerable to no single executive, manage to get along with each other and each to fit his part of the work into that of the others to arrive at a sensible result for the whole picture. Men of intelligence and good will find little difficulty in working together for a given purpose even without an organization. They do not need to be held in line or driven to do a specific task in a specific way at a specific time. They carry on because of their inner compulsion, and may in the end accomplish a far better result for that very reason. . . .

It becomes increasingly clear, therefore, that the task of the administrator must be accomplished less and less by coercion and discipline and more and more by persuasion. In other words, management of the future must look more to leadership and less to authority as the primary means of co-ordination.

. . . The more important and the more difficult part of co-ordination is to be sought not through systems of authority, but through ideas and persuasion, and to make clear the point that the absurdities of the hierarchical system of authority are made sweet and reasonable through unity of purpose. It may well be that the system of organization, the structure of authority, is primarily important in co-ordination because it makes it easy to deal with the routine affairs, and thereby lessens the strain placed upon leadership, so that it can thus devote itself more fully to the supreme task of developing consent, participation, loyalty, enthusiasm, and creative devotion.

6. CO-ORDINATION AND CHANGE

The Limits of Co-ordination

Are there limits to co-ordination? Is mankind capable of undertaking activities which though interrelated are beyond man's power of systematic co-ordination? . . .

It is clear . . . in which direction the limitations of co-ordination lie. The difficulties arise from:

1.   The uncertainty of the future, not only as to natural phenomena like rain and crops, but even more as to the behavior of individuals and of peoples;

2.   The lack of knowledge, experience, wisdom and character among leaders and their confused and conflicting ideals and objectives;

3.   The lack of administrative skill and technique;

4.   The vast number of variables involved and the incompleteness of human knowledge, particularly with regard to man and life;

5.   The lack of orderly methods of developing, considering, perfecting and adopting new ideas and programs. . . .

The Accretion of Functions

In view of the fact that organization must conform to the functions performed, attention must be given to the process by which new functions are assumed by governmental units. . . .

In view of the growth processes of governmental functions, those who are concerned with the mechanics of organization will fail to develop a satisfactory theory of organization unless they regard their basic problem as dynamic. In considering the organization of government we deal not alone with living men, but with an organism which has its own life.

The Evolution of Government

To what extent is this organism subject to the Darwinian laws of survival? It was a basic theory of classical economists that business enterprises survive only in so far as they adapt themselves to the changing economic environment, and that only the fittest survive, fitness being measured in terms of prices and profits. Whatever the truth of that hypothesis, mankind has determined not to try it out. At one end business has upset the free competitive test by monopolies and cartels, and at the other end the public has refused to let itself be pushed around freely by such combinations or to let business enterprises go to the wall in any wholesale fashion, when a whole system cannot meet the economic judgment day.

When we turn to governmental organizations we find even less "survival of the fittest." Governmental organizations seem to be extraordinarily immune to evolutionary changes. Next to the church, they are in all civilizations the most vigorous embodiments of immortality. A governmental unit is by nature a monopoly, and is thus not subject to the purifying influence of competition. It does not have a profit and loss record; its balance sheet is buoyed up by "good will"; its product is priceless and often imponderable; its deficits are met from taxes, loans and hope. Under these conditions a governmental unit can continue for many years after its utility has passed, or its form of organization or program have become obsolete. . . .

The struggle for survival in government [is] not so much a fight to the death, a test to destruction, but an endless process of adaptation to changed conditions and ideas. In this sense, governmental institutions are in continual evolution. But the process of evolution of human institutions is quite different from the process of evolution of living organisms.

The process of adaptation falls partly in the field of politics and partly in the field of administration. The two are so closely related, however, that the political aspects cannot be ignored completely even here, where we are concerned only with administrative organization. A glance at the present world situation makes it clear that the modern state faces as never before the need of rapid and radical adaptation to changed conditions. Governments which cannot make the necessary evolutionary changes will not survive. It becomes necessary, therefore, in the structure of the organization to make more elaborate provision for those agencies of management which concern themselves with the processes of adaptation. . . .

. . . In periods of change, government must strengthen those agencies which deal with administrative management, that is, with co-ordination, with planning, with personnel, with fiscal control, and with research. These services constitute the brain and will of any enterprise. It is they that need development when we pass from a regime of habit to one demanding new thinking and new acting.

NOTES

1. I.e., when *organization is the basis of co-ordination.* Wherever the central executive authority is composed of several who exercise their functions jointly by majority vote, as on a board, this is from the standpoint of organization still a "single authority"; where the central executive is in reality composed of several men acting freely and independently, then organization cannot be said to be the basis of co-ordination; it is rather the dominance of an idea and falls under the second principle stated above.

2. Henri Fayol, "Industrial and General Administration." English translation by J. A. Coubrough. International Management Association, Geneva, 1930.

3. Fayol terms the latter "unity of direction."

4. Frederick Winslow Taylor, "Shop Management." Harper and Brothers, New York and London, 1911, p. 99.

5. Of course overall efficiency by the same token rests on the purpose, not the process. For example, a report may be printed at a phenomenally low cost, but if the pamphlet has no purpose, the whole thing is a waste of effort.

informal organization and human relations

Traditional organization theory, with its emphasis on formal structure and assumptions regarding people's behavior in large-scale organizations, has proven inadequate as a basis for a science of organization and as a practical guide to managing people in organizations. By emphasizing the formal aspects, traditional theorists neglected what Charles H. Page has called "bureaucracy's other face"—informal organization.[1]

The crucial role informal groups play in organizations was identified in the twenties and thirties by a team of researchers from Harvard. The team, headed by Elton Mayo and Fritz Roethlisberger, was engaged in a study of the Hawthorne (Chicago) Works of the Western Electric Company. What began as a study of the effects of illumination on output uncovered a psychological rather than a physiological variable in organizational effectiveness. The initial findings prompted a full-scale study, with plant-wide interviews and experimental work situations, aimed at clarifying the role of informal, small group activity within the formal structure of the organization. Some of the experimental situations—the Relay Assembly Test Room and the Bank Wiring Observation Room—have become classics in social psychology. These experiments showed the development and importance of group solidarity that enabled the employees to control various aspects of their work situation despite the formal commands of the hierarchy.[2]

The Hawthorne studies sparked interest in informal groups in all kinds of organizations. The studies that followed the pioneering efforts of Mayo and Roethlisberger led to the development of a management school that saw "human relations" as the primary method by which management could weld people into an effective organization. Although the human relations movement has often been characterized as glad-handing and back-slapping in order to manipulate subordinates, the intellectual basis of the human relations movement was its concern for the effect of informal group behavior on authority within formal organizations. Research into small group behavior developed several important concepts on which more modern management practices have been based.

Peter Blau, a sociologist at Columbia University, studied informal group behavior in several public bureaucracies. In the selection reprinted in this volume, he deals with the development of informal norms that arise in direct violation of the formal rules of a law enforcement agency. Furthermore, he suggests that without the informal *modus vivendi* worked out by the participants in the organization, the objectives of the agency would be much harder to attain.

While reading the Blau piece, one might want to consider the degree to which the supervisors—the hierarchy—took part in the informal organization of the agency. What control mechanisms did the hierarchy retain over the agents? Why did the agents violate the no-consultation-with-colleagues rule? What social factors governed the agent's choice of consultants? Did the informal structure tend to support the formal structure or subvert it?

The Hawthorne studies, as well as Blau's, reveal that informal groups actually regulate, to a degree, aspects of the work situation in violation of hierarchically prescribed rules. This finding suggests a change in the notion of authority that had been implicit in the traditional organization theories. In the traditional theories, authority was assumed to come from the top of the hierarchy and flow downward. Superiors commanded; subordinates obeyed. The research into informal groups showed that the subordinates actually had quite a bit to say about whether they would obey certain orders that came down through the hierarchy. Authority began to be considered more of a relational concept than had formerly been the case.[3]

Chester I. Barnard, the late president of New Jersey Bell

Telephone Company, recognized that informal organization was inseparable from formal organization, and he noted the changed nature of authority. To Barnard, a particular communication would be considered authoritative only if the subordinate accepted it as such.[4] Communications would be accepted if they fell within the subordinate's *zone of indifference* or, as Herbert Simon later renamed it, the *zone of acceptance*.[5] The zone of indifference is that area in which subordinates accept communication from the hierarchy as legitimate. Subordinates expect their superiors to make certain demands on them. Socially defined roles govern what kinds of demands will be perceived as legitimate in a given situation. As long as the communication from a superior is viewed as consistent with the role, the subordinates will be indifferent to the communication and will obey. If, however, a superior makes an extraordinary demand—one that is not sanctioned by his role—the subordinates will not be indifferent. They will consider the demand: upon reflection, they may decide that the demand is beyond what *they* *believe* to be the legitimate power of the superior, and they will refuse to obey. They may, however, consider the demand and upon reflection decide to comply. If they do comply with a demand that was previously perceived to be beyond the role of the superior, they have, *de facto*, enlarged his role and accepted his authority. The crucial point is that the subordinate, as well as the superior, contributes to the definition of roles of both parties in any superior-subordinate interaction. This gives the subordinate an active part in determining authority within the organization—a part that had been substantially overlooked by traditional theories.

Chester I. Barnard suggests that motivation is an important part of organization theory and practical management. He posits a contribution-satisfaction equilibrium model by which people contribute to an organization in return for satisfactions. To get more cooperation from people, management must provide sufficient inducements. These inducements have the effect of broadening the zone of indifference to get more productivity from subordinates.

The reader should note the kinds of inducements with which Barnard deals. Was traditional theory interested in these variables? Can government offer such incentives as readily as private business? What is the effect of organizational size as an incentive factor according to Barnard? Do you agree? Is it possible to develop an organization-wide incentive policy that would elicit a favorable response among a large majority of organization members? If incentives fail to secure cooperation, what forms of persuasion can be effective? What is the function of the group in gaining cooperation?

NOTES

1. Attributed to Page by Peter M. Blau, *Bureaucracy in Modern Society* (New York: Random House, Inc., 1956), p. 46.

2. For an excellent summary of the Hawthorne studies see George C. Homans, "The Western Electric Researches," in Schuyler D. Hoslett, ed., *Human Factors in Management*, rev. ed. (New York: Harper and Brothers, 1951). Available as a Bobbs-Merrill reprint, number S-123.

3. Fritz J. Roethlisberger and William J. Dixon, *Management and the Worker* (Cambridge, Mass.: Harvard University Press, 1939). This book emphasizes the extent to which group attitudes affect an individual's reactions to authority.

4. Chester I. Barnard, *The Functions of the Executive* (Cambridge, Mass.: Harvard University Press, 1937) chapter 12.

5. Herbert A. Simon, *Administrative Behavior: A Study of Decision Making Processes in Administrative Organizations* (New York: The Macmillan Company, Free Press, 1965).

consultation among colleagues and informal norms

peter m. blau

. . .

Department Y, the unit under intensive study, had eighteen members. The department supervisor was in charge of sixteen agents and one clerk. The principal duties of agents were carried out in the field. Cases of firms to be investigated were assigned to them individually by the supervisor. Processing a case involved an audit of the books and records of the firm, interviews with the employer (or his representative) and a sample of employees, the determination of the existence of legal violations and of the appropriate action to be taken, and negotiations with the employer. The time spent on a case varied between half a day and several months. On the average, an agent worked seventeen hours on an investigation.

The agent had to evaluate the reliability of the information he obtained—since concealment of violations occurred, of course—and had to decide whether violations had taken place on the basis of a large and complex body of legal regulations. This was a difficult task, which often required extensive research and consultation with the supervisor or with an attorney on the agency's staff. Upon completion of a case, a full report was written. All these activities were

Peter M. Blau, The Dynamics of Bureaucracy: A Study of Interpersonal Relationships in Two Governmental Agencies, *2d ed. Copyright by the University of Chicago Press, 1955, 1963. Used with permission. Footnotes deleted.*

carried out in the office. Besides, agents sometimes interviewed employees or negotiated with employers in the office and had to attend biweekly departmental meetings as well as occasional special conferences. An average of 42 percent of their working time was spent in the office. . . .

LEGAL REGULATIONS AND OPERATING RULES

. . . Every federal agent . . . possessed a manual containing over a thousand pages of regulations, to which he constantly referred. Often this manual did not suffice, and agents consulted the volumes of administrative explications and court opinions, which occupied two library shelves. . . . The provisions of the two congressional acts that the federal agency was charged to enforce had become specified and extended through a host of legislative amendments, administrative interpretations, and court opinions setting precedent. Any of these might be pertinent to a given case. The agent's conduct had to be oriented in terms of these regulations, which defined the violations he was required to discover. . . .

. . . Although the federal manual contained operating rules as well as legal regulations, these rules were usually less specific, and most specific ones were not enforced. For example, the manual specified eleven topics to be discussed with the employer during the first interview. None of the observed agents inquired about more than six of these at that time, and the supervisor never checked conformity with this rule. As long as all the necessary information was obtained, it seemed to matter little precisely how and when it was done. . . . Federal supervisors rarely told an agent what he should do at a certain time. . . .

There was less emphasis on strict conformity with operating rules in the federal agency because control over operations was effected by a different method. Rigid and precise legal standards governed the results that agents were required to accomplish in their work. Their findings and the actions they had taken were twice checked for accuracy—by the supervisor and by the review section. Any mistake counted heavily against an agent's record. This evaluation of precision, by itself, might well have engendered overcaution or even a tendency not to report very complex violations, lest mistakes be made in dealing with them. To guard against such tendencies, success in investigations were [sic] also quantitatively evaluated.

. . . In the federal agency, quantitative records were used . . . extensively for evaluating accomplishments. . . . Thirty categories of performance, such as the number and types of violations found, were supplemented by another thirty categories based on the supervisor's standardized evaluation of every completed case. Most of these indices measured results achieved in investigations rather than techniques used. . . . These statistical records influenced ratings in the federal agency. . . . Finally, federal supervisors also tended to stress accomplishments more than conformity with procedures when they judged the qualitative factors that influenced the rating, such as "dependability."

Evaluation on the basis of the end results of operations rather than the particular means used in reaching them constrained agents to choose, on their own initiative, the most effective course of action for the attainment of clearly specified objectives. This fostered uniformity in most respects in which it was bureaucratically relevant and simultaneously permitted agents to employ diverse means in the interest of the successful performance of their duties, for instance, in order to discover a concealed violation. Operating rules, in this situation, could be largely confined to prohibiting certain methods of investigation as illegitimate, such as threatening employers in negotiations by the illicit use of authority. . . .

Specification of results promoted a professional orientation toward the discharge of responsibilities. This evaluation system therefore influenced operations without producing a feeling of being continuously hamstrung by detailed rules. Agents actually exercised a considerable amount of discretion, and the constraints that governed their conduct were experienced as self-imposed rather than arbitrary. There was no "silly" rule prescribing that fifty pages of bookkeeping records be examined in all firms, but the law specified the evidence with which the claim that a violation existed must be supported. This necessitated the examination of fifty or more pages of these records often, but not always. The agent decided rationally how to proceed in terms of the objective he was required to attain.

Operating rules, on the other hand, eliminate discretion in principle and thus restrain conduct also in cases in which there is no rational basis for it. They were experienced as more restrictive than the self-imposed constraints generated by the responsibility for achieving given results. . . . [The] agents objected to detailed operating rules, but there were [relatively few] such rules. . . . The feeling of freedom of action and the professional interest that prevailed among the agents contrasted sharply with the attitudes of most [people in an agency with many operating rules], who considered their jobs routine and confining. This difference in work satisfaction was due, at least partly, to the different control mechanisms employed.

However, the exercise of discretion that made the job more stimulating also engendered anxiety over decision-making. The agent was free to make his own decisions, but their legal validity and effectiveness determined his rating. His consequent anxious concern about the correctness of his decisions sometimes actually prevented an agent from making final commitments. The supervisor mentioned that some agents keep difficult cases on their desks instead of completing them, "being afraid to make a decision."

Official provisions were made to assist agents with their difficult cases. Decisions of specified complexity or significance—for example, if the amount of money involved exceeded a certain sum—had to be authorized by the supervisor, who, in turn, had to obtain authorization from his superiors in special cases. Similarly, if an agent encountered a problem he could not solve, he was expected to consult his supervisor, who, if he could not furnish the requested advice himself, gave the agent permission to consult a staff attorney. Agents were not allowed to consult anyone else directly, not even their colleagues.

This rule requiring agents to come to their supervisor with their problems was an integral part of the authority structure of the agency. The supervisor was responsible to his superior for the legal accuracy of all actions taken in his department. In order to be able to discharge this responsibility, he had the authority to control all official decisions of his subordinates. As a last resort, he could correct mistakes when he reviewed their cases and order agents to revise the erroneous actions they had taken. Since this involved much wasted effort and sometimes bad public relations, two other ways of exercising authority were more efficient. First, the supervisor could prevent mistakes by advising agents in difficult cases or by guiding them to expert legal consultants. The requirement that they see him when they had problems, that is, in cases in which mistakes were most likely, facilitated his control over decisions for which he was held responsible. Second, he could discourage the repetition of types of decisions he considered erroneous, because his evaluation of subordinates influenced their career chances. To use this evaluation judiciously and as an effective control device, he had to be able to place responsibility for all decisions made. This would have been impossible if a half-dozen agents had collaborated on a case. The rule prohibiting consultation with colleagues was designed to prevent such collaboration.

Agents, however, were reluctant to reveal to their supervisor their inability to solve a problem for fear that their ratings would be adversely affected. The need for assistance and the requirement that it be obtained only from the supervisor put officials under cross-pressure.

THE PATTERN OF CONSULTATION

"They are not permitted to consult other agents. If they have a problem, they have to take it up with me," said the department supervisor. Yet an agent averaged five contacts per hour with his colleagues. Hardly any of these were officially required, since each agent worked independently on the cases assigned to him. Some of them were purely private conversations, but many were discussions of their work, ranging from simple requests for information that could be answered in a sentence to consultations about complex problems.

This unofficial practice had developed in response to a need for advice from a source other than the supervisor. Anxiety over the correctness of his findings and actions, on which his rating was based, inhibited the agent in the process of making decisions and raised doubts in his mind regarding the validity of the decisions he had made. Consulting the supervisor, the only legitimate source of assistance, could not relieve the anxiety generated by concern over his opinion of an agent's competence. On the contrary, this anxiety induced agents to conceal their difficulties from the supervisor, as one of them explained: "I try to stay away from the supervisor as much as possible. The reason is that the more often you go to the supervisor, the more you show your stupidity." At best, even if an official had made correct tentative decisions, repeatedly asking the supervisor for confirmation would reveal his inability to act independently, which would also affect his rating adversely. Their need for getting advice without exposing their difficulties to the supervisor constrained agents to consult one another, in violation of the official rule.

Requests for information were a time-saving device, which must be distinguished from other consultations. An agent who did not recall a regulation or a reference often turned to ask a colleague instead of conducting a lengthy search. Since any agent might have this knowledge, depending primarily on the kinds of cases on which he had recently worked, proximity largely determined who was asked. An official requested information from his neighbors or from a colleague who passed his desk. This lack of discrimination had the result that every agent was often consulted.

When an agent had trouble solving a problem, on the other hand, he was more selective in his choice of consultant. The sixteen members of Department Y were asked with whom they usually conferred when they encountered difficulties. Seven agents were named by two or more colleagues in answer to this question, namely, all but two of the nine agents whom the supervisor considered highly competent, but none of the seven whose competence was below average.

Competence was clearly related to popularity as a consultant, but consultations were not confined to a few experts. A record was kept of all contacts between agents that lasted for three minutes or more. Most of these discussions were consultations. Two particular officials who spent at least fifteen minutes during thirty hours of observation together in such conferences are defined as a consultation pair. . . .

Most of these officials had one or two regular partners with whom they discussed problems. One partnership involved two agents whose competence, as indicated by the supervisor's rating and the estimation of colleagues, differed greatly, which suggests that one generally advised the other. Typically, however, each member of a pair was in the habit of consulting the other. All four agents without partners were experts, and three of them were also very popular consultants. These three were by no means isolated from the exchange of advice. On the contrary, they participated so widely in it that they did not spend much time with any single co-worker.

A consultation can be considered an exchange of values; both participants gain something, and both have to pay a price. The questioning agent is enabled to perform better than he could otherwise have done, without exposing his difficulties to the supervisor. By asking for advice, he implicitly pays his respect to the superior proficiency of his colleague. This acknowledgment of inferiority is the cost of receiving assistance. The consultant gains prestige, in return for which he is willing to devote some time to the consultation and permit it to disrupt his own work. The following remark of an agent illustrates this: "I like giving advice. It's flattering, I suppose, if you feel that the others come to you for advice."

The expert whose advice was often sought by colleagues obtained social evidence of his superior abilities. This increased his confidence in his own decisions and thus improved his performance as an investigator. Such a popular consultant not only needed advice on fewer occasions than did others, but he could also distribute discussions of his own problems among several colleagues, since most of them were obligated to him for his assistance. Besides, to refrain from asking any particular individual too many questions helped to maintain his reputation as an expert. Consequently, three of the most popular consultants had no regular partner.

All agents liked being consulted, but the value of any one of very many consultations became deflated for experts, and the price they paid in frequent interruptions became inflated. One of them referred to the numerous requests for his advice by saying, "I never object, although sometimes it's annoying." . . . Being approached for help was too valuable an experience to be refused, but popular consultants were not inclined to encourage further questions.

The role of the agent who frequently solicited advice was less enviable, even though he benefited most directly from this unofficial practice. Asking a colleague for guidance was less threatening than asking the supervisor, but the repeated admission by an agent of his inability to solve his own problems also undermined his self-confidence and his standing in the group. The cost of advice became prohibitive if the consultant, after the questioner had subordinated himself by asking for help, was in the least discouraging—by postponing a discussion or by revealing his impatience during one. To avoid such rejections, agents usually consulted a colleague with whom they were friendly, even if he was not an expert. One agent explained, when asked whether he ever consults a colleague whom he considers outstandingly competent: "I sometimes would like to, but I'm hesitant. I always have the feeling that I don't have the right to pick his brain. I ask the ones I know well because I don't feel any reluctance about asking them."

The establishment of partnerships of mutual consultation virtually eliminated the danger of rejections as well as the status threat implicit in asking for help, since the roles of questioner and consultant were intermittently reversed. These partnerships also enabled agents to reserve their consultations with an expert whom they did not know very well for their most complicated problems. They could therefore approach him in these cases with less fear of courting a rejection. If the complexity of a problem prevented the agent from solving it, he needed expert guidance. Often, however, anxiety over the correctness of his findings rather than lack of knowledge interfered with his ability to arrive at decisions. In this situation, the counsel of a colleague who was not outstandingly competent could furnish the reassurance that facilitated decision-making.

The prevailing practice of consulting colleagues removed the agent from the isolation in which he otherwise would have been, since his work on his own cases officially required hardly any contact with co-workers. The evidence it supplied that he was not alone in having difficulties and the knowledge it provided that advice could be obtained without revealing his troubles to the supervisor lessened his anxiety about making decisions. The repeated experience of being consulted did so even more effectively. By reducing such anxiety, this unofficial practice made the job less strenuous for agents and improved their ability to make accurate decisions in general and not only in those cases where a consultation took place.

However, consulting others also had disadvantages. It was a source of possible conflict with the supervisor, since it violated an official rule. Although the supervisor tolerated consultations, he did express his disapproval of agents "who are shopping around for the answers to their questions." Moreover, admitting ignorance by asking many questions lowered the group's estimation of an agent and his own self-confidence. The more competent an official was, the greater was his reluctance to admit inability to solve a problem. But even experts needed assistance in making difficult decisions.

CONSULTATION IN DISGUISE

An agent who worked on an interesting case and encountered strange problems often told his fellow-agents about it. All members of the department liked these discussions and considered them educational. One expressed her disappointment that superiors sometimes discouraged them by saying: "I wish they would not frown upon it. I used to like our gab-fests. You used to learn so much discussing cases somebody came across, which you would never get. I guess they feel that you waste too much time that way." The fact that agents devoted their free time to such discussions—lunch periods were filled with them, despite occasional protests, "No shop talk!"—indicates that they were enjoyed. Officials found it interesting to hear how unusual problems were solved, perhaps after suggesting a possible solution themselves.

Generally, the discussant did not solicit the opinions of his listeners. For instance, an agent explained that one of the experts occasionally discussed a case with him: "He mentions a problem once in a while, because he finds it interesting. I'm sure that he's not going to ask *my* opinion. Usually, you don't want the opinion of somebody else in these discussions. What you're doing is thinking out loud." Even when no advice was expected and none was given, these presentations of complex cases assisted the speaker in solving his problems. They were consultations in disguise.

Making decisions in an investigation involved the co-ordination of many pieces of information, the selection of the appropriate regulations from a large body of such regulations, and the appraisal of the specific data in terms of these legal principles. Anxiety resulted in "blocking" of ideas and associations, which increased the difficulties inherent in this intellectual process. The agent who attempted to arrive at decisions while sitting alone at his desk defined the situation as preparing the case for submission to the supervisor. His anxiety, engendered by the supervisor's evaluation of his decisions, interfered most with clear thinking in this situation. Instead of trying to make important official decisions, an agent could discuss the interesting aspects of his case with one of his colleagues. This situation, defined as a discussion among friends, did not evoke anxiety. On the contrary, it destroyed the anxiety that pervaded the decision-making process.

The listener was not merely a friend but a fellow-specialist in solving the problems that occurred in investigations. This created the possibility of interruption, if the suggested interpretation required correction. A listener might remind the speaker that he forgot to take some factor into account or that the data lend themselves to alternative conclusions. The assent implicit in the absence of interruptions and in attentive listening destroyed the doubts that continuously arose in the process of making many minor decisions in order to arrive at a conclusion. The admiration for the clever solution of the problem advanced, expressed the speaker's confidence in his partial solutions while groping for the final one. By reducing his anxiety, "thinking out loud" enabled an official to associate relevant pieces of information and pertinent regulations and thus arrive at decisions which he might not have thought of while alone.

These discussions of problems were functional substitutes for consultations. They served the same functions for the discussant without having the same disadvantages for him. An explanation of a complex case did not violate the rule against asking other agents for advice, and it did not threaten the speaker's prestige or his self-confidence. In contrast to asking a question, presenting an interesting discussion *enhanced* the respect of his colleagues for an agent. Of course, this was the case only if his conclusions were correct; presenting false conclusions that were corrected by his listeners hurt an agent's standing in the group. Agents who were not confident of their abilities, therefore, did not feel so free as experts to present their own solutions of problems. Besides, experts more often worked on intricate cases with unusual problems that others found interesting. Consequently, they, the very agents most reluctant to admit ignorance by asking for advice, were in the best position to use this substitute for consultations.

The recognition of both participants in a consultation that one provided an intellectual service to the other raised the status of the consultant and subordinated or obligated the questioner to him. These were the inducements for the consultant to give advice and, simultaneously, the cost incurred by the questioner for receiving it. Discussions of interesting problems, on the other hand, were not recognized as providing a service to the speaker, and he did not start them because he experienced a need for *advice*. Manifestly, both he and the listeners, who sometimes commented, participated in these discussions because they were stimulating. The fact that they facilitated his solving of problems was disguised from the speaker as well as from his listeners; this was a latent function of such discussions.

In the absence of awareness that a service was furnished, no need existed for the speaker to reciprocate for the help he did, in fact, obtain. He did not subordinate or obligate himself to listeners. Such inducements were unnecessary for finding an audience, since interest in the problem and its solution supplied sufficient motivation for listening. This constituted the major advantage of consultations in disguise over direct consultations. We find . . . that the extraneous factors that motivate an interaction pattern that is *not intended* to, but does, fulfil a given function make it more efficient than a different pattern *intended* to fulfil this same function. Only a service intentionally rendered creates obligations, which make it costly. . . .

The practice of consulting co-workers, directly or in disguised form, served social, as well as psychological, functions. First, it transformed an aggregate of individuals who happened to have the same supervisor into a cohesive group. The recurrent experience of being dependent on the group, whose members furnished needed help, and of being appreciated by the others in the group, as indicated by their solicitations for assistance, created strong mutual bonds. Requests for information, which were indiscriminately made of any agent near by, permitted all agents, even the least competent ones, to experience being needed by several other members of the department. Social cohesion, in turn, contributed to operations in a variety of ways. . . .

Second, consultation among colleagues made more effective law enforcement possible because it improved the quality of the decisions of agents. Every agent knew that he could obtain help with solving problems whenever he needed it. This knowledge, reinforced by the feeling of being an integrated member of a cohesive group, decreased anxiety about making decisions. Simultaneously, being often approached for advice raised the self-confidence of an investigator. The very existence of this practice enhanced the ability of all agents, experts as well as others, to make decisions independently, even when they were alone in the field.

Third, discussions of problems increased the agent's interest in his work and his knowledge about it. They provided, not only opportunities for learning, from the examples of experts, how intricate problems can be solved, but also incentives for becoming more skilful in this task, since the presentation of an ingenious solution raised an agent's standing in the group. These stimulating discussions, moreover, contributed to the great interest that agents took in their work and their professional pride in being responsible for such complex duties. Most federal officials, in contrast to those in the state agency, considered the interesting and important nature of their tasks the most attractive feature of their job. Such work satisfaction furnishes inducements for exerting greater efforts. Its existence, and that of social cohesion, are perhaps particularly important for the American civil servant, who does not enjoy the emoluments of high status and authority that fortify the *esprit de corps* of his European counterpart, the *Herr Geheimrat*.

Fourth, the pattern of consultations stabilized the relationships among the members of the department and forestalled conflict. It gave agents accurate knowledge of the differences in proficiency among them, as indicated by the close correspondence between his colleagues' ranking of an agent's competence and that of the supervisor, who had evaluated every case. . . . Besides, officials *socially* acknowledged the superior ability of others in the process of asking for advice and in the course of listening admiringly, sometimes in a small group, to presentations of clever solutions of problems. This reduced the chances of friction when agents were differently rewarded for their performance. A high rating, or even a promotion, was less likely to create resentment against the supervisor or the agent involved, since his superior competence had been socially recognized in advance. Indeed, promotion expectations in this department were most realistic. Only two agents expected to become supervisors within ten years, the same ones who were considered to be the two most competent members of Department Y by all co-workers and by the supervisor.

The mechanisms through which these functions were fulfilled also entailed dysfunctions. Thus this pattern of interaction tended to reinforce competence differentials in the process of making them known. The high esteem of agents frequently consulted reinforced their self-confidence as investigators at the expense of lessened self-confidence on the part of others. Furthermore, by creating social cohesion, this pattern also generated resistance to the frequent transfers of personnel from one department to another. Agents disliked being transferred because they felt loyal to their departmental group and because it required adaptation to new consultation relationships. Finally, this practice weakened the authority of the supervisor. It decreased not only the frequency with which agents consulted him but also their respect for his judgment, which they compared unfavorably with that of their most competent colleagues. The comment of one agent is typical: "If you can't get an answer from [either one of two agents], the likelihood of getting an answer from any supervisor is remote." It is quite possible that the anxiety evoked by consulting the supervisor, and its absence in consultations with colleagues, produced a bias in favor of the advice received from peers. In any case, the fact that his judgment did not command their full respect diminished the supervisor's control over subordinates and made it more difficult for him to discharge his responsibilities. . . .

UNOFFICIAL NORMS

Statistical records of performance enabled the supervisor in Department Y to set production quotas for his subordinates. He expected every agent to complete eight cases a month, to find violations in half of them, and to obtain the employer's agreement to make voluntary adjustments in at least two-thirds of these. The repeated emphasis on these standards and invidious comparisons of one agent's record with those of others were intended to encourage speedy and effective work.

This method of supervision generated some competition between agents. How close they had come to meeting the production standards constituted "the prime topic of discussion," said one agent, exaggerating somewhat; and another confirmed this in principle: "That's what you usually talk about when you're kidding. For example, one month I had *nine* cases. [Simon] was kidding me about it."

This remark indicates the existence of unofficial norms that curbed competitive tendencies. Officials who produced too much were warned by being teased. If one did not heed this warning and persistently exceeded the group's limits, he was ostracized. These norms induced agents, who had strong incentives to perform well, to conceal their accomplishments from colleagues, as one of them noted:

All agents tend to run themselves down, I've found out. . . .
(What do you mean?) They try to make themselves appear less good than they are. . . . I may say that out of eight cases this month, I [obtained agreements for voluntary adjustments] in four, and he'll say, "*Really?!*" Now, he may have just as many or more than I do, and just say this to make me feel good. That's what I mean when I say, the agents run themselves down.

A highly competent agent admitted that he underemphasized the quality of his performance in his discussions with co-workers:

There's the tendency to tone down the amount of work you've done.
I know I do. You don't want to seem like an eager beaver.

(How do you do this?) There's a tendency to play up the poorer
aspects of your work, and to keep quiet about the better ones. If I have
several cases in a row where I don't find anything, I'll mention that.

Agents were ambivalent about their own productivity standards,
but they were in unequivocal agreement concerning other unofficial norms, notably the taboo on reporting offers of bribes. . . .

STANDARDS OF PRODUCTIVITY AMONG WHITE-COLLAR WORKERS

. . . [T]he agents in Department Y hardly competed with one
another at all. . . . [T]he co-operative practice of consulting with
co-workers engendered a cohesive situation, which was fertile soil
for the development of social norms to check the rivalry for outstanding performance that superiors encouraged. Actually, none of
the members of Department Y exceeded the group's standards to
the extent of invoking the serious disapproval of his colleagues, although this had happened in the past, as one agent reported: "We
had some agents here for a short while who set up terrific production
standards. They worked very fast, and I don't think they did a good
job; but they set up impossible production records."

Compared with the clear-cut restrictions of output that are often
found among factory workers, however, the production standards
among agents appear vague and ineffective. Condemnation of an
individual for excessive performance was so rare because large
differences in productivity were tolerated. Furthermore, these group
norms were very elastic, as indicated by the reaction of agents
when their new supervisor raised the monthly quota from six to
eight. Despite considerable grumbling, there was no concerted effort
to sabotage the new quota. Most agents met it, and their norms adjusted themselves to it.

The effort of these white-collar workers to standardize productivity was half-hearted, at best, because they were conflicted about
it. Remaining true to type as middle-class individuals, they believed
that superior ability, ambition, and efficient performance should be
rewarded. Enforcing the laws under the agency's jurisdiction, the
objectives of which they highly approved, was considered too important a task to be discouraged. In the process of consulting, more-

over, agents had learned to respect and appreciate the proficiency of experts who willingly helped them solve difficult problems. Attitudes such as these made it well-nigh impossible to condemn excellent performance; yet social cohesion required that competitive endeavors to excel be suppressed. The solution to this dilemma was a set of unofficial norms that served not so much to restrict productivity as to freeze the established differentials in performance.

The practice of working overtime without compensation, to which some officials resorted who had trouble meeting the production quota, was generally disapproved. One agent said: "There was some discussion of an agent who took cases home to work on. It was looked upon with scorn." Four members of Department Y, all of whom had a low rating, reported in the interview that they took work home on occasion, and one added, "I don't think there is an agent who doesn't." This is unlikely, but it is quite possible that more agents than acknowledged it engaged in this practice. Since such excessive efforts were frowned upon, agents tended to conceal them from their co-workers, and probably also from the observer. It was, significantly, a trainee who had made the mistake of admitting to colleagues that he worked overtime. . . .

The less competent agents condemned this practice as unfair to the rest of the group. One of them stated: "It would make one agent look very good in comparison with the others. I don't think that's fair. Maybe he's interested in his work, or maybe he does it for selfish motives. But it puts all the other agents in a bad light." The more competent officials did not think that a member of the department put the others at a disadvantage by working overtime. Nevertheless, they, too, discouraged this practice, if only by their disrespect for those who engaged in it. This is indicated by their very similar answers, exemplified here by one, when asked, "Does this [the fact that an agent works at home] hurt the others?" "No. Only those who aren't competent tend to do this. Generally, it is only the incompetent agent who responds to this kind of pressure."

Most agents thought ill of colleagues who worked after office hours, although their standing as agents determined the form in which they expressed their disapproval. This censure of working overtime can be considered a functional equivalent of restriction of output among manual workers which was compatible with the professional orientation of these white-collar workers. Their identification with professional standards and their respect for experts did not allow agents to object to superior performance. These attitudes permitted, however, and even fostered disrespect for the person who tried to conceal his inferior ability by devoting more time to the job than was required. By discouraging agents from raising their production beyond the level that they could maintain during regular working hours, this group prevented progressive rivalry of this kind from undermining social cohesion.

The unofficial norm against working overtime minimized competitive conflicts, just as restriction of output in a factory does; but, in contrast to such standardization of productivity, it reinforced the differences in the performance of agents. It deterred those who were less skilled from devoting extra hours to their work in order to match the productivity of their more proficient colleagues. This norm, although it applied equally to all, was inequitable in its effects; it benefited particularly the expert who worked fast, since it protected his superior standing in the department.

THE TABOO ON REPORTING OFFERS OF BRIBES

Agent Croner had uncovered serious violations in a firm. The manager of this firm brought employee Smith to the agency, whose testimony was intended to show that the alleged violations had not taken place. In a cleverly conducted cross-examination, Mr. Croner forced Mr. Smith to admit that his statements were untrue and that the violations had in fact occurred. Upon leaving, Mr. Smith whispered to Mr. Croner, in a foreign language that he knew the latter understood, asking whether they could talk about this informally. Mr. Croner answered loudly in English, "No, nothing can be done; this is what the law says." Such a "feeler," more or less persistently pursued, is the typical starting point of a bribe. And such a blunt rejection usually ends the incident, despite an unequivocal rule that all offers of bribes must be reported to higher authorities for possible prosecution.

Right after this incident, the observer asked Mr. Croner what agents generally do about clients who offer bribes.

CRONER: We do what I just did. We never get bribes offered, because we usually stop it before we get an offer. [Turning to his neighbor:] Bert, come over here. [To the observer:] You don't mind if I call him over; I like him. [To the other agent:] What do you do about bribe offers, Bert?

BERT LEHMANN: Squelch it right away; you stop his talking, and that's all.

OBSERVER: That's very interesting. You never turn a man in?

LEHMANN: There's no possibility of turning a man in. It doesn't get to that point. Nobody offers you a bribe. The only thing they sometimes do is to make some vague suggestions. Then you stop it, and no bribe is offered to you. If you don't, you would have to enter into the proposition, and tell him that you're interested. For instance, once a man asked me whether we could talk it over outside. I knew what that was. So I said, "No; why should we go outside?" If somebody makes an offer like that, you would have to enter into collusion with him before you could report it. You would have to accept his suggestion, and meet him some place, and say that you will take the money. If you do that, you're just as guilty as he is.

Clients recurrently made offers of bribes, and some were quite direct, but all agents were strongly opposed to reporting such offers for prosecution, regardless of their attitudes toward clients. They not only failed to make such reports but considered it *wrong* to do so. The taboo on reporting attempted bribes was the strongest unofficial norm of the group. When the observer questioned it by asking whether prosecuting employers who tried to bribe officials would not show the public how honest civil servants are, agents became aggressive and defended the righteousness of the norm in emotional language, for example, by saying, "We don't like squealers!"

Strong mores are rarely violated. . . . [One] violator of this unofficial taboo, a member of Department Y, questioned his own wisdom in having reported the attempt at bribery. He explained that he had received such offers before but had merely discouraged them. Only the special circumstances in this case, the repeated and insistent way in which the offer had been made in the presence of third persons, had induced him to report it. He added that he would not report an offer of a bribe again under any condition—"It's too unpleasant." Even the deviant agreed with the fundamental validity of the norm.

The major reason for this agent's change of attitude was that the group had responded to his violation of an important norm by ostracizing him. One of his colleagues explained, referring to this person without naming him: "One fellow did turn in a guy once. After that, nobody in the office talked to him for a year." This was not literally true, of course, but the others confirmed that he had been ostracized. He himself said: "Nobody talked to me directly, criticizing me for it, but you can feel it if your fellow-agents disapprove of you." Several years later, this agent continued to occupy an isolated position in the group. . . .

Being offered a bribe constituted a special tactical advantage for an agent. An employer who had violated one law was caught in the act of compounding his guilt by violating another one. He could no longer claim ignorance or inadvertence as an excuse for his violation. Agents exploited this situation to strengthen their position in negotiations. This is implied by the following remark concerning offers of small sums of money: "There's no sense in turning in a man for a small thing like that. You assume the role of the judge, and tell him what's right." Such a superordinate position, created by putting the briber in his place and maintained by his fear that this incorruptible public official might report him for prosecution, made it much easier to induce him to make retroactive adjustments. Refusing but not reporting bribes enabled agents more effectively to carry out their duties, which they considered important and on the basis of which they were evaluated.

Since bribe offers helped agents in their work, there existed a perennial temptation, consciously or unconsciously, to provoke employers to make such overtures. Of course, we do not know, and neither do these agents, to what extent their attitudes invited the many offers of bribes that they, according to their own statements, received. In any case, to preserve the advantageous position into which such an offer had put an agent, he had to reject it outright rather than appear hesitant in anticipation of reporting it for prosecution.

The fact that failing to report bribes facilitated the agent's task can explain only why this was rarely done but not why there was a social norm prohibiting it. The existence of this norm suggests that this act might actually have some advantages for the actor and must therefore be proscribed if it also has disadvantages for the rest of the group. . . .

THE ENFORCEMENT OF GROUP NORMS

The unofficial norms of work groups in a bureaucratic organization are, of course, not labeled as such. Their existence is revealed only by their characteristics, which may be briefly summarized:

1. *Acceptance by all members of the group,* regardless of differences in attitudes on related subjects. Some agents were very friendly, and others were stern or domineering, toward clients; some refused even the offer of a cigar, and others considered the acceptance of small favors, such as invitations to lunch, legitimate; but they all condemned the reporting of bribes. Even the violator of the taboo agreed with it in principle, and explained his violation as resulting from exceptional circumstances. (For less basic norms, this agreement existed only on the verbal level, and agents tried to hide their violations from colleagues.)

2. *Endeavors to conceal violations,* since they are considered to be shameful, not only from other members of the group, but also from outsiders; indeed, in this case, the reticence extends to violations of colleagues. Several agents refused to talk to the observer about the cases in which bribes had been reported, and most of the others did not mention the names of the two officials who had made the reports. Typically, it was the badly integrated official who named violators of norms. The counterpart of this concealment, stemming from the same assumption of the intrinsic shamefulness of these acts, is the use of the statement that a person has committed such an act as a deliberate insult. Thus an agent climaxed his derogatory remarks about a colleague by saying that he had even "denounced an employer" who had offered him a bribe.

3. *Questioning provokes hostility* and emotional reactions. Many agents became resentful or aggressive when the observer asked why bribes are not reported, and defended the taboo with irrational phrases, such as "We don't like squealers."

4. *Myths develop* with the theme that it is advantageous to conform. For example: "I'll tell you of one case. . . . He did exactly what you say. He went into a bar with a guy who had promised him money. He was supposed to give it to him in the bar. Then the F.B.I. came in, and they actually came in just like in the movies: the sirens were blasting. They happened to be late, and could only get there on time by using their sirens. And they came in with their guns, asking, 'Who is offering a bribe here?' By that time, the client had said, 'Excuse me, I have to go to the washroom,' and left the place. You know what happened? The F.B.I. didn't say it had made a mistake. It wrote to the [commissioner] telling him that the agent had handled the case badly. So, you can get into all kinds of trouble if you turn a man in."

5. *Ostracism is the penalty* only for violations of the most basic norms. Since the agent who had reported a bribe was cold-shouldered, none of the other members of Department Y made such reports, despite demands from superiors to do so. This one violation had provided the group with an opportunity to demonstrate to potential deviants the dire consequences of disobedience, and thus to assure conformity. . . .

Ostracism is only the most extreme form of a much more frequent phenomenon: a reduction in the degree of friendliness with which one person treats another, an almost automatic reaction to an associate's behavior that arouses one's displeasure. . . .

In addition to these sanctions, which found largely inadvertent expression in daily interaction, there also existed *specific* social sanctions for deviant behavior, such as ridiculing an agent, shaming him, or manifesting aggression in other forms. The departmental meeting or any other gathering of several officials provided an opportunity for punishing a deviant. Pair relationships usually were transformed into group situations before an individual who had violated a norm was penalized. For instance, when an agent asked a colleague to do him a favor, he was refused with the words, "Why ask me? There are lots of good men around. Ask them!" The first agent merely turned away in disgust. However, two others, who had overheard this exchange, called across the room, "Yes, but you're the best one" and "You asked the right man!" Now, the agent who had made the request turned back and joined several others in laughing at the culprit, who remained silent. The penalty for lack of co-operation—sarcasm and laughter—had not been administered so long as only one person confronted the deviant.

Specific sanctions were typically administered in group situations and not in the relative privacy of the pair relationship. . . .

Interactions of this type provide an individual who has violated a taboo with a brief but concentrated experience of what it is like to be ostracized. Two agents showed the observer that his opinions conflicted with theirs and rejected him, by making aggressive remarks, for this reason. Simultaneously, they presented him, through their agreement, with a demonstration of the desirability of being accepted by others. Even the observer, not a genuine part of the group, found this disconcerting. If several colleagues treated a member of the departmental group in this way—for example, by laughing together at aggressive remarks directed against him—he was momentarily put into the worst state of anomie: being alone and feeling disoriented, while witnessing the cohesiveness of others. This threat constituted a strong inducement to surrender unorthodox opinions and to cease deviant practices. . . .

Social sanctions were administered not only when a member of the group violated a norm but in the case of some individuals much more frequently. The fact that deviants are more often the subject of the group's aggression than their conduct warrants is well known; this is, after all, what is generally meant by a "scapegoat." One isolate in Department Y, in particular, could scarcely make a remark in the presence of several colleagues without being ridiculed or reprimanded. When he gave an earnest explanation, the others found reasons to laugh at him; when he made a joke about something, he was seriously told that this was no laughing matter. But his statements were neither so funny nor so tasteless as they were made out to be.

The isolate's continued presence in the group was a constant threat to the authority of its norms. His isolated position often prevented the group from penalizing his deviant acts. Since the others rarely included him in their informal gatherings, there was usually no occasion to administer specific social sanctions immediately after he had violated a norm. Neither could they become much less friendly toward an individual with whom they had only few and superficial contacts. The fact that the isolate's deviant action often went unpunished helps to explain his great tendency to violate group standards and also the frequent aggression of others against him. In the opinion of his colleagues, such an individual deserved, at all times, more punishment than he had actually received. Consequently, they seized every opportunity that presented itself to penalize the isolate. . . .

the economy
of incentives

chester i. barnard

It has already been demonstrated that an essential element of organizations is the willingness of persons to contribute their individual efforts to the cooperative system. The power of cooperation, which is often spectacularly great when contrasted with that even of large numbers of individuals unorganized, is nevertheless dependent upon the willingness of individuals to cooperate and to contribute their efforts to the cooperative system. The contributions of personal efforts which constitute the energies of organizations are yielded by individuals because of incentives. The egotistical motives of self-preservation and of self-satisfaction are dominating forces; on the whole, organizations can exist only when consistent with the satisfaction of these motives, unless, alternatively, they can change these motives. The individual is always the basic strategic factor in organization. Regardless of his history or his obligations he must be induced to cooperate, or there can be no cooperation.

It needs no further introduction to suggest that the subject of incentives is fundamental in formal organizations and in conscious efforts to organize. Inadequate incentives mean dissolution, or changes of organization purpose, or failure of cooperation. Hence, in

Chapter IX. Reprinted by permission of the publishers from Chester I. Barnard, The Functions of the Executive, *Cambridge, Mass.: Harvard University Press, Copyright, 1938, 1968, by the President and Fellows of Harvard College; 1966 by Grace F. Noera Barnard.*

all sorts of organizations the affording of adequate incentives becomes the most definitely emphasized task in their existence. It is
probably in this aspect of executive work that failure is most pro-
nounced, though the causes may be due either to inadequate understanding or to the breakdown of the effectiveness of organization.

I

The net satisfactions which induce a man to contribute his efforts
to an organization result from the positive advantages as against the
disadvantages which are entailed. It follows that a net advantage
may be increased or a negative advantage made positive either by
increasing the number or the strength of the positive inducements
or by reducing the number or the strength of the disadvantages. It
often occurs that the positive advantages are few and meager, but
the burdens involved are also negligible, so that there is a strong net
advantage. Many "social" organizations are able to exist under such
a state of affairs. Conversely, when the burdens involved are numerous or heavy, the offsetting positive advantages must be either
numerous or powerful.

Hence, from the viewpoint of the organization requiring or seeking contributions from individuals, the problem of effective incentives may be either one of finding positive incentives or of reducing
or eliminating negative incentives or burdens. For example, employment may be made attractive either by reducing the work
required—say, by shortening hours or supplying tools or power,
that is, by making conditions of employment less onerous—or by
increasing positive inducement, such as wages.

In practice, although there are many cases where it is clear which
side of the "equation" is being adjusted, on the whole specific practices and conditions affect both sides simultaneously or it is impossible to determine which they affect. Most specific factors in
so-called working conditions may be viewed either as making employment positively attractive or as making work less onerous. We
shall, therefore, make no attempt to treat specific inducements as
increasing advantages or as decreasing disadvantages; but this
underlying aspect is to be kept in mind.

More important than this is the distinction between the objective
and the subjective aspects of incentives. Certain common positive
incentives, such as material goods and in some senses money, clearly

have an objective existence; and this is true also of negative incentives like working hours, conditions of work. Given a man of a certain state of mind, of certain attitudes, or governed by certain motives, he can be induced to contribute to an organization by a given combination of these objective incentives, positive or negative. It often is the case, however, that the organization is unable to offer objective incentives that will serve as an inducement to that state of mind, or to those attitudes, or to one governed by those motives. The only alternative then available is to change the state of mind, or attitudes, or motives, so that the available objective incentives can become effective.

An organization can secure the efforts necessary to its existence, then, either by the objective inducements it provides or by changing states of mind. It seems to me improbable that any organization can exist as a practical matter which does not employ both methods in combination. In some organizations the emphasis is on the offering of objective incentives—this is true of most industrial organizations. In others the preponderance is on the state of mind—this is true of most patriotic and religious organizations.

We shall call the processes of offering objective incentives "the method of incentives"; and the processes of changing subjective attitudes "the method of persuasion." Using these new terms, let us repeat what we have said: In commercial organizations the professed emphasis is apparently almost wholly on the side of the method of incentives. In religious and political organizations the professed emphasis is apparently almost wholly on the side of persuasion. But in fact, especially if account be taken of the different kinds of contributions required from different individuals, both methods are used in all types of organizations. Moreover, the centrifugal forces of individualism and the competition between organizations for individual contributions result in both methods being ineffective, with few exceptions, for more than short periods or a few years.

I. The Method of Incentives

We shall first discuss the method of incentives. It will facilitate our consideration of the subject if at the outset we distinguish two classes of incentives; first those that are specific and can be specifically offered to an individual; and second, those that are general, not personal, that cannot be specifically offered. We shall call the first class specific inducements, the second general incentives.

The specific inducements that may be offered are of several classes, for example: (a) material inducements; (b) personal non-material opportunities; (c) desirable physical conditions; (d) ideal benefactions. General incentives afforded are, for example: (e) associational attractiveness; (f) adaptation of conditions to habitual methods and attitudes; (g) the opportunity of enlarged participation; (h) the condition of communion. Each of these classes of incentives is known under various names, and the list does not purport to be complete, since our purpose now is illustrative. But to accomplish this purpose it is necessary briefly to discuss the incentives named.

(a) Material inducements are money, things, or physical conditions that are offered to the individual as inducements to accepting employment, compensation for service, reward for contribution. Under a money economy and the highly specialized production of material goods, the range and profusion of material inducements are very great. The complexity of schedules of money compensation, the difficulty of securing the monetary means of compensation, and the power of exchange which money gives in organized markets, have served to exaggerate the importance of money in particular and material inducements in general as incentives to personal contributions to organized effort. It goes without elaboration that where a large part of the time of an individual is devoted to one organization, the physiological necessities—food, shelter, clothing—require that material inducements should be present in most cases; but these requirements are so limited that they are satisfied with small quantities. The unaided power of material incentives, when the minimum necessities are satisfied, in my opinion is exceedingly limited as to most men, depending almost entirely for its development upon persuasion. Notwithstanding the great emphasis upon material incentives in modern times and especially in current affairs, there is no doubt in my mind that, unaided by other motives, they constitute weak incentives beyond the level of the bare physiological necessities.

To many this view will not be readily acceptable. The emphasis upon material rewards has been a natural result of the success of technological developments—relative to other incentives it is the material things which have been progressively easier to produce, and therefore to offer. Hence there has been a forced cultivation of the love of material things among those above the level of subsistence. Since existing incentives seem always inadequate to the degree of cooperation and of social integration theoretically possible and ideally desirable, the success of the sciences and the arts of material production would have been partly ineffective, and in turn would have been partly impossible, without inculcating the desire of the material. The most significant result of this situation has been the expansion of population, most of which has been necessarily at the bare subsistence level, at which level material inducements are, on the whole, powerful incentives. This has perpetuated the illusion that beyond this subsistence level material incentives are also the most effective.

A concurrent result has been the creation of sentiments in individuals that they *ought* to want material things. The inculcation of "proper" ambitions in youth have greatly stressed material possessions as an evidence of good citizenship, social adequacy, etc. Hence, when underlying and governing motives have not been satisfied, there has been strong influence to rationalize the default as one of material compensation, and not to be conscious of the controlling motives or at least not to admit them.

Yet it seems to me to be a matter of common experience that material rewards are ineffective beyond the subsistence level excepting to a very limited proportion of men; that most men neither work harder for more material things, nor can be induced thereby to devote more than a fraction of their possible contribution to organized effort. It is likewise a matter of both present experience and past history that many of the most effective and powerful organizations are built up on incentives in which the materialistic elements, above bare subsistence, are either relatively lacking or absolutely absent. Military organizations have been relatively lacking in material incentives. The greater part of the work of political organizations is without material incentive. Religious organizations are characterized on the whole by material sacrifice. It seems to me to be definitely a general fact that even in purely commercial organizations material incentives are so weak as to be almost negligible except when reinforced by other incentives, and then only because of wholesale general persuasion in the form of salesmanship and advertising.

It will be noted that the reference has been to material incentives rather than to money. What has been said requires some, but not great, qualification with reference to money as an incentive—solely for the reason that money in our economy may be used as the indirect means of satisfying non-materialistic motives—philanthropic, artistic, intellectual, and religious motives for example—and because money income becomes an index of social status, personal development, etc.

(b) Inducements of a personal, non-materialistic character are of great importance to secure cooperative effort above the minimum material rewards essential to subsistence. The opportunities for distinction, prestige, personal power, and the attainment of dominating position are much more important than material rewards in the development of all sorts of organizations, including commercial organizations. In various ways this fact applies to many types of human beings, including those of limited ability and children. Even in strictly commercial organizations, where it is least supposed to be true, money without distinction, prestige, position, is so utterly ineffective that it is rare that greater income can be made to serve even temporarily as an inducement if accompanied by suppression of prestige. At least for short periods inferior material rewards are often accepted if assurance of distinction is present; and usually the presumption is that material rewards ought to follow or arise from or even are made necessary by the attainment of distinction and prestige. There is unlimited experience to show that among many men, and especially among women, the real value of differences of money rewards lies in the recognition or distinction assumed to be conferred thereby, or to be procured therewith—one of the reasons why differentials either in money income or in material possessions are a source of jealousy and disruption if not accompanied by other factors of distinction.

(c) Desirable physical conditions of work are often important conscious, and more often important unconscious, inducements to cooperation.

(d) Ideal benefactions as inducements to cooperation are among the most powerful and the most neglected. By ideal benefaction I mean the capacity of organizations to satisfy personal ideals usually relating to non-material, future, or altruistic relations. They include pride of workmanship, sense of adequacy, altruistic service for family or others, loyalty to organization in patriotism, etc., aesthetic and religious feeling. They also include the opportunities for the satisfaction of the motives of hate and revenge, often the controlling factor in adherence to and intensity of effort in some organizations.

All of these inducements—material rewards, personal non-material opportunities, desirable physical conditions, and ideal benefactions—may be and frequently are definitely offered as inducements to contribute to organizations. But there are other conditions which cannot usually be definitely offered, and which are known or recognized by their absence in particular cases. Of these I consider associational attractiveness as exceedingly, and often critically, important.

(e) By associational attractiveness I mean social compatibility. It is in many cases obvious that racial hostility, class antagonism, and national enmities absolutely prevent cooperation, in others decrease its effectiveness, and in still others make it impossible to secure cooperation except by great strengthening of other incentives. But it seems clear that the question of personal compatibility or incompatibility is much more far-reaching in limiting cooperative effort than is recognized, because an intimate knowledge of particular organizations is usually necessary to understand its precise character. When such an intimate knowledge exists, personal compatibility or incompatibility is so thoroughly sensed, and the related problems are so difficult to deal with, that only in special or critical cases is conscious attention given to them. But they can be neglected only at peril of disruption. Men often will not work at all, and will rarely work well, under other incentives if the social situation *from their point of view* is unsatisfactory. Thus often men of inferior education cannot work well with those of superior education, and vice versa. Differences not merely of race, nation, religion, but of customs, morals, social status, education, ambition, are frequently controlling. Hence, a powerful incentive to the effort of almost all men is favorable associational conditions from their viewpoint.

Personal aversions based upon racial, national, color, and class differences often seem distinctly pernicious; but on the whole they are, in the immediate sense, I believe, based upon a sound feeling of organization necessities. For when there is incompatibility or even merely lack of compatibility, both formal communication and especially communication through informal organization become difficult and sometimes impossible.

(f) Another incentive of the general type is that of customary working conditions and conformity to habitual practices and attitudes. This is made obvious by the universal practice, in all kinds of organization, of rejecting recruits trained in different methods or possessing "foreign" attitudes. It is taken for granted that men will not or cannot do well by strange methods or under strange conditions. What is not so obvious is that men will frequently not attempt to cooperate if they recognize that such methods or conditions are to be accepted.

(g) Another indirect incentive that we may regard as of general and often of controlling importance is the opportunity for the feeling of enlarged participation in the course of events. It affects all classes of men under some conditions. It is sometimes, though not necessarily, related to love of personal distinction and prestige. Its realization is the feeling of importance of result of effort because of the importance of the cooperative effort as a whole. Thus, *other things being equal,* many men prefer association with large organizations, organizations which they regard as useful, or organizations they regard as effective, as against those they consider small, useless, ineffective.

(h) The most intangible and subtle of incentives is that which I have called the condition of communion. It is related to social compatibility, but is essentially different. It is the feeling of personal comfort in social relations that is sometimes called solidarity, social integration, the gregarious instinct, or social security (in the original, not in its present debased economic, sense). It is the opportunity for comradeship, for mutual support in personal attitudes. The need for communion is a basis of informal organization that is essential to the operation of every formal organization. It is likewise the basis for informal organization within but hostile to formal organization.

It is unnecessary for our purpose to exhaust the list of inducements and incentives to cooperative contributions of individuals to organization. Enough has been said to suggest that the subject of incentives is important and complex when viewed in its objective aspects. One fact of interest now is that different men are moved by different incentives or combinations of incentives, and by different incentives or combinations at different times. Men are unstable in their desires, a fact partly reflecting the instability of their environments. A second fact is that organizations are probably never able to offer *all* the incentives that move men to cooperative effort, and are usually unable to offer adequate incentives. To the reasons for this fact we shall advert later; but a result of it to which we shall turn our attention now is the necessity of persuasion.

II. The Method of Persuasion

If an organization is unable to afford incentives adequate to the personal contributions it requires it will perish unless it can by persuasion so change the desires of enough men that the incentives it can offer will be adequate. Persuasion in the broad sense in which I am here using the word includes: (a) the creation of coercive conditions; (b) the rationalization of opportunity; (c) the inculcation of motives.

(a) Coercion is employed both to exclude and to secure the contribution of individuals to an organization. Exclusion is often intended to be exclusion permanently and nothing more. It is an aspect of competition or hostility between organizations or between organizations and individuals with which we shall not further be concerned, except to note that exclusion of undesirables is a necessary method of maintaining organization efficiency. But forced exclusion is also employed as a means of persuasion *by example,* to create fear among those not directly affected, so that they will be disposed to render to an organization certain contributions. It presents realistically the alternative either of making these contributions or of foregoing the advantages of association. The grades of exclusion are numerous, beginning with homicide, outlawing, ostracism, corporal punishment, incarceration, withholding of specific benefits, discharge, etc.

Contributions secured by force seem to have been often a necessary process of cooperation. Thus slavery is the creation of conditions by force under which bare subsistence and protection are made sufficient incentives to give certain contributions to the organization; although often it has been the result of conditions not purposely created, that is, slavery has been sometimes a voluntary means to being admitted to benefits of cooperation otherwise withheld. However, usually slavery is evidence of an unstable efficiency, except when it can be combined with other incentives (as in forced military service). But it has undoubtedly often been an effective process of persuasion to those not directly affected. Those who observe homicide, ostracism, outlawing, incarceration, discharge, and other expressions of the power of organizations to persuade by force have unquestionably been affected in their views of the adequacy of offered incentives. Nevertheless, I suppose it is generally accepted that no superior permanent or very complex system of cooperation can be supported to a great extent merely by coercion.

(b) The rationalization of opportunity is a method of persuasion of much greater importance in most modern activities. Even under political and economic regimes in which coercion of individuals is at least temporarily and in some degree the basic process of persuasion, as in Russia, Germany, and Italy, it is observed that the processes of rationalization of other incentives, that is, propaganda, are carried on more extensively than anywhere else.

The rationalization of incentives occurs in two degrees; the general rationalization that is an expression of social organization as a whole and has chiefly occurred in connection with religious and political organizations, and the specific rationalization that consists in attempting to convince individuals or groups that they "ought," "it is to their interest," to perform services or conform to requirements of specific organizations.

The general rationalization of incentives on a noteworthy scale has occurred many times. The rationalization of religious motives as a basis of the Crusades is one of the most striking. The rationalization of communist doctrine in Russia is another. The rationalization of hate as a means of increasing organization (national) "solidarity" is well known. One of the most interesting of these general rationalizations is that of materialistic progress, to which we have already referred. It is an important basis of the characteristic forms of modern western organization. In its most general form it consists in the cult of science as a means to material ends, the glorification of inventions and inventive talent, including patent legislation; and the exaltation of the exploitation of land, forests, mineral resources, and of the means of transportation. In its more obvious current forms it consists in extensive and intensive salesmanship, advertising, and propaganda concerning the satisfactions to be had from the use of material products.

It is the pleasure of many idealists to decry this rationalization of the material. If materialism is to be made an incentive to cooperation as an alternative to other incentives, there is grave reason to question its social value except as it may be the process whereby many millions are enabled to survive and live on a bare subsistence level who otherwise would have perished. But if it is regarded as in the nature of making an *additional* incentive effective, with the result of more effective social cooperation, its justification is not, in my opinion, questionable. It is then the process by which, to use current economic phraseology, purchasing power in material things and services is created. In everyday language, people will not work for what they are not convinced is "worth while"; if the conviction that material things are worth while detracts from other non-material things as incentives it may be harmful; but if it succeeds in capturing waste[d] effort or wasted time or in minimizing harmful incentives, such as hate, it is clearly advantageous.

Specific rationalization of incentives is the process of personal appeal to "join" an organization, to accept a job or position, to undertake a service, to contribute to a cause. It is the process of proselyting or recruiting that is commonly observed in connection with industrial, military, political, and religious organizations. It consists in emphasizing opportunities for satisfaction that are offered, usually in contrast with those available otherwise; and in attempting to elicit interest in those incentives which are most easily or most outstandingly afforded.

The background of the individual to whom incentives are rationalized consists of his physiological requirements, his geographical and social location, and the general rationalization and especially the social influences to which he has previously been subjected by his society, his government, and his church.

Thus specific rationalization is concerned usually with a small marginal area of choice and with competition. This background differs so widely among individuals that at any given time only a few individuals are deemed to be within range of specific rationalization; and for those that are within that range there are wide differences in the composition of incentives that will be effective.

(c) The form of persuasion that is most important is the inculcation of motives. In its formal aspects this is a process of deliberate education of the young, and propaganda for adults. Thus the persuasion of religious incentives, except at comparatively infrequent intervals, is chiefly accomplished by religious instruction of children. Similarly, the inculcation of ideas of patriotism and much of the other incentives to cooperation are a part of the family and general educational process.

Associated with these formal processes are those which are informal and indirect. Precept, example, suggestion, imitation and emulation, habitual attitudes, chiefly condition the motives and the emotional response of individuals to incentives. These are the controlling and fundamental conditions of whole peoples and of groups and classes with respect to the power of incentives. They furnish the greatest limitations to which organizations must adapt their processes both of offering incentives and of persuading individuals.

This brief discussion of the incentives has been a necessary introduction to the considerations that are important to our study of the subject of organization and the executive functions. The processes concerned are each of them difficult in themselves, and are subject to highly developed techniques and skills. Their importance as a whole arises from the inherent difficulty that organizations experience either in supplying incentives or in exercising persuasion. The most appropriate phrase to apply to this inherent difficulty is "economy of incentives"; but it should be understood that "economy" is used in a broad sense and refers not merely to material or monetary economy.

II

In the economy of incentives we are concerned with the net effects of the income and outgo of things resulting from the production of objective incentives and the exercise of persuasion. An organization which makes material things the principal incentive will be unable long to offer this kind of incentive if it is unable to secure at least as much material or money as it pays out. This is the ordinary economic aspect which is well understood. But the same principle applies to other incentives. The possibilities of offering non-material opportunities, desirable conditions, ideal benefactions, desirable associations, stability of practice, enlarged participation, or communion advantages are limited and usually insufficient, so that the utmost economy is ordinarily essential not only in the material sense but in the broader sense as well. The limitations are not alone due to the relationship of the organization to the external physical environment, but also to its relationship to the social environment, and to its internal efficiency.

A complete exposition of the economy of incentives would among other things involve some duplication of the theories of general economics, rewritten from the point of view of organization. This is not the place to attempt such an exposition; but as the economy of incentives as a whole in terms of organization is not usually stressed in economic theory and is certainly not well understood, I shall attempt to indicate the outlines of the theory. It will be convenient to do this with reference to organizations of three radically different purposes: (a) an industrial organization; (b) a political organization; and (c) a religious organization.

(a) In an industrial organization the purpose is the production of material goods, or services. For the sake of simplicity we may assume that it requires no capital. It secures material production by applying the energies of men to the physical environment. These energies will result in a gross production; but if the inducements offered to secure these energies are themselves material; and are sufficient, then it will pay out of its production something on this account. If the amount paid out is no more than the production the organization can survive; but if the amount paid out is more than the production, it must cease, since it cannot then continue to offer inducements.

Whether this occurs depends upon the combined effect of four factors; the difficulties of the environment, the effectiveness of organization effort, the internal efficiency of organization, and the amount of inducements paid. Obviously many cooperative efforts fail because the environment is too resistant, others because the organization is ineffective, others because internal losses are large, others because the price paid for services is too large. Within the range of ordinary experience, these are mutually dependent variables, or mutually interacting factors. Under very favorable environmental conditions, relative ineffectiveness and relative internal inefficiency with high outgo for inducements are possible. Under unfavorable conditions, effectiveness, efficiency, and low inducements are necessary.

In most cases the limitations of conditions, of effectiveness, and of efficiency permit only limited material inducements; and both effectiveness and efficiency require an output of individual energies that cannot be elicited from most men by material inducements in any event. Hence, in practice other inducements also must be offered. But in such an organization such inducements in some degree, and usually to a considerable degree, require again material inducements. Thus, satisfactory physical conditions of work mean material inducements to factors not directly productive; satisfactory social conditions mean the rejection of some of those best able to contribute to the material production and acceptance of some less able. Almost every type of incentive that can be, or is, necessary will itself in some degree call for material outgo, so that the question is one of choice of methods and degree of emphasis upon different incentives to find the most efficient combination of incentives determined from the material viewpoint. Hence, the various incentives are in competition with each other even from the material point of view.

But the economy of incentives in an industrial organization only begins with the analysis of incentives from the standpoint of material; that is, dollars and cents, costs. The non-material incentives often conflict with each other or are incompatible. Thus opportunity for personal prestige as an incentive for one person necessarily involves a relative depression of others; so that if this incentive is emphasized as to one person, it must be in conjunction with other persons to whom personal prestige is relatively an unimportant inducement.

The difficulties of finding the workable balance of incentives is so great that recourse must be had to persuasion. But persuasion in connection with an industrial effort itself involves material outgo. Thus if coercion is the available method of persuasion, the maintenance of force for this purpose is involved; and if the contribution that can be secured by coercion is limited, as it usually is, except for short periods, the cost of coercion exceeds its effect. The limited efficiencies of slavery systems is an example.

If the method of persuasion is rationalization, either in the form of general propaganda or that of specific argument to individuals (including processes of "selection"), again the overhead cost is usually not negligible. When the general social conditioning is favorable, of course, it is a windfall like favorable physical environment.

(b) A political organization is not ordinarily productive in the materialistic sense. The motives which lie at its roots are ideal benefactions and community satisfactions. Such organizations appear not to survive long unless they can afford these incentives; yet it is obvious that every extensive political organization requires the use of "inferior" incentives. Of these, opportunity for personal prestige and material rewards are most prominent. Hence the necessity, under all forms of political organization, for obtaining great supplies of material inducements for use either in the form of direct payments or of "paying jobs." Accordingly, a striking characteristic of political organizations has been the necessity for securing material contributions from "members" either to capture the opportunities to secure additional material (through taxation) or for direct payment (as in campaigns). But here again the balancing of incentives is necessary. For the limitations of material resources, the impossibility of giving more than is received, the discrimination between recipients as respects either material benefits or prestige granted, all tend either to destroy the vital idealism upon which political organization is based or to minimize the *general* material advantages which are perhaps an alternative basis of political organization in many cases.

It is hardly necessary to add that persuasion in its many forms is an important aspect of political recruiting—and that much of the material expenditure goes for this purpose; but this thereby decreases the material available as an incentive to intensive efforts of the "faithful."

(c) In religious organizations the predominant incentives appear to be ideal benefactions and the communion of "kindred spirits," although inferior incentives no doubt often are effective. The fundamental contributions required of members are intensity of faith and loyalty to organization. A most important effort of religious organizations has been persuasion, known as missionary or proselyting effort. But both the maintenance of organization and missionary effort (and coercion when this is used) require material means, so that superficially, and often primarily, members are required by various methods to make material contributions to permit great material expenditures. The material aspects of religious organizations have been often prominent and always inescapable. As a result, the combination and adjustment of incentives in religious organizations appear even more delicate and difficult to administer than in political, military, or industrial organizations. Consider, for example, the conflict between sacrifice by individuals on one hand as a means of intensifying faith and loyalty—which it does in many cases—and sacrifice as a deterrent to adherence and membership, and the resulting dilemma as respects both quality and numbers of communicants. Or the necessity for prestige and display—which are both individual and group incentives—and humility, which is a contrary ideal benefaction.

It will be evident, perhaps, without more elaborate illustration, that in every type of organization, for whatever purpose, several incentives are necessary, and some degree of persuasion likewise, in order to secure and maintain the contributions to organization that are required. It will also be clear that, excepting in rare instances, the difficulties of securing the means of offering incentives, of avoiding conflict of incentives, and of making effective persuasive efforts, are inherently great; and that the determination of the precise combination of incentives and of persuasion that will be both effective and feasible is a matter of great delicacy. Indeed, it is so delicate and complex that rarely, if ever, is the scheme of incentives determinable in advance of application. It can only evolve; and the questions relating to it become chiefly those of strategic factors from time to time in the course of the life of the organization. It is also true, of course, that the scheme of incentives is probably the most unstable of the elements of the cooperative system, since invariably external conditions affect the possibilities of material incentives; and human motives are likewise highly variable. Thus incentives represent the final residual of all the conflicting forces involved in organization, a very slight change in underlying forces often making a great change in the power of incentives; and yet it is only by the incentives that the effective balancing of these forces is to be secured, if it can be secured at all.

Two general consequences of this inherent instability are to be noted. One is the innate propensity of all organizations to expand. The maintenance of incentives, particularly those relating to prestige, pride of association, and community satisfaction, calls for growth, enlargement, extension. It is, I think, the basic and, in a sense, the legitimate reason for bureaucratic aggrandizement in corporate, governmental, labor, university, and church organizations everywhere observed. To grow seems to offer opportunity for the realization of all kinds of active incentives—as may be observed by the repeated emphasis in all organizations upon size as an index of the existence of desirable incentives, or the alternative rationalization of other incentives when size is small or growth is discouraged. The overreaching which arises from this cause is the source of destruction of organizations otherwise successful, since growth often so upsets the economy of incentives, through its reactions upon the effectiveness and efficiency of organization, that it is no longer possible to make them adequate.

A second and more important result of the inherent difficulty of securing an adequate scheme of incentives is the highly selective character of the organizational recruiting practice. This has two aspects, the acceptance of desirable and the rejection of undesirable contributions or contributors; and its chief process is the maintenance of differential incentives. Since all incentives are costly to organization, and the costs tend to prevent its survival, and since the balancing of organization outgo and income is initially to be regarded as impossible without the utmost economy, the distribution of incentives must be proportioned to the value and effectiveness of the various contributions sought.

This is only too much accepted as respects material incentives, that is, material things or money payment. No enduring or complex formal organization of any kind seems to have existed without differential material payments, though material compensation may be indirect to a considerable extent. This seems true up to the present even though contrary to the expressed attitude of the organization or not in harmony with its major purpose, as often in the case of churches and socialistic states.

The same doctrine applies in principle and practice even more to non-material incentives. The hierarchy of positions, with gradation of honors and privileges, which is the universal accompaniment of all complex organization, is essential to the adjustment of non-material incentives to induce the services of the most able individuals or the most valuable potential contributors to organization, and it is likewise necessary to the maintenance of pride of organization, community sense, etc., which are important general incentives to all classes of contributors.

organizational
humanism

Human relations research broadened traditional organization theory to take note of the human factors in management, and through the fifties human relations organizational theory supported the pillars upon which traditional theory rested. These pillars are the division of labor, the hierarchical and functional processes, structure, and the span of control.[1] Human relations had been concerned with monotony, alienation, and other problems relating to specialization of work. Authority through the hierarchy and in conflict with functional expertise was a major concern of human relations researchers. Problems of structure and span of control in human relations research were viewed as problems of the individuals who occupied specific roles in organizations. The human relations school accepted the goal of efficiency implicit in traditional organization theory and sought to indicate ways by which management could manipulate human factors to mold the workers to better fit the needs of the organization.

Toward the end of the fifties, however, theorists began to delve behind the more superficial aspects of human activity in organizations, and to deal with the nature of work itself, internalized motivation, and what appeared to be a basic incompatibility between the individual and the organization. The focus was no longer on the organization but on the individual and how his personal growth would affect the organization. This change in emphasis from short-term organizational goals to deep concern for the individual and for the longer-range goals of the organization was the key difference between human relations and organizational humanism.

Chris Argyris, one of the most influential behavioral scientists connected with organizational humanism, sought to delineate the inherent conflict between the individual and the organization. Argyris suggested that healthy personality development takes place along the following seven "developmental dimensions": from passive to active; from dependence to independence; from limited behavior patterns to more complex ones; from casual interests to deep interests; from short time perspectives to long ones; from subordinate roles to peer roles; and from lack of awareness of self to self-awareness. Although Argyris recognized that the world would be a difficult place if everyone progressed toward the more developed end of each continuum, he thought that individuals should have the chance to progress as far as their intelligence and inclinations would permit.

Argyris noted, however, that the traditional type of bureaucratic organization tended to work against the development of mature personalities along the seven developmental dimensions. In large formal organizations individuals have minimal control over their work situation, are expected to be passive and have a short time perspective, and are permitted to develop only a few superficial skills. Furthermore, the organization expects individuals to produce under the conditions that lead to psychological failure.[2]

The organizational humanists, although deeply concerned with the role of the individual, are still concerned with the effectiveness of the overall organization. They claim that an organization that is made up of unhealthy personalities cannot be healthy. An atmosphere conducive to individual growth is necessary. Organizational democracy provides such an atmosphere.

This democratic component of the organizational humanists' thought is brought out most clearly by Warren Bennis and Philip Slater. To Bennis and Slater, democracy is a system of values "which people are *internally* compelled to affirm."[3] Among these values are the following:[4]

1. Full and free *communication*, regardless of rank and power.

2. A reliance on *consensus*, rather than the more customary forms of coercion or compromise to manage conflict

3. The idea that *influence* is based on technical competence and knowledge rather than on the vagaries of personal whims or prerogatives of power.

4. An atmosphere that permits and even encourages emotional expression as well as task-oriented acts.

5. A basically human bias, one that accepts the inevitability of conflict between the organization and the individual, but that is willing to cope with and mediate this conflict on rational grounds.

Organizational humanists have great faith in the inner resources of individuals and a positive view of human nature. These assumptions suggest vastly different organizational structures and management behavior than those suggested by the contrary assumptions of traditional theory. The late Douglas McGregor, a college president and successful industrial consultant, sought to spell out an alternative role for management under the assumptions of organizational humanism. Using Abraham Maslow's theory of motivation—the hierarchy of needs—McGregor criticized traditional management practices and suggested new approaches. Often Theory X, the archetype traditional theory, and Theory Y, the organizational humanism approach, have been labeled as "hard" and "soft," respectively, but there is nothing soft about McGregor's insistence that managers operating in a Theory Y environment be held responsible for their results.[5]

The Theory X versus Theory Y formulation sparked research initially aimed at finding *the* best way for motivating people in organizations. Such research quickly evolved into a search for situations in which one or the other of these theories might be useful. Such "contingency theory" has developed the view that change-oriented, unstructured operations like scientific research respond better to the Theory Y approach, whereas routine operations are more effectively managed in a Theory X environment.[6]

When reading the McGregor selection reprinted below, one should deal critically with Maslow's hierarchy of needs theory. Does it seem valid? Can it be proven or disproven? Are only unsatisfied needs motivators? Does Theory Y necessarily stand or fall on the intellectual soundness of the hierarchy of needs? At what levels in a hierarchy might one try a Theory Y approach? How do organizations in the real world attempt to deal with motivation?

Frederick Herzberg discusses this last question. In the article reprinted in this volume, he forcefully explains what motivation is not, then goes on to suggest what might really motivate employees according to his motivator-hygiene theory.[7] A kick in the pants (KITA), whether positive or negative, is not a motivator. Although many of his more caustic comments are aimed at human relations practitioners, what other schools of organization theory does he confront? In Herzberg's view, what is the function of money as a motivating factor? What is his view of the nature of work? Would he agree with those motivational techniques suggested by McGregor?

NOTES

1. William G. Scott, "Organization Theory: An Overview and an Appraisal," *Journal of the Academy of Management* 4, no. 1 (April, 1961): 4, 7–27. I have substituted the term "hierarchical" for Scott's term "scalar." The term "organizational humanism" is derived from Scott's discussion of "industrial humanism" in "Organizational Government: Prospects for a Truly Participative System," *Public Administrative Review* 29, no. 1 (January/February, 1969): 44–45. Among the people identified with the organizational humanists are Chris Argyris, Robert Blake, Warren Bennis, Rensis Likert, Jane Mouton, and Douglas McGregor.

2. Chris Argyris, *Personality and Organization* (New York: Harper & Row, Publishers, 1957) fully develops the argument. The discussion of the developmental dimensions has appeared in several journals. Among them, "Being Human and Being Organized," *Transaction* 1, no. 5 (July, 1964): 1, 3–6.

3. Warren G. Bennis and Philip E. Slater, *The Temporary Society* (New York: Harper & Row, Publishers, 1968), p. 4. (Emphasis added.)

4. Ibid., p. 4. (Emphasis in the original.)

5. Douglas McGregor, *The Human Side of Enterprise* (New York: McGraw-Hill Book Company, 1960).

6. John J. Morse and Jay W. Lorsch, "Beyond Theory Y," *Harvard Business Review* 48, no. 3 (May/June, 1970): 61–68.

7. The theory came out of Frederick Herzberg, Bernard Mausner, and Barbara B. Snyderman, *The Motivation to Work* (New York: John Wiley & Sons, Inc., 1959).

the human side
of enterprise

douglas mcgregor

It has become trite to say that the most significant developments of the next quarter century will take place not in the physical but in the social sciences, that industry—the economic organ of society—has the fundamental know-how to utilize physical science and technology for the material benefit of mankind, and that we must now learn how to utilize the social sciences to make our human organizations truly effective.

Many people agree in principle with such statements; but so far they represent a pious hope—and little else. Consider with me, if you will, something of what may be involved when we attempt to transform the hope into reality.

I

Let me begin with an analogy. A quarter century ago basic conceptions of the nature of matter and energy had changed profoundly from what they had been since Newton's time. The physical scientists

Reprinted from Leadership and Motivation, *Essays of Douglas McGregor, edited by Warren G. Bennis and Edgar H. Schein, with the collaboration of Caroline McGregor by permission of The M.I.T. Press, Cambridge, Massachusetts. First published in* Adventure in Thought and Action, *Proceedings of the Fifth Anniversary Convocation of the School of Industrial Management, Massachusetts Institute of Technology, Cambridge, Mass.: April 9, 1957; and reprinted in* The Management Review, *1957, 46, no. 11, 22–28.*

were persuaded that under proper conditions new and hitherto unimagined sources of energy could be made available to mankind.

We know what has happened since then. First came the bomb. Then, during the past decade, have come many other attempts to exploit these scientific discoveries—some successful, some not.

The point of my analogy, however, is that the application of theory in this field is a slow and costly matter. We expect it always to be thus. No one is impatient with the scientist because he cannot tell industry how to build a simple, cheap, all-purpose source of atomic energy today. That it will take at least another decade and the investment of billions of dollars to achieve results which are economically competitive with present sources of power is understood and accepted.

It is transparently pretentious to suggest any *direct* similarity between the developments in the physical sciences leading to the harnessing of atomic energy and potential developments in the social sciences. Nevertheless, the analogy is not as absurd as it might appear to be at first glance.

To a lesser degree, and in a much more tentative fashion, we are in a position in the social sciences today like that of the physical sciences with respect to atomic energy in the thirties. We know that past conceptions of the nature of man are inadequate and in many ways incorrect. We are becoming quite certain that, under proper conditions, unimagined resources of creative human energy could become available within the organizational setting.

We cannot tell industrial management how to apply this new knowledge in simple, economic ways. We know it will require years of exploration, much costly development research, and a substantial amount of creative imagination on the part of management to discover how to apply this growing knowledge to the organization of human effort in industry.

May I ask that you keep this analogy in mind—overdrawn and pretentious though it may be—as a framework for what I have to say. . . .

Management's Task: Conventional View

The conventional conception of management's task in harnessing human energy to organizational requirements can be stated broadly in terms of three propositions. In order to avoid the complications introduced by a label, I shall call this set of propositions "Theory X":

1. Management is responsible for organizing the elements of productive enterprise—money, materials, equipment, people—in the interest of economic ends.

2. With respect to people, this is a process of directing their efforts, motivating them, controlling their actions, modifying their behavior to fit the needs of the organization.

3. Without this active intervention by management, people would be passive—even resistant—to organizational needs. They must therefore be persuaded, rewarded, punished, controlled—their activities must be directed. This is management's task—in managing subordinate managers or workers. We often sum it up by saying that management consists of getting things done through other people.

Behind this conventional theory there are several additional beliefs —less explicit, but widespread:

4. The average man is by nature indolent—he works as little as possible.

5. He lacks ambition, dislikes responsibility, prefers to be led.

6. He is inherently self-centered, indifferent to organizational needs.

7. He is by nature resistant to change.

8. He is gullible, not very bright, the ready dupe of the charlatan and the demagogue.

The human side of economic enterprise today is fashioned from propositions and beliefs such as these. Conventional organization structures, managerial policies, practices, and programs reflect these assumptions.

In accomplishing its task—with these assumptions as guides— management has conceived of a range of possibilities between two extremes.

The Hard or the Soft Approach?

At one extreme, management can be "hard" or "strong." The methods for directing behavior involve coercion and threat (usually disguised), close supervision, tight controls over behavior. At the

other extreme, management can be "soft" or "weak." The methods for
directing behavior involve being permissive, satisfying people's demands, achieving harmony. Then they will be tractable, accept
direction.

This range has been fairly completely explored during the past
half century, and management has learned some things from the exploration. There are difficulties in the "hard" approach. Force breeds
counter-forces: restriction of output, antagonism, militant unionism,
subtle but effective sabotage of management objectives. This approach is especially difficult during times of full employment.

There are also difficulties in the "soft" approach. It leads frequently
to the abdication of management—to harmony, perhaps, but to
indifferent performance. People take advantage of the soft approach.
They continually expect more, but they give less and less.

Currently, the popular theme is "firm but fair." This is an attempt
to gain the advantages of both the hard and the soft approaches. It is
reminiscent of Teddy Roosevelt's "speak softly and carry a big stick."

Is the Conventional View Correct?

The findings which are beginning to emerge from the social
sciences challenge this whole set of beliefs about man and human
nature and about the task of management. The evidence is far from
conclusive, certainly, but it is suggestive. It comes from the laboratory, the clinic, the schoolroom, the home, and even to a limited
extent from industry itself.

The social scientist does not deny that human behavior in industrial organization today is approximately what management per-
ceives it to be. He has, in fact, observed it and studied it fairly
extensively. But he is pretty sure that this behavior is *not* a consequence of man's inherent nature. It is a consequence rather of the
nature of industrial organizations, of management philosophy,
policy, and practice. The conventional approach of Theory X is
based on mistaken notions of what is cause and what is effect.

"Well," you ask, "what then is the *true* nature of man? What
evidence leads the social scientist to deny what is obvious?" And, if
I am not mistaken, you are also thinking, "Tell me—simply, and
without a lot of scientific verbiage—what you think you know that
is so unusual. Give me—without a lot of intellectual claptrap and
theoretical nonsense—some practical ideas which will enable me to

improve the situation in my organization. And remember, I'm faced with increasing costs and narrowing profit margins. I want proof that such ideas won't result simply in new and costly human relations frills. I want practical results, and I want them now."

If these are your wishes, you are going to be disappointed. Such requests can no more be met by the social scientist today than could comparable ones with respect to atomic energy be met by the physicist fifteen years ago. I can, however, indicate a few of the reasons for asserting that conventional assumptions about the human side of enterprise are inadequate. And I can suggest—tentatively—some of the propositions that will comprise a more adequate theory of the management of people. The magnitude of the task that confronts us will then, I think, be apparent.

II

Perhaps the best way to indicate why the conventional approach of management is inadequate is to consider the subject of motivation. In discussing this subject I will draw heavily on the work of my colleague, Abraham Maslow of Brandeis University. His is the most fruitful approach I know. Naturally, what I have to say will be overgeneralized and will ignore important qualifications. In the time at our disposal, this is inevitable.

Physiological and Safety Needs

Man is a wanting animal—as soon as one of his needs is satisfied, another appears in its place. This process is unending. It continues from birth to death.

Man's needs are organized in a series of levels—a hierarchy of importance. At the lowest level, but preeminent in importance when they are thwarted, are his physiological needs. Man lives by bread alone, when there is no bread. Unless the circumstances are unusual, his needs for love, for status, for recognition are inoperative when his stomach has been empty for a while. But when he eats regularly and adequately, hunger ceases to be an important need. The sated man has hunger only in the sense that a full bottle has emptiness. The same is true of the other physiological needs of man—for rest, exercise, shelter, protection from the elements.

A satisfied need is not a motivator of behavior! This is a fact of profound significance. It is a fact which is regularly ignored in the conventional approach to the management of people. I shall return to it later. For the moment, one example will make my point. Consider your own need for air. Except as you are deprived of it, it has no appreciable motivating effect upon your behavior.

When the physiological needs are reasonably satisfied, needs at the next higher level begin to dominate man's behavior—to motivate him. These are called safety needs. They are needs for protection against danger, threat, deprivation. Some people mistakenly refer to these as needs for security. However, unless man is in a dependent relationship where he fears arbitrary deprivation, he does not demand security. The need is for the "fairest possible break." When he is confident of this, he is more than willing to take risks. But when he feels threatened or dependent, his greatest need is for guarantees, for protection, for security.

The fact needs little emphasis that since every industrial employee is in a dependent relationship, safety needs may assume considerable importance. Arbitrary management actions, behavior which arouses uncertainty with respect to continued employment or which reflects favoritism or discrimination, unpredictable administration of policy —these can be powerful motivators of the safety needs in the employment relationship *at every level* from worker to vice president.

Social Needs

When man's physiological needs are satisfied and he is no longer fearful about his physical welfare, his social needs become important motivators of his behavior—for belonging, for association, for acceptance by his fellows, for giving and receiving friendship and love.

Management knows today of the existence of these needs, but it often assumes quite wrongly that they represent a threat to the organization. Many studies have demonstrated that the tightly knit, cohesive work group may, under proper conditions, be far more effective than an equal number of separate individuals in achieving organizational goals.

Yet management, fearing group hostility to its own objectives, often goes to considerable lengths to control and direct human efforts in ways that are inimical to the natural "groupiness" of human beings. When man's social needs—and perhaps his safety needs, too —are thus thwarted, he behaves in ways which tend to defeat organizational objectives. He becomes resistant, antagonistic, unco-operative. But this behavior is a consequence, not a cause.

Ego Needs

Above the social needs—in the sense that they do not become motivators until lower needs are reasonably satisfied—are the needs of greatest significance to management and to man himself. They are the egoistic needs, and they are of two kinds:

1. Those needs that relate to one's self-esteem—needs for self-confidence, for independence, for achievement, for competence, for knowledge.
2. Those needs that relate to one's reputation—needs for status, for recognition, for appreciation, for the deserved respect of one's fellows.

Unlike the lower needs, these are rarely satisfied; man seeks in-definitely for more satisfaction of these needs once they have become important to him. But they do not appear in any significant way until physiological, safety, and social needs are all reasonably satisfied.

The typical industrial organization offers few opportunities for the satisfaction of these egoistic needs to people at lower levels in the hierarchy. The conventional methods of organizing work, particu-larly in mass production industries, give little heed to these aspects of human motivation. If the practices of scientific management were deliberately calculated to thwart these needs—which, of course, they are not—they could hardly accomplish this purpose better than they do.

Self-fulfillment Needs

Finally—a capstone, as it were, on the hierarchy of man's needs—there are what we may call the needs for self-fulfillment. These are the needs for realizing one's own potentialities, for continued self-development, for being creative in the broadest sense of that term.

It is clear that the conditions of modern life give only limited opportunity for these relatively weak needs to obtain expression. The deprivation most people experience with respect to other lower-level needs diverts their energies into the struggle to satisfy *those* needs, and the needs for self-fulfillment remain dormant.

III

Now, briefly, a few general comments about motivation:

We recognize readily enough that a man suffering from a severe dietary deficiency is sick. The deprivation of physiological needs has behavioral consequences. The same is true—although less well recognized—of deprivation of higher-level needs. The man whose needs for safety, association, independence, or status are thwarted is sick just as surely as is he who has rickets. And his sickness will be mistaken if we attribute his resultant passivity, his hostility, his refusal to accept responsibility to his inherent "human nature." These forms of behavior are *symptoms* of illness—of deprivation of his social and egoistic needs.

The man whose lower-level needs are satisfied is not motivated to satisfy those needs any longer. For practical purposes they exist no longer. (Remember my point about your need for air.) Management often asks, "Why aren't people more productive? We pay good wages, provide good working conditions, have excellent fringe benefits and steady employment. Yet people do not seem to be willing to put forth more than minimum effort."

The fact that management has provided for these physiological and safety needs has shifted the motivational emphasis to the social and perhaps to the egoistic needs. Unless there are opportunities *at work* to satisfy these higher-level needs, people will be deprived; and their behavior will reflect this deprivation. Under such conditions, if management continues to focus its attention on physiological needs, its efforts are bound to be ineffective.

People *will* make insistent demands for more money under these conditions. It becomes more important than ever to buy the material goods and services which can provide limited satisfaction of the thwarted needs. Although money has only limited value in satisfying many higher-level needs, it can become the focus of interest if it is the *only* means available.

The Carrot and Stick Approach

The carrot and stick theory of motivation (like Newtonian physical theory) works reasonably well under certain circumstances. The *means* for satisfying man's physiological and (within limits) his safety needs can be provided or withheld by management. Employment itself is such a means, and so are wages, working conditions, and benefits. By these means the individual can be controlled so long as he is struggling for subsistence. Man lives for bread alone when there is no bread.

But the carrot and stick theory does not work at all once man has reached an adequate subsistence level and is motivated primarily by higher needs. Management cannot provide a man with self-respect, or with the respect of his fellows, or with the satisfaction of needs for self-fulfillment. It can create conditions such that he is encouraged and enabled to seek such satisfactions *for himself,* or it can thwart him by failing to create those conditions.

But this creation of conditions is not "control." It is not a good device for directing behavior. And so management finds itself in an odd position. The high standard of living created by our modern technological know-how provides quite adequately for the satisfaction of physiological and safety needs. The only significant exception is where management practices have not created confidence in a "fair break"—and thus where safety needs are thwarted. But by making possible the satisfaction of low-level needs, management has deprived itself of the ability to use as motivators the devices on which conventional theory has taught it to rely—rewards, promises, incentives, or threats and other coercive devices.

Neither Hard nor Soft

The philosophy of management by direction and control—*regardless of whether it is hard or soft*—is inadequate to motivate because the human needs on which this approach relies are today unimportant motivators of behavior. Direction and control are essentially useless in motivating people whose important needs are social and egoistic. Both the hard and the soft approach fail today because they are simply irrelevant to the situation.

People, deprived of opportunities to satisfy at work the needs which are now important to them, behave exactly as we might predict—with indolence, passivity, resistance to change, lack of responsibility, willingness to follow the demagogue, unreasonable demands for economic benefits. It would seem that we are caught in a web of our own weaving.

In summary, then, of these comments about motivation:

Management by direction and control—whether implemented

with the hard, the soft, or the firm but fair approach—fails under today's conditions to provide effective motivation of human efforts toward organizational objectives. It fails because direction and control are useless methods of motivating people whose physiological and safety needs are reasonably satisfied and whose social, egoistic, and self-fulfillment needs are predominant.

IV

For these and many other reasons, we require a different theory of the task of managing people based on more adequate assumptions about human nature and human motivation. I am going to be so bold as to suggest the broad dimensions of such a theory. Call it "Theory Y," if you will.

1. Management is responsible for organizing the elements of productive enterprise—money, materials, equipment, people—in the interest of economic ends.

2. People are *not* by nature passive or resistant to organizational needs. They have become so as a result of experience in organizations.

3. The motivation, the potential for development, the capacity for assuming responsibility, the readiness to direct behavior toward organizational goals are all present in people. Management does not put them there. It is a responsibility of management to make it possible for people to recognize and develop these human characteristics for themselves.

4. The essential task of management is to arrange organizational conditions and methods of operation so that people can achieve their own goals *best* by directing *their own* efforts toward organizational objectives.

This is a process primarily of creating opportunities, releasing potential, removing obstacles, encouraging growth, providing guidance. It is what Peter Drucker has called "management by objectives" in contrast to "management by control."

And I hasten to add that it does *not* involve the abdication of management, the absence of leadership, the lowering of standards, or the other characteristics usually associated with the "soft" approach under Theory X. Much on the contrary. It is no more possible to create an organization today which will be a fully effective application of this theory than it was to build an atomic power plant in 1945. There are many formidable obstacles to overcome.

Some Difficulties

The conditions imposed by conventional organization theory and by the approach of scientific management for the past half century have tied men to limited jobs which do not utilize their capabilities, have discouraged the acceptance of responsibility, have encouraged passivity, have eliminated meaning from work. Man's habits, attitudes, expectations—his whole conception of membership in an industrial organization—have been conditioned by his experience under these circumstances. Change in the direction of Theory Y will be slow, and it will require extensive modification of the attitudes of management and workers alike.

People today are accustomed to being directed, manipulated, controlled in industrial organizations and to finding satisfaction for their social, egoistic, and self-fulfillment needs away from the job. This is true of much of management as well as of workers. Genuine "industrial citizenship"—to borrow again a term from Drucker—is a remote and unrealistic idea, the meaning of which has not even been considered by most members of industrial organizations.

Another way of saying this is that Theory X places exclusive reliance upon external control of human behavior, while Theory Y relies heavily on self-control and self-direction. It is worth noting that this difference is the difference between treating people as children and treating them as mature adults. After generations of the former, we cannot expect to shift to the latter overnight.

V

Before we are overwhelmed by the obstacles, let us remember that the application of theory is always slow. Progress is usually achieved in small steps.

Consider with me a few innovative ideas which are entirely consistent with Theory Y and which are today being applied with some success:

Decentralization and Delegation

These are ways of freeing people from the too-close control of conventional organization, giving them a degree of freedom to direct their own activities, to assume responsibility, and, importantly, to satisfy their egoistic needs. In this connection, the flat organization of Sears, Roebuck and Company provides an interesting example. It forces "management by objectives" since it enlarges the number of people reporting to a manager until he cannot direct and control them in the conventional manner.

Job Enlargement

This concept, pioneered by I.B.M. and Detroit Edison, is quite consistent with Theory Y. It encourages the acceptance of responsibility at the bottom of the organization; it provides opportunities for satisfying social and egoistic needs. In fact, the reorganization of work at the factory level offers one of the more challenging opportunities for innovation consistent with Theory Y. The studies by A.T.M. Wilson and his associates of British coal mining and Indian textile manufacture have added appreciably to our understanding of work organization. Moreover, the economic and psychological results achieved by this work have been substantial.

Participation and Consultative Management

Under proper conditions these results provide encouragement to people to direct their creative energies toward organizational objectives, give them some voice in decisions that affect them, provide significant opportunities for the satisfaction of social and egoistic needs. I need only mention the Scanlon Plan as the outstanding embodiment of these ideas in practice.

The not infrequent failure of such ideas as these to work as well as expected is often attributable to the fact that a management has "bought the idea" but applied it within the framework of Theory X and its assumptions.

Delegation is not an effective way of exercising management by control. Participation becomes a farce when it is applied as a sales gimmick or a device for kidding people into thinking they are important. Only the management that has confidence in human capacities and is itself directed toward organizational objectives rather than toward the preservation of personal power can grasp the implications of this emerging theory. Such management will find and apply successfully other innovative ideas as we move slowly toward the full implementation of a theory like Y.

Performance Appraisal

Before I stop, let me mention one other practical application of Theory Y which—while still highly tentative—may well have important consequences. This has to do with performance appraisal within the ranks of management. Even a cursory examination of conventional programs of performance appraisal will reveal how completely consistent they are with Theory X. In fact, most such programs tend to treat the individual as though he were a product under inspection on the assembly line.

Take the typical plan: substitute "product" for "subordinate being appraised," substitute "inspector" for "superior making the appraisal," substitute "rework" for "training or development," and, except for the attributes being judged, the human appraisal process will be virtually indistinguishable from the product inspection process.

A few companies—among them General Mills, Ansul Chemical, and General Electric—have been experimenting with approaches which involve the individual in setting "targets" or objectives *for himself* and in a *self*-evaluation of performance semi-annually or annually. Of course, the superior plays an important leadership role in this process—one, in fact, which demands substantially more competence than the conventional approach. The role is, however, considerably more congenial to many managers than the role of "judge" or "inspector" which is forced upon them by conventional performance. Above all, the individual is encouraged to take a greater responsibility for planning and appraising his own contribution to organizational objectives; and the accompanying effects on egoistic and self-fulfillment needs are substantial. This approach to performance appraisal represents one more innovative idea being explored by a few managements who are moving toward the implementation of Theory Y.

VI

And now I am back where I began. I share the belief that we could realize substantial improvements in the effectiveness of industrial organizations during the next decade or two. Moreover, I believe the social sciences can contribute much to such developments. We are only beginning to grasp the implications of the growing body of knowledge in these fields. But if this conviction is to become a reality instead of a pious hope, we will need to view the process much as we view the process of releasing the energy of the atom for constructive human ends—as a slow, costly, sometimes discouraging approach toward a goal which would seem to many to be quite unrealistic.

The ingenuity and the perseverance of industrial management in the pursuit of economic ends have changed many scientific and technological dreams into commonplace realities. It is now becoming clear that the application of these same talents to the human side of enterprise will not only enhance substantially these materialistic achievements but will bring us one step closer to "the good society." Shall we get on with the job?

one more time:
how do you
motivate employees?

frederick herzberg

. . .

The psychology of motivation is tremendously complex, and what has been unraveled with any degree of assurance is small indeed. But the dismal ratio of knowledge to speculation has not dampened the enthusiasm for new forms of snake oil that are constantly coming on the market, many of them with academic testimonials. Doubtless this article will have no depressing impact on the market for snake oil, but since the ideas expressed in it have been tested in many corporations and other organizations, it will help—I hope—to re-dress the imbalance in the aforementioned ratio.

"MOTIVATING" WITH KITA

. . .

What is the simplest, surest, and most direct way of getting some-one to do something? Ask him? But if he responds that he does not want to do it, then that calls for a psychological consultation to determine the reason for his obstinacy. Tell him? His response shows

From Frederick Herzberg, "One More Time: How Do You Motivate Em-ployees?" Harvard Business Review 46, no. 1 (January–February, 1968): 53–62. Copyright © 1967 by the President and Fellows of Harvard College; all rights reserved.

that he does not understand you, and now an expert in communication methods has to be brought in to show you how to get through to him. Give him a monetary incentive? I do not need to remind the reader of the complexity and difficulty involved in setting up and administering an incentive system. Show him? This means a costly training program. We need a simple way.

Every audience contains the "direct action" manager who shouts, "Kick him!" And this type of manager is right. The surest and least circumlocuted way of getting someone to do something is to kick him in the pants—give him what might be called the KITA.

There are various forms of KITA, and here are some of them:

Negative Physical KITA. This is a literal application of the term and was frequently used in the past. It has, however, three major drawbacks: (1) it is inelegant; (2) it contradicts the precious image of benevolence that most organizations cherish; and (3) since it is a physical attack, it directly stimulates the autonomic nervous system, and this often results in negative feedback—the employee may just kick you in return. These factors give rise to certain taboos against negative physical KITA.

The psychologist has come to the rescue of those who are no longer permitted to use negative physical KITA. He has uncovered infinite sources of psychological vulnerabilities and the appropriate methods to play tunes on them. "He took my rug away"; "I wonder what he meant by that"; "The boss is always going around me"—these symptomatic expressions of ego sores that have been rubbed raw are the result of application of:

Negative Psychological KITA. This has several advantages over negative physical KITA. First, the cruelty is not visible; the bleeding is internal and comes much later. Second, since it affects the higher cortical centers of the brain with its inhibitory powers, it reduces the possibility of physical backlash. Third, since the number of psychological pains that a person can feel is almost infinite, the direction and site possibilities of the KITA are increased many times. Fourth, the person administering the kick can manage to be above it all and let the system accomplish the dirty work. Fifth, those who practice it receive some ego satisfaction (one-upmanship), whereas they would find drawing blood abhorrent. Finally, if the employee does complain, he can always be accused of being paranoid, since there is no tangible evidence of an actual attack.

Now, what does negative KITA accomplish? If I kick you in the rear (physically or psychologically), who is motivated? *I* am motivated; *you* move! Negative KITA does not lead to motivation, but to movement. So:

Positive KITA. Let us consider motivation. If I say to you, "Do this for me or the company, and in return I will give you a reward, an incentive, more status, a promotion, all the quid pro quos that exist in the industrial organization," am I motivating you? The overwhelming opinion I receive from management people is, "Yes, this is motivation."

I have a year-old Schnauzer. When it was a small puppy and I wanted it to move, I kicked it in the rear and it moved. Now that I have finished its obedience training, I hold up a dog biscuit when I want the Schnauzer to move. In this instance, who is motivated—I or the dog? The dog wants the biscuit, but it is I who want it to move. Again, I am the one who is motivated, and the dog is the one who moves. In this instance all I did was apply KITA frontally; I exerted a pull instead of a push. When industry wishes to use such positive KITAs, it has available an incredible number and variety of dog biscuits (jelly beans for humans) to wave in front of the employee to get him to jump.

Why is it that managerial audiences are quick to see that negative KITA is *not* motivation, while they are almost unanimous in their judgment that positive KITA *is* motivation? It is because negative KITA is rape, and positive KITA is seduction. But it is infinitely worse to be seduced than to be raped; the latter is an unfortunate occurrence, while the former signifies that you were a party to your own downfall. This is why positive KITA is so popular: it is a tradition; it is in the American way. The organization does not have to kick you; you kick yourself.

Myths about Motivation

Why is KITA not motivation? If I kick my dog (from the front or the back), he will move. And when I want him to move again, what must I do? I must kick him again. Similarly, I can charge a man's battery, and then recharge it, and recharge it again. But it is only when he has his own generator that we can talk about motivation. He then needs no outside stimulation. He *wants* to do it.

With this in mind, we can review some positive KITA personnel practices that were developed as attempts to instill "motivation":

1. *Reducing time spent at work*—This represents a marvelous way of motivating people to work—getting them off the job! We have reduced (formally and informally) the time spent on the job over the last 50 or 60 years until we are finally on the way to the "6½-day weekend." An interesting variant of this approach is the development of off-hour recreation programs. The philosophy here seems to be that those who play together, work together. The fact is that motivated people seek more hours of work, not fewer.

2. *Spiraling wages*—Have these motivated people? Yes, to seek the next wage increase. Some medievalists still can be heard to say that a good depression will get employees moving. They feel that if rising wages don't or won't do the job, perhaps reducing them will.

3. *Fringe benefits*—Industry has outdone the most welfare-minded of welfare states in dispensing cradle-to-the-grave succor. One company I know of had an informal "fringe benefit of the month club" going for a while. The cost of fringe benefits in this country has reached approximately 25% of the wage dollar, and we still cry for motivation.

People spend less time working for more money and more security than ever before, and the trend cannot be reversed. These benefits are no longer rewards; they are rights. A 6-day week is inhuman, a 10-hour day is exploitation, extended medical coverage is a basic decency, and stock options are the salvation of American initiative. Unless the ante is continuously raised, the psychological reaction of employees is that the company is turning back the clock.

When industry began to realize that both the economic nerve and the lazy nerve of their employees had insatiable appetites, it started to listen to the behavioral scientists who, more out of a humanist tradition than from scientific study, criticized management for not knowing how to deal with people. The next KITA easily followed.

4. *Human relations training*—Over 30 years of teaching and, in many instances, of practicing psychological approaches to handling people have resulted in costly human relations programs and, in the end, the same question: How do you motivate workers? Here, too, escalations have taken place. Thirty years ago it was necessary to request, "Please don't spit on the floor." Today the same admonition requires three "please"s before the employee feels that his superior has demonstrated the psychologically proper attitudes toward him.

The failure of human relations training to produce motivation led to the conclusion that the supervisor or manager himself was not psychologically true to himself in his practice of interpersonal decency. So an advanced form of human relations KITA, sensitivity training, was unfolded.

5. *Sensitivity training*—Do you really, really understand yourself? Do you really, really, really trust the other man? Do you really, really, really, really cooperate? The failure of sensitivity training is now being explained, by those who have become opportunistic exploiters of the technique, as a failure to really (five times) conduct proper sensitivity training courses.

With the realization that there are only temporary gains from comfort and economic and interpersonal KITA, personnel managers concluded that the fault lay not in what they were doing, but in the employee's failure to appreciate what they were doing. This opened up the field of communications, a whole new area of "scientifically" sanctioned KITA.

6. *Communications*—The professor of communications was invited to join the faculty of management training programs and help in making employees understand what management was doing for them. House organs, briefing sessions, supervisory instruction on the importance of communication, and all sorts of propaganda have proliferated until today there is even an International Council of Industrial Editors. But no motivation resulted, and the obvious thought occurred that perhaps management was not hearing what the employees were saying. That led to the next KITA.

7. *Two-way communication*—Management ordered morale surveys, suggestion plans, and group participation programs. Then both employees and management were communicating and listening to each other more than ever, but without much improvement in motivation.

The behavioral scientists began to take another look at their conceptions and their data, and they took human relations one step further. A glimmer of truth was beginning to show through in the writings of the so-called higher-order-need psychologists. People, so they said, want to actualize themselves. Unfortunately, the "actualizing" psychologists got mixed up with the human relations psychologists, and a new KITA emerged.

8. *Job participation*—Though it may not have been the theoretical intention, job participation often became a "give them the big picture" approach. For example, if a man is tightening 10,000 nuts a day on an assembly line with a torque wrench, tell him he is building a Chevrolet. Another approach had the goal of giving the employee a *feeling* that he is determining, in some measure, what he does on his job. The goal was to provide a *sense* of achievement rather than a substantive achievement in his task. Real achievement, of course, requires a task that makes it possible.

But still there was no motivation. This led to the inevitable conclusion that the employees must be sick, and therefore to the next KITA.

9. *Employee counseling*—The initial use of this form of KITA in a systematic fashion can be credited to the Hawthorne experiment of the Western Electric Company during the early 1930s. At that time, it was found that the employees harbored irrational feelings that were interfering with the rational operation of the factory. Counseling in this instance was a means of letting the employees unburden themselves by talking to someone about their problems. Although the counseling techniques were primitive, the program was large indeed.

The counseling approach suffered as a result of experiences during World War II, when the programs themselves were found to be interfering with the operation of the organizations; the counselors had forgotten their role of benevolent listeners and were attempting to do something about the problems that they heard about. Psychological counseling, however, has managed to survive the negative impact of World War II experiences and today is beginning to flourish with renewed sophistication. But, alas, many of these programs, like all the others, do not seem to have lessened the pressure of demands to find out how to motivate workers.

Since KITA results only in short-term movement, it is safe to predict that the cost of these programs will increase steadily and new varieties will be developed as old positive KITAs reach their satiation points.

HYGIENE VS. MOTIVATORS

Let me rephrase the perennial question this way: How do you install a generator in an employee? A brief review of my motivation-hygiene theory of job attitudes is required before theoretical and practical suggestions can be offered. The theory was first drawn from an examination of events in the lives of engineers and accountants. At least 16 other investigations, using a wide variety of populations (including some in the Communist countries), have since been completed, making the original research one of the most replicated studies in the field of job attitudes.

The findings of these studies, along with corroboration from many other investigations using different procedures, suggest that the factors involved in producing job satisfaction (and motivation) are separate and distinct from the factors that lead to job dissatisfaction. Since separate factors need to be considered, depending on whether job satisfaction or job dissatisfaction is being examined, it follows that these two feelings are not opposites of each other. The opposite of job satisfaction is not job dissatisfaction but, rather, *no* job satisfaction; and, similarly, the opposite of job dissatisfaction is not job satisfaction, but *no* job dissatisfaction.

Stating the concept presents a problem in semantics, for we normally think of satisfaction and dissatisfaction as opposites—i.e., what is not satisfying must be dissatisfying, and vice versa. But when it comes to understanding the behavior of people in their jobs, more than a play on words is involved.

Two different needs of man are involved here. One set of needs can be thought of as stemming from his animal nature—the built-in drive to avoid pain from the environment, plus all the learned drives which become conditioned to the basic biological needs. For example, hunger, a basic biological drive, makes it necessary to earn money, and then money becomes a specific drive. The other set of needs relates to that unique human characteristic, the ability to achieve and, through achievement, to experience psychological growth. The stimuli for the growth needs are tasks that induce growth; in the industrial setting, they are the *job content*. Contrariwise, the stimuli inducing pain-avoidance behavior are found in the *job environment*.

The growth or *motivator* factors that are intrinsic to the job are: achievement, recognition for achievement, the work itself, responsibility, and growth or advancement. The dissatisfaction-avoidance or *hygiene* (KITA) factors that are extrinsic to the job include: company policy and administration, supervision, interpersonal relationships, working conditions, salary, status, and security.

A composite of the factors that are. involved in causing job satisfaction and job dissatisfaction, drawn from samples of 1,685 employees, is shown in Exhibit 1. The results indicate that motivators were the primary cause of satisfaction, and hygiene factors the primary cause of unhappiness on the job. The employees, studied in 12 different investigations, included lower-level supervisors, professional women, agricultural administrators, men about to retire from management positions, hospital maintenance personnel, manufacturing supervisors, nurses, food handlers, military officers, engineers, scientists, housekeepers, teachers, technicians, female assemblers, accountants, Finnish foremen, and Hungarian engineers.

They were asked what job events had occurred in their work that had led to extreme satisfaction or extreme dissatisfaction on

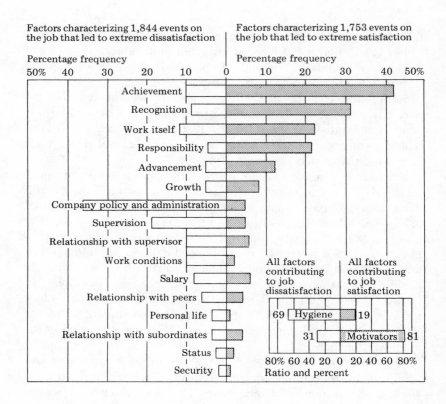

Factors characterizing 1,844 events on the job that led to extreme dissatisfaction

Factors characterizing 1,753 events on the job that led to extreme satisfaction

Percentage frequency
50% 40 30 20 10 0 10 20 30 40 50%

Achievement
Recognition
Work itself
Responsibility
Advancement
Growth
Company policy and administration
Supervision
Relationship with supervisor
Work conditions
Salary
Relationship with peers
Personal life
Relationship with subordinates
Status
Security

All factors contributing to job dissatisfaction

All factors contributing to job satisfaction

69 | Hygiene | 19
31 | Motivators | 81

80% 60 40 20 0 20 40 60 80%
Ratio and percent

EXHIBIT 1

Factors Affecting Job Attitudes, As Reported in 12 Investigations

their part. Their responses are broken down in the exhibit into percentages of total "positive" job events and of total "negative" job events. (The figures total more than 100 per cent on both the "hygiene" and "motivators" sides because often at least two factors can be attributed to a single event; advancement, for instance, often accompanies assumption of responsibility.)

To illustrate, a typical response involving achievement that had a negative effect for the employee was, "I was unhappy because I didn't do the job successfully." A typical response in the small number of positive job events in the Company Policy and Administration grouping was, "I was happy because the company reorganized the section so that I didn't report any longer to the guy I didn't get along with."

As the lower right-hand part of the exhibit shows, of all the factors contributing to job satisfaction, 81 per cent were motivators. And of all the factors contributing to the employees' dissatisfaction over their work, 69 per cent involved hygiene elements.

External Triangle

There are three general philosophies of personnel management. The first is based on organizational theory, the second on industrial engineering, and the third on behavioral science.

The organizational theorist believes that human needs are either so irrational or so varied and adjustable to specific situations that the major function of personnel management is to be as pragmatic as the occasion demands. If jobs are organized in a proper manner, he reasons the result will be the most efficient job structure, and the most favorable job attitudes will follow as a matter of course.

The industrial engineer holds that man is mechanistically oriented and economically motivated and his needs are best met by attuning the individual to the most efficient work process. The goal of personnel management therefore should be to concoct the most appropriate incentive system and to design the specific working conditions in a way that facilitates the most efficient use of the human machine. By structuring jobs in a manner that leads to the most efficient operation, the engineer believes that he can obtain the optimal organization of work and the proper work attitudes.

The behavioral scientist focuses on group sentiments, attitudes of individual employees, and the organization's social and psychological climate. According to his persuasion, he emphasizes one or more of the various hygiene and motivator needs. His approach to personnel management generally emphasizes some form of human relations education, in the hope of instilling healthy employee attitudes and an organizational climate which he considers to be felicitous to human values. He believes that proper attitudes will lead to efficient job and organizational structure.

There is always a lively debate as to the over-all effectiveness of the approaches of the organizational theorist and the industrial engineer. Manifestly they have achieved much. But the nagging question for the behavioral scientist has been: What is the cost in human problems that eventually cause more expense to the organization— for instance, turnover, absenteeism, errors, violation of safety rules, strikes, restriction of output, higher wages, and greater fringe benefits? On the other hand, the behavioral scientist is hard put to document much manifest improvement in personnel management, using his approach.

The three philosophies can be depicted as a triangle, as is done in Exhibit 2, with each persuasion claiming the apex angle. The motivation-hygiene theory claims the same angle as industrial engineering, but for opposite goals. Rather than rationalizing the work to increase efficiency, the theory suggests that work be *enriched* to bring about effective utilization of personnel. Such a systematic attempt to motivate employees by manipulating the motivator factors is just beginning.

The term *job enrichment* describes this embryonic movement. An older term, job enlargement, should be avoided because it is associated with past failures stemming from a misunderstanding of the problem. Job enrichment provides the opportunity for the employee's psychological growth, while job enlargement merely

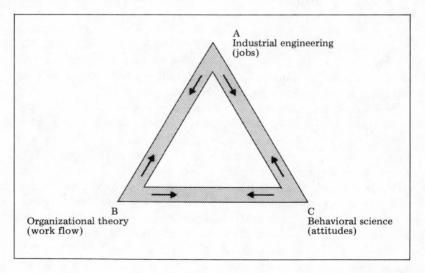

EXHIBIT 2

"Triangle" of Philosophies of Personnel Management

makes a job structurally bigger. Since scientific job enrichment is very new, this article only suggests the principles and practical steps that have recently emerged from several successful experiments in industry.

Job Loading

In attempting to enrich an employee's job, management often succeeds in reducing the man's personal contribution, rather than giving him an opportunity for growth in his accustomed job. Such an endeavor, which I shall call horizontal job loading (as opposed to vertical loading, or providing motivator factors), has been the problem of earlier job enlargement programs. This activity merely enlarges the meaninglessness of the job. Some examples of this approach, and their effect, are:

● Challenging the employee by increasing the amount of production expected of him. If he tightens 10,000 bolts a day, see if he can tighten 20,000 bolts a day. The arithmetic involved shows that multiplying zero by zero still equals zero.

● Adding another meaningless task to the existing one, usually some routine clerical activity. The arithmetic here is adding zero to zero.

● Rotating the assignments of a number of jobs that need to be enriched. This means washing dishes for a while, then washing silverware. The arithmetic is substituting one zero for another zero.

● Removing the most difficult parts of the assignment in order to free the worker to accomplish more of the less challenging assignments. This traditional industrial engineering approach amounts to subtraction in the hope of accomplishing addition.

These are common forms of horizontal loading that frequently come up in preliminary brainstorming sessions on job enrichment. The principles of vertical loading have not all been worked out as yet, and they remain rather general, but I have furnished seven useful starting points for consideration in Exhibit 3.

A Successful Application

An example from a highly successful job enrichment experiment can illustrate the distinction between horizontal and vertical load-

EXHIBIT 3

Principles of Vertical Job Loading

Principle	Motivators Involved
A. Removing some controls while retaining accountability	Responsibility and personal achievement
B. Increasing the accountability of individuals for own work	Responsibility and recognition
C. Giving a person a complete natural unit of work (module, division, area, and so on)	Responsibility, achievement, and recognition
D. Granting additional authority to an employee in his activity; job freedom	Responsibility, achievement, and recognition
E. Making periodic reports directly available to the worker himself rather than to the supervisor	Internal recognition
F. Introducing new and more difficult tasks not previously handled	Growth and learning
G. Assigning individuals specific or specialized tasks, enabling them to become experts	Responsibility, growth, and advancement

ing of a job. The subjects of this study were the stockholder correspondents employed by a very large corporation. Seemingly, the task required of these carefully selected and highly trained correspondents was quite complex and challenging. But almost all indexes of performance and job attitudes were low, and exit interviewing confirmed that the challenge of the job existed merely as words.

A job enrichment project was initiated in the form of an experiment with one group, designated as an achieving unit, having its job enriched by the principles described in Exhibit 3. A control group continued to do its job in the traditional way. (There were also two "uncommitted" groups of correspondents formed to measure the so-called Hawthorne Effect—that is, to gauge whether productivity and attitudes toward the job changed artificially merely because employees sensed that the company was paying more attention to them in doing something different or novel. The results for these groups were substantially the same as for the control group, and for the sake of simplicity I do not deal with them in this summary.) No changes in hygiene were introduced for either group other than those that would have been made anyway, such as normal pay increases.

The changes for the achieving unit were introduced in the first two months, averaging one per week of the seven motivators listed in Exhibit 3. At the end of six months the members of the achieving unit were found to be outperforming their counterparts in the control group, and in addition indicated a marked increase in their liking for their jobs. Other results showed that the achieving group had lower absenteeism and, subsequently, a much higher rate of promotion. . . .

STEPS TO JOB ENRICHMENT

Now that the motivator idea has been described in practice, here are the steps that managers should take in instituting the principle with their employees:

1. Select those jobs in which (a) the investment in industrial engineering does not make changes too costly, (b) attitudes are poor, (c) hygiene is becoming very costly, and (d) motivation will make a difference in performance.

2. Approach these jobs with the conviction that they can be changed. Years of tradition have led managers to believe that the content of the jobs is sacrosanct and the only scope of action that they have is in ways of stimulating people.

3. Brainstorm a list of changes that may enrich the jobs, without concern for their practicality.

4. Screen the list to eliminate suggestions that involve hygiene, rather than actual motivation.

5. Screen the list for generalities, such as "give them more responsibility," that are rarely followed in practice. This might seem obvious, but the motivator words have never left industry; the substance has just been rationalized and organized out. Words like "responsibility," "growth," "achievement," and "challenge," for example, have been elevated to the lyrics of the patriotic anthem for all organizations. It is the old problem typified by the pledge of allegiance to the flag being more important than contributions to the country—of following the form, rather than the substance.

EXHIBIT 4

Enlargement vs. Enrichment of Correspondents' Task in Company Experiment

Horizontal Loading Suggestions (rejected)	Vertical Loading Suggestions (adopted)	Principle
Firm quotas could be set for letters to be answered each day, using a rate which would be hard to reach.	Subject matter experts were appointed within each unit for other members of the unit to consult with before seeking supervisory help. (The supervisor had been answering all specialized and difficult questions.)	G
The women could type the letters themselves, as well as compose them, or take on any other clerical functions.	Correspondents signed their own names on letters. (The supervisor had been signing all letters.)	B
All difficult or complex inquiries could be channeled to a few women so that the remainder could achieve high rates of output. These jobs could be exchanged from time to time.	The work of the more experienced correspondents was proofread less frequently by supervisors and was done at the correspondents' desks, dropping verification from 100% to 10%. (Previously, all correspondents' letters had been checked by the supervisor.)	A
	Production was discussed, but only in terms such as "a full day's work is expected." As time went on, this was no longer mentioned. (Before, the group had been constantly reminded of the number of letters that needed to be answered.)	D
	Outgoing mail went directly to the mailroom without going over supervisors' desks. (The letters had always been routed through the supervisors.)	A
The women could be rotated through units handling different customers, and then sent back to their own units.	Correspondents were encouraged to answer letters in a more personalized way. (Reliance on the form-letter approach had been standard practice.)	C
	Each correspondent was held personally responsible for the quality and accuracy of letters. (This responsibility had been the province of the supervisor and the verifier.)	B, E

6. Screen the list to eliminate any *horizontal* loading suggestions.

7. Avoid direct participation by the employees whose jobs are to be enriched. Ideas they have expressed previously certainly constitute a valuable source for recommended changes, but their direct involvement contaminates the process with human relations *hygiene* and, more specifically, gives them only a *sense* of making a contribution. The job is to be changed, and it is the content that will produce the motivation, not attitudes about being involved or the challenge inherent in setting up a job. That process will be over shortly, and it is what the employees will be doing from then on that will determine their motivation. A sense of participation will result only in short-term movement.

8. In the initial attempts at job enrichment, set up a controlled experiment. At least two equivalent groups should be chosen, one an experimental unit in which the motivators are systematically introduced over a period of time, and the other one a control group in which no changes are made. For both groups, hygiene should be allowed to follow its natural course for the duration of the experiment. Pre- and post-installation tests of performance and job attitudes are necessary to evaluate the effectiveness of the job enrichment program. The attitude test must be limited to motivator items in order to divorce the employee's view of the job he is given from all the surrounding hygiene feelings that he might have.

9. Be prepared for a drop in performance in the experimental group the first few weeks. The changeover to a new job may lead to a temporary reduction in efficiency.

10. Expect your first-line supervisors to experience some anxiety and hostility over the changes you are making. The anxiety comes from their fear that the changes will result in poorer performance for their unit. Hostility will arise when the employees start assuming what the supervisors regard as their own responsibility for performance. The supervisor without checking duties to perform may then be left with little to do.

After a successful experiment, however, the supervisor usually discovers the supervisory and managerial functions he has neglected, or which were never his because all his time was given over to checking the work of his subordinates. For example, in the R&D division of one large chemical company I know of, the supervisors of the laboratory assistants were theoretically responsible for their training and evaluation. These functions, however, had come to be performed in a routine, unsubstantial fashion. After the job enrichment program, during which the supervisors were not merely passive observers of the assistants' performance, the supervisors actually were devoting their time to reviewing performance and administering thorough training.

What has been called an employee-centered style of supervision will come about not through education of supervisors, but by changing the jobs that they do.

CONCLUDING NOTE

Job enrichment will not be a one-time proposition, but a continuous management function. The initial changes, however, should last for a very long period of time. There are a number of reasons for this:

- The changes should bring the job up to the level of challenge commensurate with the skill that was hired.
- Those who have still more ability eventually will be able to demonstrate it better and win promotion to higher-level jobs.
- The very nature of motivators, as opposed to hygiene factors, is that they have a much longer-term effect on employees' attitudes. Perhaps the job will have to be enriched again, but this will not occur as frequently as the need for hygiene.

Not all jobs can be enriched, nor do all jobs need to be enriched. If only a small percentage of the time and money that is now devoted to hygiene, however, were given to job enrichment efforts, the return in human satisfaction and economic gain would be one of the largest dividends that industry and society have ever reaped through their efforts at better personnel management.

The argument for job enrichment can be summed up quite simply: If you have someone on a job, use him. If you can't use him on the job, get rid of him, either via automation or by selecting someone with lesser ability. If you can't use him and you can't get rid of him, you will have a motivation problem.

decision-making theory

Organizations exist to accomplish things, and to accomplish things, the people within an organization must make choices among various alternatives. The factors that they consider and the means they use to assess these factors comprise the heart of decision-making theory as it applies to organizations—especially public organizations.

As William J. Gore has pointed out, a "decision refers to the consideration of the consequences of some act before undertaking it."[1] Consideration is a rational process that unites perceptions of reality and possible consequences with the values that the decision maker places on those consequences. The perceptions of reality that an organization has are dependent upon the information available to it and its manipulation of that information.

Ideally an organization wants to get a picture of reality that approaches reality itself and not one distorted far out of proportion. John Kenneth Galbraith has suggested that organizations have a natural tendency to develop and act on false pictures of reality: "What is done and what is believed are, first and naturally, what serve the goals of the bureaucracy itself."[2] An organization that is to cope with changes in the environment must be able to act flexibly on accurate information. If an organization is a prisoner to its own "bureaucratic truths," it will not be able to deal with change in a positive way.

There are several ways through which an organization attempts to keep its information processes open to reality. Organizational humanism is one way. A Theory Y atmosphere is one in which many views of reality can be suggested, debated, and assessed on their merits and freed from some of the inhibitions of the hierarchy that encourage the propagation of "bureaucratic truths." Supposedly, the views that more closely reflect the true situation will survive. Management science is another way. Management science is the general term covering the application of modern technology to all planes of organizational activity, but especially to information gathering and manipulation. Among the tools associated with this area of management science are computers, systems analysis, and operations research. Still another way that organizations seek to obtain an accurate picture of reality is through contact with other organizations that deal in the same or related functional areas. The aim of all these methods is to get a better view of the real world so that better decisions can be made.

It is this question of how organizations represent the real world that has engendered several decision-making theories. Charles E. Lindblom, the distinguished political economist at Yale, discusses two theories. One he calls the rational-comprehensive theory. Basically, this is the scientific method of problem solving. Lindblom claims that this method, despite modern technology, cannot adequately deal with complex questions because of man's limitations —"the boundaries of rationality," as Herbert Simon has called it.[3] Furthermore, the scientific method of problem-solving assumes agreement on goals—agreement on what the problem is—and this assumption generally does not apply to complex public policy issues.

As an alternative to rational-comprehensive analysis, Lindblom suggests the method of successive limited comparisons. This incremental approach is a practical decision-making method for public policy questions because of its use of the process of *partisan mutual adjustment*.[4] Partisan mutual adjustment is an overtly political means for getting information and making decisions; various interests make demands on the organization and bargain with it and with other interests who are making contradictory demands. It can also be viewed as an attempt by the organization to maintain a liaison with reality through outside organizations. Partisan mutual adjustment, working through increments of change, is pluralism in action. As such it is subject to the most telling criticisms of pluralism—which groups are involved in the bargaining and what are the power positions of these groups in society.[5]

Herbert Simon, a strong advocate of management science, has suggested that decision makers do not engage in comprehensive analysis because they are satisfied with less information and analysis than the rational-comprehensive model posits. Decision makers do not seek to maximize the goodness of any decision. They "satisfice." They are satisfied by a certain level of goodness in their decisions.[6] Taking this into account, has Lindblom presented analysis as a straw man? Is there a place for analysis in the bargaining process? What kinds of change and responses to change can we expect from the incremental strategy? If people can agree on goals and computers can handle the data, are there any arguments for the incremental approach of partisan mutual adjustment?

Even though Lindblom included several reservations in his piece, the thrust of "Muddling Through" denigrates analysis and sanctifies incrementalism. As such, it gives aid and comfort to anti-change, anti-innovation forces. Furthermore, it unrealistically ignores the middle ground where economic criteria and analytic methods can be integrated with political criteria.

Amitai Etzioni has given the theoretical justification for this middle way between pure economic rationality and pure political rationality. Using a satellite-based weather observation system as an analogy to observing social phenomena, Etzioni suggested how a "mixed-scanning" technique might work:

The rationalistic approach would seek an exhaustive survey of weather conditions by using cameras capable of detailed observations and by scheduling reviews of the entire sky as often as possible. This would yield an avalanche of details, costly to analyze and likely to overwhelm our action capacities. . . . Incrementalism would focus on those areas in which similar patterns developed in the recent past and, perhaps, on a few nearby regions; it would thus ignore all formations which might deserve attention if they arose in unexpected areas.

A mixed-scanning strategy would include elements of both approaches by employing two cameras: a broad-angle camera that would cover all parts of the sky but not in great detail, and a second one which would zero in on those areas revealed by the first camera to require a more in-depth examination. While mixed-scanning might miss areas in which only a detailed camera could reveal trouble, it is less likely than incrementalism to miss obvious trouble spots in unfamiliar areas.[7]

The common sense of a mixed-scanning approach has, indeed, been characteristic of many aspects of policy making since the mid-1960s. The polar positions of decision theory have not changed, but there is an operational accommodation between the two. Very few people would claim that rational-comprehensive decision making is possible on such major political issues as racism, poverty, the economy, or even national security. Similarly, few people would completely discount the role that systematic planning and analysis can have in clarifying certain aspects of these pressing problems.

E. S. Quade of the Rand Corporation sees a strong future for analytic work on policy problems, yet he is aware of the limitations on the craft.[8] The piece reprinted here was originally written to introduce decision makers to the kind of analysis that was to be the heart of the Planning-Programming-Budgeting System (PPBS). PPBS, it was hoped in the mid-1960s, was supposed to enable the government to make better decisions by identifying national goals, uncovering alternative ways to achieve them, and correctly costing out these alternatives. Although PPBS was quietly phased out in the early 1970s, analysis of public policy problems has survived.

Quade suggests specific ways in which one can engage in analysis of public problems. Is he overly optimistic? Does he understate the limitations of the method? Can you think of any examples where policy analysis has actually changed a major policy decision? How can analysis be integrated with politics in decision making? What problems might there be?

NOTES

1. William J. Gore, *Administrative Decision-Making: A Heuristic Model* (New York: John Wiley & Sons, Inc., 1964), p. 19.

2. John Kenneth Galbraith, *How to Control the Military* (New York: New American Library Inc., Signet Books, 1969), p. 16. "Bureaucratic truth" is also Galbraith's term.

3. James G. March and Herbert A. Simon, *Organizations* (New York: John Wiley & Sons, Inc., 1958), p. 171 and chapter 6.

4. Charles E. Lindblom, *The Intelligence of Democracy* (New York: The Macmillan Company, The Free Press, 1965).

5. For an excellent collection of essays indicting pluralism, see William E. Connolly, ed., *The Bias of Pluralism* (New York: Atherton, 1969).

6. March and Simon, *Organizations*, pp. 140–41, 169.

7. Amitai Etzioni, "Mixed-Scanning: a 'Third' Approach to Decision Making," *Public Administration Review* 27, no. 5 (December, 1967): 388.

8. For a more complete argument, see E. S. Quade, *Analysis for Public Decisions* (New York: American Elsevier Publishing Company, 1975).

the science of
"muddling through"

charles e. lindblom

Suppose an administrator is given responsibility for formulating policy with respect to inflation. He might start by trying to list all related values in order of importance, e.g., full employment, reasonable business profit, protection of small savings, prevention of a stock market crash. Then all possible policy outcomes could be rated as more or less efficient in attaining a maximum of these values. This would of course require a prodigious inquiry into values held by members of society and an equally prodigious set of calculations on how much of each value is equal to how much of each other value. He could then proceed to outline all possible policy alternatives. In a third step, he would undertake systematic comparison of his multitude of alternatives to determine which attains the greatest amount of values.

In comparing policies, he would take advantage of any theory available that generalized about classes of policies. In considering inflation, for example, he would compare all policies in the light of the theory of prices. Since no alternatives are beyond his investigation, he would consider strict central control and the abolition of all prices and markets on the one hand and elimination of all public controls with reliance completely on the free market on the other,

Reprinted from Public Administration Review 19 (Spring, 1959): 79–88, *by permission of author and publisher.*

both in the light of whatever theoretical generalizations he could find on such hypothetical economies.

Finally, he would try to make the choice that would in fact maximize his values.

An alternative line of attack would be to set as his principal objective, either explicitly or without conscious thought, the relatively simple goal of keeping prices level. This objective might be compromised or complicated by only a few other goals, such as full employment. He would in fact disregard most other social values as beyond his present interest, and he would for the moment not even attempt to rank the few values that he regarded as immediately relevant. Were he pressed, he would quickly admit that he was ignoring many related values and many possible important consequences of his policies.

As a second step, he would outline those relatively few policy alternatives that occurred to him. He would then compare them. In comparing his limited number of alternatives, most of them familiar from past controversies, he would not ordinarily find a body of theory precise enough to carry him through a comparison of their respective consequences. Instead he would rely heavily on the record of past experience with small policy steps to predict the consequences of similar steps extended into the future.

Moreover, he would find that the policy alternatives combined objectives or values in different ways. For example, one policy might offer price level stability at the cost of some risk of unemployment; another might offer less price stability but also less risk of unemployment. Hence, the next step in his approach—the final selection— would combine into one the choice among values and the choice among instruments for reaching values. It would not, as in the first method of policy-making, approximate a more mechanical process of choosing the means that best satisfied goals that were previously clarified and ranked. Because practitioners of the second approach expect to achieve their goals only partially, they would expect to repeat endlessly the sequence just described, as conditions and aspirations changed and as accuracy of prediction improved.

BY ROOT OR BY BRANCH

For complex problems, the first of these two approaches is of course impossible. Although such an approach can be described, it cannot be practiced except for relatively simple problems and even then only in a somewhat modified form. It assumes intellectual capacities and sources of information that men simply do not possess, and it is even more absurd as an approach to policy when the time and money that can be allocated to a policy problem is limited, as is always the case. Of particular importance to public administrators is the fact that public agencies are in effect usually instructed not to practice the first method. That is to say, their prescribed functions and constraints—the politically or legally possible—restrict their attention to relatively few values and relatively few alternative policies among the countless alternatives that might be imagined. It is the second method that is practiced.

Curiously, however, the literatures of decision-making, policy formulation, planning, and public administration formalize the first approach rather than the second, leaving public administrators who handle complex decisions in the position of practicing what few preach. For emphasis I run some risk of overstatement. True enough, the literature is well aware of limits on man's capacities and of the inevitability that policies will be approached in some such style as the second. But attempts to formalize rational policy formulation —to lay out explicitly the necessary steps in the process—usually describe the first approach and not the second.[1]

The common tendency to describe policy formulation even for complex problems as though it followed the first approach has been strengthened by the attention given to, and successes enjoyed by, operations research, statistical decision theory, and systems analysis. The hallmarks of these procedures, typical of the first approach, are clarity of objective, explicitness of evaluation, a high degree of comprehensiveness of overview, and, wherever possible, quantification of values for mathematical analysis. But these advanced procedures remain largely the appropriate techniques of relatively small-scale problem-solving where the total number of variables to be considered is small and value problems restricted. Charles Hitch, head of the Economics Division of RAND Corporation, one of the leading centers for application of these techniques, has written:

I would make the empirical generalization from my experience at RAND and elsewhere that operations research is the art of sub-optimizing, i.e., of solving some lower-level problems, and that difficulties increase and our special competence diminishes by an order of magnitude with every level of decision making we attempt to ascend. The sort of simple explicit model which operations researchers are so proficient in using can certainly reflect most of the significant factors influencing traffic control on the George Washington Bridge, but the proportion of the relevant reality which we can represent by any such model or models in studying, say, a major foreign-policy decision, appears to be almost trivial.[2]

Accordingly, I propose in this paper to clarify and formalize the second method, much neglected in the literature. This might be described as the method of *successive limited comparisons*. I will contrast it with the first approach, which might be called the rational-comprehensive method.[3] More impressionistically and briefly—and therefore generally used in this article—they could be characterized as the branch method and root method, the former continually building out from the current situation, step-by-step and by small degrees; the latter starting from fundamentals anew each time, building on the past only as experience is embodied in a theory, and always prepared to start completely from the ground up.

Let us put the characteristics of the two methods side by side in simplest terms.

Rational-Comprehensive (Root)	Successive Limited Comparisons (Branch)
1a. Clarification of values or objectives distinct from and usually prerequisite to empirical analysis of alternative policies.	1b. Selection of value goals and empirical analysis of the needed action are not distinct from one another but are closely intertwined.
2a. Policy-formulation is therefore approached through means-end analysis: First the ends are isolated, then the means to achieve them are sought.	2b. Since means and ends are not distinct, means-end analysis is often inappropriate or limited.
3a. The test of a "good" policy is that is can be shown to be the most appropriate means to desired ends.	3b. The test of a "good" policy is typically that various analysts find themselves directly agreeing on a policy (without their agreeing that it is the most appropriate means to an agreed objective).

Rational-Comprehensive (Root)	Successive Limited Comparisons (Branch)
4a. Analysis is comprehensive; every important relevant factor is taken into account.	4b. Analysis is drastically limited: i) Important possible outcomes are neglected. ii) Important alternative potential policies are neglected. iii) Important affected values are neglected.
5a. Theory is often heavily relied upon.	5b. A succession of comparisons greatly reduces or eliminates reliance on theory.

Assuming that the root method is familiar and understandable, we proceed directly to clarification of its alternative by contrast. In explaining the second, we shall be describing how most administrators do in fact approach complex questions, for the root method, the "best" way as a blueprint or model, is in fact not workable for complex policy questions, and administrators are forced to use the method of successive limited comparisons.

INTERTWINING EVALUATION AND EMPIRICAL ANALYSIS (1b)

The quickest way to understand how values are handled in the method of successive limited comparisons is to see how the root method often breaks down in *its* handling of values or objectives. The idea that values should be clarified, and in advance of the examination of alternative policies, is appealing. But what happens when we attempt it for complex social problems? The first difficulty is that on many critical values or objectives, citizens disagree, congressmen disagree, and public administrators disagree. Even where a fairly specific objective is prescribed for the administrator, there remains considerable room for disagreement on sub-objectives. Consider, for example, the conflict with respect to locating public housing, described in Meyerson and Banfield's study of the Chicago Housing Authority[4]—disagreement which occurred despite the clear objective of providing a certain number of public housing units in the city. Similarly conflicting are objectives in highway location, traffic control, minimum wage administration, development of tourist facilities in national parks, or insect control.

Administrators cannot escape these conflicts by ascertaining the majority's preference, for preferences have not been registered on most issues; indeed, there often *are* no preferences in the absence of public discussion sufficient to bring an issue to the attention of the electorate. Furthermore, there is a question of whether intensity of feeling should be considered as well as the number of persons preferring each alternative. By the impossibility of doing otherwise, administrators often are reduced to deciding policy without clarifying objectives first.

Even when an administrator resolves to follow his own values as a criterion for decisions, he often will not know how to rank them when they conflict with one another, as they usually do. Suppose, for example, that an administrator must relocate tenants living in tenements scheduled for destruction. One objective is to empty the buildings fairly promptly, another is to find suitable accommodation for persons displaced, another is to avoid friction with residents in other areas in which a large influx would be unwelcome, another is to deal with all concerned through persuasion if possible, and so on.

How does one state even to himself the relative importance of these partially conflicting values? A simple ranking of them is not enough; one needs ideally to know how much of one value is worth sacrificing for some of another value. The answer is that typically the administrator chooses—and must choose—directly among policies in which these values are combined in different ways. He cannot first clarify his values and then choose among policies.

A more subtle third point underlies both the first two. Social objectives do not always have the same relative values. One objective may be highly prized in one circumstance, another in another circumstance. If, for example, an administrator values highly both the dispatch with which his agency can carry through its projects *and* good public relations, it matters little which of the two possibly conflicting values he favors in some abstract or general sense. Policy questions arise in forms which put to administrators such a question as: Given the degree to which we are or are not already achieving the values of dispatch and the values of good public relations, is it worth sacrificing a little speed for a happier clientele, or is it better to risk offending the clientele so that we can get on with our work? The answer to such a question varies with circumstances.

The value problem is, as the example shows, always a problem of adjustments at a margin. But there is no practicable way to state marginal objectives or values except in terms of particular policies. That one value is preferred to another in one decision situation does not mean that it will be preferred in another decision situation in which it can be had only at great sacrifice of another value. Attempts to rank or order values in general and abstract terms so that they do not shift from decision to decision end up by ignoring the relevant marginal preferences. The significance of this third point thus goes very far. Even if all administrators had at hand an agreed set of values, objectives, and constraints, and an agreed ranking of these values, objectives, and constraints, their marginal values in actual choice situations would be impossible to formulate.

Unable consequently to formulate the relevant values first and then choose among policies to achieve them, administrators must choose directly among alternative policies that offer different marginal combinations of values. Somewhat paradoxically, the only practicable way to disclose one's relevant marginal values even to oneself is to describe the policy one chooses to achieve them. Except roughly and vaguely, I know of no way to describe—or even to understand—what my relative evaluations are for, say, freedom and security, speed and accuracy in governmental decisions, or low taxes and better schools than to describe my preferences among specific policy choices that might be made between the alternatives in each of the pairs.

In summary, two aspects of the process by which values are actually handled can be distinguished. The first is clear: evaluation and empirical analysis are intertwined; that is, one chooses among values and among policies at one and the same time. Put a little more elaborately, one simultaneously chooses a policy to attain certain objectives and chooses the objectives themselves. The second aspect is related but distinct: the administrator focuses his attention on marginal or incremental values. Whether he is aware of it or not, he does not find general formulations of objectives very helpful and in fact makes specific marginal or incremental comparisons. Two policies, X and Y, confront him. Both promise the same degree of attainment of objectives a, b, c, d, and e. But X promises him somewhat more of f than does Y, while Y promises him somewhat more of g than does X. In choosing between them, he is in fact offered the alternative of a marginal or incremental amount of f at the expense of a marginal or incremental amount of g. The only values that are relevant to his choice are these increments by which the two policies differ; and, when he finally chooses between the two marginal values, he does so by making a choice between policies.[5]

As to whether the attempt to clarify objectives in advance of policy selection is more or less rational than the close intertwining of marginal evaluation and empirical analysis, the principal difference established is that for complex problems the first is impossible and irrelevant, and the second is both possible and relevant. The second is possible because the administrator need not try to analyze any values except the values by which alternative policies differ and need not be concerned with them except as they differ marginally. His need for information on values or objectives is drastically reduced as compared with the root method; and his capacity for grasping, comprehending, and relating values to one another is not strained beyond the breaking point.

RELATIONS BETWEEN MEANS AND ENDS (2b)

Decision-making is ordinarily formalized as a means-ends relationship: means are conceived to be evaluated and chosen in the light of ends finally selected independently of and prior to the choice of means. This is the means-ends relationship of the root method. But it follows from all that has just been said that such a means-ends relationship is possible only to the extent that values are agreed upon, are reconcilable, and are stable at the margin. Typically, therefore, such a means-ends relationship is absent from the branch method, where means and ends are simultaneously chosen.

Yet any departure from the means-ends relationship of the root method will strike some readers as inconceivable. For it will appear to them that only in such a relationship is it possible to determine whether one policy choice is better or worse than another. How can an administrator know whether he has made a wise or foolish decision if he is without prior values or objectives by which to judge his decisions? The answer to this question calls up the third distinctive difference between root and branch methods: how to decide the best policy.

THE TEST OF "GOOD" POLICY (3b)

In the root method, a decision is "correct," "good," or "rational" if it can be shown to attain some specified objective, where the objective can be specified without simply describing the decision itself. Where objectives are defined only through the marginal or incremental approach to values described above, it is still sometimes possible to test whether a policy does in fact attain the desired objectives; but a precise statement of the objectives takes the form of a description of the policy chosen or some alternative to it. To show that a policy is mistaken one cannot offer an abstract argument that important objectives are not achieved; one must instead argue that another policy is more to be preferred.

So far, the departure from customary ways of looking at problem-solving is not troublesome, for many administrators will be quick to agree that the most effective discussion of the correctness of policy does take the form of comparison with other policies that might have been chosen. But what of the situation in which administrators cannot agree on values or objectives, either abstractly or in marginal terms? What then is the test of "good" policy? For the root method, there is no test. Agreement on objectives failing, there is no standard of "correctness." For the method of successive limited comparisons, the test is agreement on policy itself, which remains possible even when agreement on values is not.

It has been suggested that continuing agreement in Congress on the desirability of extending old age insurance stems from liberal desires to strengthen the welfare programs of the federal government and from conservative desires to reduce union demands for private pension plans. If so, this is an excellent demonstration of the ease with which individuals of different ideologies often can agree on concrete policy. Labor mediators report a similar phenomenon: the contestants cannot agree on criteria for settling their disputes but can agree on specific proposals. Similarly, when one administrator's objective turns out to be another's means, they often can agree on policy.

Agreement on policy thus becomes the only practicable test of the policy's correctness. And for one administrator to seek to win the other over to agreement on ends as well would accomplish nothing and create quite unnecessary controversy.

If agreement directly on policy as a test for "best" policy seems a poor substitute for testing the policy against its objectives, it ought to be remembered that objectives themselves have no ultimate validity other than they are agreed upon. Hence agreement is the test of "best" policy in both methods. But where the root method requires agreement on what elements in the decision constitute objectives and on which of these objectives should be sought, the branch method falls back on agreement wherever it can be found.

In an important sense, therefore, it is not irrational for an administrator to defend a policy as good without being able to specify what it is good for.

NON-COMPREHENSIVE ANALYSIS (4b)

Ideally, rational-comprehensive analysis leaves out nothing important. But it is impossible to take everything important into consideration unless "important" is so narrowly defined that analysis is in fact quite limited. Limits on human intellectual capacities and on available information set definite limits to man's capacity to be comprehensive. In actual fact, therefore, no one can practice the rational-comprehensive method for really complex problems, and every administrator faced with a sufficiently complex problem must find ways drastically to simplify.

An administrator assisting in the formulation of agricultural economic policy cannot in the first place be competent on all possible policies. He cannot even comprehend one policy entirely. In planning a soil bank program, he cannot successfully anticipate the impact of higher or lower farm income on, say, urbanization—the possible consequent loosening of family ties, possible consequent eventual need for revisions in social security and further implications for tax problems arising out of new federal responsibilities for social security and municipal responsibilities for urban services. Nor, to follow another line of repercussions, can he work through the soil bank program's effects on prices for agricultural products in foreign markets and consequent implications for foreign relations, including those arising out of economic rivalry between the United States and the U.S.S.R.

In the method of successive limited comparisons, simplification is systematically achieved in two principal ways. First, it is achieved through limitation of policy comparisons to those policies that differ in relatively small degree from policies presently in effect. Such a limitation immediately reduces the number of alternatives to be investigated and also drastically simplifies the character of the investigation of each. For it is not necessary to undertake fundamental inquiry into an alternative and its consequences; it is necessary only to study those respects in which the proposed alternative and its consequences differ from the status quo. The empirical comparison of marginal differences among alternative policies that differ only marginally is, of course, a counterpart to the incremental or marginal comparison of values discussed above.[6]

Relevance as Well as Realism

It is a matter of common observation that in Western democracies public administrators and policy analysts in general do largely limit their analyses to incremental or marginal differences in policies that are chosen to differ only incrementally. They do not do so, however, solely because they desperately need some way to simplify their problems; they also do so in order to be relevant. Democracies change their policies almost entirely through incremental adjustments. Policy does not move in leaps and bounds.

The incremental character of political change in the United States has often been remarked. The two major political parties agree on fundamentals; they offer alternative policies to the voters only on relatively small points of difference. Both parties favor full employment, but they define it somewhat differently; both favor the development of water power resources, but in slightly different ways; and both favor unemployment compensation, but not the same level of benefits. Similarly, shifts of policy within a party take place largely through a series of relatively small changes, as can be seen in their only gradual acceptance of the idea of governmental responsibility for support of the unemployed, a change in party positions beginning in the early 30s and culminating in a sense in the Employment Act of 1946.

Party behavior is in turn rooted in public attitudes, and political theorists cannot conceive of democracy's surviving in the United States in the absence of fundamental agreement on potentially disruptive issues, with consequent limitation of policy debates to relatively small differences in policy.

Since the policies ignored by the administrator are politically impossible and so irrelevant, the simplification of analysis achieved by concentrating on policies that differ only incrementally is not a capricious kind of simplification. In addition, it can be argued that, given the limits on knowledge within which policy-makers are confined, simplifying by limiting the focus to small variations from present policy makes the most of available knowledge. Because policies being considered are like present and past policies, the administrator can obtain information and claim some insight. Nonincremental policy proposals are therefore typically not only politically irrelevant but also unpredictable in their consequences.

The second method of simplification of analysis is the practice of ignoring important possible consequences of possible policies, as well as the values attached to the neglected consequences. If this appears to disclose a shocking shortcoming of successive limited comparisons, it can be replied that, even if the exclusions are random, policies may nevertheless be more intelligently formulated than through futile attempts to achieve a comprehensiveness beyond human capacity. Actually, however, the exclusions, seeming arbitrary or random from one point of view, need be neither.

Achieving a Degree of Comprehensiveness

Suppose that each value neglected by one policy-making agency were a major concern of at least one other agency. In that case, a helpful division of labor would be achieved, and no agency need find its task beyond its capacities. The shortcomings of such a system would be that one agency might destroy a value either before another agency could be activated to safeguard it or in spite of another agency's efforts. But the possibility that important values may be lost is present in any form of organization, even where agencies attempt to comprehend in planning more than is humanly possible.

The virtue of such a hypothetical division of labor is that every important interest or value has its watchdog. And these watchdogs can protect the interests in their jurisdiction in two quite different ways: first, by redressing damages done by other agencies; and, second, by anticipating and heading off injury before it occurs.

In a society like that of the United States in which individuals are free to combine to pursue almost any possible common interest they might have and in which government agencies are sensitive to the pressures of these groups, the system described is approximated. Almost every interest has its watchdog. Without claiming that every interest has a sufficiently powerful watchdog, it can be argued that our system often can assure a more comprehensive regard for the values of the whole society than any attempt at intellectual comprehensiveness.

In the United States, for example, no part of government attempts a comprehensive overview of policy on income distribution. A policy nevertheless evolves, and one responding to a wide variety of interests. A process of mutual adjustment among farm groups, labor unions, municipalities and school boards, tax authorities, and government agencies with responsibilities in the fields of housing, health, highways, national parks, fire, and police accomplishes a distribution of income in which particular income problems neglected at one point in the decision processes become central at another point.

Mutual adjustment is more pervasive than the explicit forms it takes in negotiation between groups; it persists through the mutual impacts of groups upon each other even where they are not in communication. For all the imperfections and latent dangers in this ubiquitous process of mutual adjustment, it will often accomplish an adaptation of policies to a wider range of interests than could be done by one group centrally.

Note, too, how the incremental pattern of policy-making fits with the multiple pressure pattern. For when decisions are only incremental—closely related to known policies, it is easier for one group to anticipate the kind of moves another might make and easier too for it to make correction for injury already accomplished.[7]

Even partisanship and narrowness, to use pejorative terms, will sometimes be assets to rational decision-making, for they can doubly insure that what one agency neglects, another will not; they specialize personnel to distinct points of view. The claim is valid that effective rational coordination of the federal administration, if possible to achieve at all, would require an agreed set of values[8]—if "rational" is defined as the practice of the root method of decision-making. But a high degree of administrative coordination occurs as each agency adjusts its policies to the concerns of the other agencies in the process of fragmented decision-making I have just described.

For all the apparent shortcomings of the incremental approach to policy alternatives with its arbitrary exclusion coupled with fragmentation, when compared to the root method, the branch method often looks far superior. In the root method, the inevitable exclusion of factors is accidental, unsystematic, and not defensible by any argument so far developed, while in the branch method the exclusions are deliberate, systematic, and defensible. Ideally, of course, the root method does not exclude; in practice it must.

Nor does the branch method necessarily neglect long-run considerations and objectives. It is clear that important values must be omitted in considering policy, and sometimes the only way long-run objectives can be given adequate attention is through the neglect of short-run considerations. But the values omitted can be either long-run or short-run.

SUCCESSION OF COMPARISONS (5b)

The final distinctive element in the branch method is that the comparisons, together with the policy choice, proceed in a chronological series. Policy is not made once and for all; it is made and re-made endlessly. Policy-making is a process of successive approximation to some desired objectives in which what is desired itself continues to change under reconsideration.

Making policy is at best a very rough process. Neither social scientists, nor politicians, nor public administrators yet know enough about the social world to avoid repeated error in predicting the consequences of policy moves. A wise policy-maker consequently expects that his policies will achieve only part of what he hopes and at the same time will produce unanticipated consequences he would have preferred to avoid. If he proceeds through a *succession* of incremental changes, he avoids serious lasting mistakes in several ways.

In the first place, past sequences of policy steps have given him knowledge about the probable consequences of further similar steps. Second, he need not attempt big jumps toward his goals that would require predictions beyond his or anyone else's knowledge, because he never expects his policy to be a final resolution of a problem. His decision is only one step, one that if successful can quickly be followed by another. Third, he is in effect able to test his previous predictions as he moves on to each further step. Lastly, he often can remedy a past error fairly quickly—more quickly than if policy proceeded through more distinct steps widely spaced in time.

Compare this comparative analysis of incremental changes with the aspiration to employ theory in the root method. Man cannot think without classifying, without subsuming one experience under a more general category of experiences. The attempt to push categorization as far as possible and to find general propositions which can be applied to specific situations is what I refer to with the word "theory." Where root analysis often leans heavily on theory in this sense, the branch method does not.

The assumption of root analysts is that theory is the most systematic and economical way to bring relevant knowledge to bear on a specific problem. Granting the assumption, an unhappy fact is that we do not have adequate theory to apply to problems in any policy area, although theory is more adequate in some areas—monetary policy, for example—than in others. Comparative analysis, as in the branch method, is sometimes a systematic alternative to theory.

Suppose an administrator must choose among a small group of policies that differ only incrementally from each other and from present policy. He might aspire to "understand" each of the alternatives—for example, to know all the consequences of each aspect of each policy. If so, he would indeed require theory. In fact, however, he would usually decide that, *for policy-making purposes,* he need know, as explained above, only the consequences of each of those aspects of the policies in which they differed from one another. For this much more modest aspiration, he requires no theory (although it might be helpful, if available), for he can proceed to isolate probable differences by examining the differences in consequences associated with past differences in policies, a feasible program because he can take his observations from a long sequence of incremental changes.

For example, without a more comprehensive social theory about juvenile delinquency than scholars have yet produced, one cannot possibly understand the ways in which a variety of public policies— say on education, housing, recreation, employment, race relations, and policing—might encourage or discourage delinquency. And one needs such an understanding if he undertakes the comprehensive overview of the problem prescribed in the models of the root method. If, however, one merely wants to mobilize knowledge sufficient to assist in a choice among a small group of similar policies—alternative policies on juvenile court procedures, for example—he can do so by comparative analysis of the results of similar past policy moves.

THEORISTS AND PRACTITIONERS

This difference explains—in some cases at least—why the administrator often feels that the outside expert or academic problem-solver is sometimes not helpful and why they in turn often urge more theory on him. And it explains why an administrator often feels more confident when "flying by the seat of his pants" than when following the advice of theorists. Theorists often ask the administrator to go the long way round to the solution of his problems, in effect ask him to follow the best canons of the scientific method, when the administrator knows that the best available theory will work less well than more modest incremental comparisons. Theorists do not realize that the administrator is often in fact practicing a systematic method. It would be foolish to push this explanation too far, for sometimes practical decision-makers are pursuing neither a theoretical approach nor successive comparisons, nor any other systematic method.

It may be worth emphasizing that theory is sometimes of extremely limited helpfulness in policy-making for at least two rather different reasons. It is greedy for facts; it can be constructed only through a great collection of observations. And it is typically insufficiently precise for application to a policy process that moves through small changes. In contrast, the comparative method both economizes on the need for facts and directs the analyst's attention to just those facts that are relevant to the fine choices faced by the decision-maker.

With respect to precision of theory, economic theory serves as an example. It predicts that an economy without money or prices would in certain specified ways misallocate resources, but this finding pertains to an alternative far removed from the kind of policies on which administrators need help. On the other hand, it is not precise enough to predict the consequences of policies restricting business mergers, and this is the kind of issue on which the administrators need help. Only in relatively restricted areas does economic theory achieve sufficient precision to go far in resolving policy questions; its helpfulness in policy-making is always so limited that it requires supplementation through comparative analysis.

SUCCESSIVE COMPARISON AS A SYSTEM

Successive limited comparisons is, then, indeed a method or system; it is not a failure of method for which administrators ought to apologize. None the less, its imperfections, which have not been explored in this paper, are many. For example, the method is without a built-in safeguard for all relevant values, and it also may lead the decision-maker to overlook excellent policies for no other reason than that they are not suggested by the chain of successive policy steps leading up to the present. Hence, it ought to be said that under this method, as well as under some of the most sophisticated variants of the root method—operations research, for example—policies will continue to be as foolish as they are wise.

Why then bother to describe the method in all the above detail? Because it is in fact a common method of policy formulation, and is, for complex problems, the principal reliance of administrators as well as of other policy analysts.[9] And because it will be superior to any other decision-making method available for complex problems in many circumstances, certainly superior to a futile attempt at superhuman comprehensiveness. The reaction of the public administrator to the exposition of method doubtless will be less a discovery of a new method than a better acquaintance with an old. But by becoming more conscious of their practice of this method, administrators might practice it with more skill and know when to extend or constrict its use. (That they sometimes practice it effectively and sometimes not may explain the extremes of opinion on "muddling through," which is both praised as a highly sophisticated form of problem-solving and denounced as no method at all. For I suspect that in so far as there is a system in what is known as "muddling through," this method is it.)

One of the noteworthy incidental consequences of clarification of the method is the light it throws on the suspicion an administrator sometimes entertains that a consultant or adviser is not speaking relevantly and responsibly when in fact by all ordinary objective evidence he is. The trouble lies in the fact that most of us approach policy problems within a framework given by our view of a chain of successive policy choices made up to the present. One's thinking about appropriate policies with respect, say, to urban traffic control is greatly influenced by one's knowledge of the incremental steps taken up to the present. An administrator enjoys an intimate knowledge of his past sequences that "outsiders" do not share, and his thinking and that of the "outsider" will consequently be different in ways that may puzzle both. Both may appear to be talking intelligently, yet each may find the other unsatisfactory. The relevance of the policy chain of succession is even more clear when an American tries to discuss, say, antitrust policy with a Swiss, for the chains of policy in the two countries are strikingly different and the two individuals consequently have organized their knowledge in quite different ways.

If this phenomenon is a barrier to communication, an understanding of it promises an enrichment of intellectual interaction in policy formulation. Once the source of difference is understood, it will sometimes be stimulating for an administrator to seek out a policy analyst whose recent experience is with a policy chain different from his own.

This raises again a question only briefly discussed above on the merits of like-mindedness among government administrators. While much of organization theory argues the virtues of common values and agreed organizational objectives, for complex problems in which the root method is inapplicable, agencies will want among their own personnel two types of diversification: administrators whose thinking is organized by reference to policy chains other than those familiar to most members of the organization and, even more commonly, administrators whose professional or personal values or interests create diversity of view (perhaps coming from different specialties, social classes, geographical areas) so that, even within a single agency, decision-making can be fragmented and parts of the agency can serve as watchdogs for other parts.

NOTES

1. James G. March and Herbert A. Simon similarly characterize the literature. They also take some important steps, as have Simon's recent articles, to describe a less heroic model of policy-making. See *Organizations* (John Wiley and Sons, 1958), p. 137.

2. "Operations Research and National Planning—A Dissent," 5 *Operations Research* 718 (October, 1957). Hitch's dissent is from particular points made in the article to which his paper is a reply; his claim that operations research is for low-level problems is widely accepted.

For examples of the kind of problems to which operations research is applied, see C.W. Churchman, R.L. Ackoff and E.L. Arnoff, *Introduction to Operations Research* (John Wiley and Sons, 1957); and J.F. Mc-Closkey and J.M. Coppinger (eds.), *Operations Research for Management,* Vol. II (The Johns Hopkins Press, 1956).

3. I am assuming that administrators often make policy and advise in the making of policy and am treating decision-making and policy-making as synonymous for purposes of this paper.

4. Martin Meyerson and Edward C. Banfield, *Politics, Planning and the Public Interest* (The Free Press, 1955).

5. The line of argument is, of course, an extension of the theory of

market choice, especially the theory of consumer choice, to public policy choices.

6. A more precise definition of incremental policies and a discussion of whether a change that appears "small" to one observer might be seen differently by another is to be found in my "Policy Analysis," 48 *American Economic Review* 298 (June, 1958).

7. The link between the practice of the method of successive limited comparisons and mutual adjustment of interests in a highly fragmented decision-making process adds a new facet to pluralist theories of government and administration.

8. Herbert Simon, Donald W. Smithburg, and Victor A. Thompson, *Public Administration* (Alfred A. Knopf, 1950), p. 434.

9. Elsewhere I have explored this same method of policy formulation as practiced by academic analysts of policy ("Policy Analysis," 48 *American Economic Review* 298 [June, 1958]). Although it has been here presented as a method for public administrators, it is no less necessary to analysts more removed from immediate policy questions despite their tendencies to describe their own analytical efforts as though they were the rational-comprehensive method with an especially heavy use of theory. Similarly, this same method is inevitably resorted to in personal problem-solving, where means and ends are sometimes impossible to separate, where aspirations or objectives undergo constant development, and where drastic simplification of the complexity of the real world is urgent if problems are to be solved in the time that can be given to them. To an economist accustomed to dealing with the marginal or incremental concept in market processes, the central idea in the method is that both evaluation and empirical analysis are incremental. Accordingly I have referred to the method elsewhere as "the incremental method."

systems analysis techniques for public policy problems

e. s. quade

INTRODUCTION

Broadly speaking, any orderly analytic study designed to help a decision-maker identify a preferred course of action from among possible alternatives might be termed a systems analysis. As commonly used in the defense community, the phrase "systems analysis" refers to formal inquiries intended to advise a decision-maker on the policy choices involved in such matters as weapon development, force posture design, or the determination of strategic objectives. A typical analysis might tackle the question of what might be the possible characteristics of a new strategic bomber and whether one should be developed; whether tactical air wings, carrier task forces, or neither could be substituted for United States ground divisions in Europe; or whether we should modify the test-ban treaty now that the Chinese Communists have nuclear weapons and, if so, how.

Originally entitled "Systems Analysis Techniques for Planning-Programming-Budgeting," Report P-3322 (Santa Monica, California: The Rand Corporation, March, 1966); reprinted by permission of the author and publisher. Any views expressed in this paper are those of the author. They should not be interpreted as reflecting the views of the Rand Corporation or the official opinion or policy of any of its governmental or private research sponsors. Papers are reproduced by the Rand Corporation as a courtesy to the members of its staff.

151

Systems analysis represents an approach to, or way of looking at, complex problems of choice under uncertainty that should have utility in the Planning–Programming–Budgeting (PPB) process. Our purpose is to discuss the question of extending military systems analysis to the civilian activities of the government, to point out some of the limitations of analysis in this role, and to call attention to techniques that seem likely to be particularly useful. I will interpret the term "technique" broadly enough to range from proven mathematical algorithms to certain broad principles that often seem to be associated with successful analysis.

Some fifteen years ago a similar extension raised quite some doubt. When weapons system analysts (particularly those at The Rand Corporation) began to include the formulation of national security policy and strategy as part of their field of interest, experienced "military analysts" in the Pentagon and elsewhere were not encouraging. They held that the tools, techniques, and concepts of operations analysis, as practiced in World War II, or of weapons system optimization and selection—in which analysts had been reasonably successful—would not carry over, that strategy and policy planning were arts and would remain so.

Fortunately, these skeptics were only partially right. It is true that additional concepts and methodologies significantly different from those of earlier analysis had to be developed. But there has been substantial progress, and the years since 1961 have seen a marked increase in the extent to which analyses of policy and strategy have influenced decision-makers on the broadest issues of national defense.

Today's contemplated extension to PPB is long overdue and possibly even more radical. Systems analysis has barely entered the domain of the social sciences. Here, in urban planning, in education, in welfare, and in other nonmilitary activities, as Olaf Helmer remarks in his perceptive essay:

We are faced with an abundance of challenges: how to keep the peace, how to alleviate the hardships of social change, how to provide food and comfort for the inaffluent, how to improve the social institutions and the values of the affluent, how to cope with revolutionary innovations, and so on.[1]

Since systems analysis represents an approach to, or way of looking at, any problem of choice under uncertainty, it should be able to help with these problems.

Actually, systematic analysis of *routine* operations is widespread throughout the civil government as well as in commerce, industry, and the military. Here analysis takes its most mathematical form and, in a certain sense, its most fruitful role. For example, it may help to determine how Post Office pickup trucks should be routed to collect mail from deposit boxes, or whether computers should be rented or purchased to handle warehouse inventories, or what type of all-weather landing system should be installed in new commercial aircraft. Such problems are typically an attempt to increase the efficiency of a man-machine system in a situation where it is clear what "more efficient" means. The analysis can often be reduced to the application of a well understood mathematical discipline such as linear programming or queuing theory to a generic "model," which, by a specification of its parameters, can be made to fit a wide variety of operations. An "optimum" solution is then obtained by means of a systematic computational routine. The queuing model, for example, is relevant to many aspects of the operations of the Post Office, airports, service facilities, maintenance shops, and so on. In many instances such models may actually tell the client what his decision or plan ought to be. Analysis of this type is usually called operations research or management science rather than systems analysis, however.

There are, however, other decisions or problems, civilian as well as military, where computational techniques can help only with subproblems. Typical decisions of this latter type might be the determination of how much of the federal budget should be allocated to economic development and what fraction of that should be spent on South America; or whether the needs of interstate transportation are better served by improved high-speed rail transport or by higher performance highway turnpikes; or if there is some legislative action that might end the growth of juvenile delinquency. Such problems will normally involve more than the efficient allocation of resources among alternative uses; they are not "solvable" in the same sense as efficiency problems in which one can maximize some "payoff" function that clearly expresses what one is trying to accomplish. Here, rather, the objectives or goals of the action to be taken must be determined first. Decision problems associated with program budgeting are mainly of this type—where the difficulty lies in deciding what ought to be done as well as in how to do it, where it is not clear what "more efficient" means, and where many of the factors in the problem elude quantification. The final program recommendation will thus remain in part a matter of faith and judgment. Studies to help with these problems are systems analyses rather than operations research.[2]

Every systems analysis involves, at one stage, a comparison of alternative courses of action in terms of their costs and their effectiveness in attaining a specified objective. Usually this comparison takes the form of an attempt to designate the alternative that will minimize the costs, subject to some fixed performance requirement (something like reduce unemployment to less than 2 percent in two years, or add a certain number of miles to the interstate highway system); or conversely, it is an attempt to maximize some physical measure of performance subject to a budget constraint. Such evaluations are called cost-effectiveness analyses.[3] Since they often receive the lion's share of attention, the entire study also is frequently called a cost-effectiveness analysis. But this label puts too much emphasis on just one aspect of the decision process. In analyses designed to furnish broad policy advice, other facets of the problem are of greater significance than the comparison of alternatives: the specification of sensible objectives, the determination of a satisfactory way to measure performance, the influence of considerations that cannot be quantified, or the design of better alternatives.

THE ESSENCE OF THE METHOD

What is there about the analytic approach that makes it better or more useful than other ways to furnish advice—than, say, an expert or a committee? In areas such as urban redevelopment or welfare planning, where there is no accepted theoretical foundation, advice obtained from experts working individually or as a committee must depend largely on judgment and intuition. *So must the advice from systems analysis.* But the virtue of such analysis is that it permits the judgment and intuition of the experts in relevant fields to be combined systematically and efficiently. The essence of the method is to construct and operate within a "model," a simplified abstraction of the real situation appropriate to the question. Such a model, which may take such varied forms as a computer simulation, an operational game, or even a purely verbal "scenario," introduces a precise structure and terminology that serve primarily as an effective means of communication, enabling the participants in the study to exercise their judgment and intuition in a concrete context and in proper relation to others. Moreover, through feed-back from the model (the results of computation, the countermoves in the game, or the critique of the scenario), the experts have a chance to revise early judgments and thus arrive at a clearer understanding of the problem and its context, and perhaps of their subject matter.[4]

The Process of Analysis

The fundamental importance of the model is seen in its relation to the other elements of analysis.[5] There are five all told, and each is present in every analysis of choice and should always be explicitly identified.

1. *The objective (or objectives)*. Systems analysis is undertaken primarily to help choose a policy or course of action. The first and most important task of the analyst is to discover what the decision-maker's objectives are (or should be) and then how to measure the extent to which these objectives are, in fact, attained by various choices. This done, strategies, policies, or possible actions can be examined, compared, and recommended on the basis of how well and how cheaply they can accomplish these objectives.

2. *The alternatives*. The alternatives are the means by which it is hoped the objectives can be attained. They may be policies or strategies or specific actions or instrumentalities and they need not be obvious substitutes for each other or perform the same specific function. Thus, education, anti-poverty measures, police protection, and slum clearance may all be alternatives in combating juvenile delinquency.

3. *The costs*. The choice of a particular alternative for accomplishing the objectives implies that certain specific resources can no longer be used for other purposes. These are the costs. For a future time period, most costs can be measured in money, but their true measure is in terms of the opportunities they preclude. Thus, if the goal is to lower traffic fatalities, the irritation and delay caused to motorists by schemes that lower automobile speed in a particular location must be considered as costs, for such irritation and delay may cause more speeding elsewhere.

4. *A model (or models)*. A model is a simplified, stylized representation of the real world that abstracts the cause-and-effect relationships essential to the question studied. The means of representa-

tion may range from a set of mathematical equations or a computer program to a purely verbal description of the situation, in which intuition alone is used to predict the consequences of various choices. In systems analysis, or any analysis of choice, the role of the model (or models, for it may be inappropriate or absurd to attempt to incorporate all the aspects of a problem in a single formulation) is to estimate for each alternative the costs that would be incurred and the extent to which the objectives would be attained.

5. *A criterion.* A criterion is a rule or standard by which to rank the alternatives in order of desirability. It provides a means for weighing cost against effectiveness.

The process of analysis takes place in three overlapping stages. In the first, the formulation stage, the issues are clarified, the extent of the inquiry limited, and the elements identified. In the second, the search stage, information is gathered and alternatives generated. The third stage is evaluation.

To start the process of evaluation or comparison (see Figure 1), the various *alternatives* (which may have to be discovered or invented as part of the analysis) are examined by means of the *models*. The models tell us what consequences or outcomes can be expected to follow from each alternative; that is, what the *costs*

FIGURE 1

The Structure of Analysis

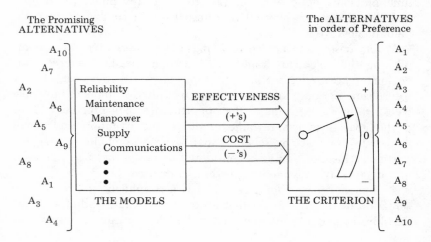

The Promising
ALTERNATIVES

The ALTERNATIVES
in order of Preference

are and the extent to which each *objective* is attained. A *criterion* can then be used to weigh the costs against performance, and thus the alternatives can be arranged in the order of preference.

Unfortunately, things are seldom tidy: too often the objectives are multiple, conflicting, and obscure; alternatives are not adequate to attain the objectives; the measures of effectiveness do not really measure the extent to which the objectives are attained; the predictions from the model are full of uncertainties; and other criteria that look almost as plausible as the one chosen may lead to a different order of preference. When this happens, we must take another approach. A single attempt or pass at a problem is seldom enough. (See Figure 2.) The key of successful analysis is a continuous cycle of formulating the problem, selecting objectives, designing alternatives, collecting data, building models, weighing cost against performance, testing for sensitivity, questioning assumptions and data, re-examining the objectives, opening new alternatives, building better models, and so on, until satisfaction is obtained or time or money force a cut-off.

In brief, a systems analysis attempts to look at the entire problem and look at it in its proper context. Characteristically, it will involve a systematic investigation of the decision-maker's objectives and of the relevant criteria; a comparison—quantitative insofar as possible—of the cost, effectiveness, risk, and timing associated with each alternative policy or strategy for achieving the objectives; and an attempt to design better alternatives and select other goals if those examined are found wanting.

Note that there is nothing really new about the procedures I have just sketched. They have been used, more or less successfully, by managers throughout government and industry since ancient times. The need for considering cost relative to performance must have occurred to the earliest planner. Systems analysis is thus not a catchword to suggest we are doing something new; at most, we are doing something better. What may be novel though, is that this sort of analysis is an attempt to look at the entire problem systematically with emphasis on explicitness, on quantification, and on the recognition of uncertainty. Also novel are the schemes or models used to explore the consequences of various choices and to eliminate inferior action in situations where the relationships cannot be represented adequately by a mathematical model.

Note that there is nothing in these procedures that guarantees

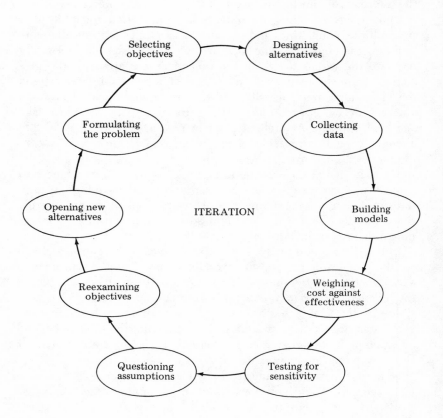

FIGURE 2
The Key to Analysis

the advice from the analysis to be good. They do not preclude the possibility that we are addressing the wrong problem or have allowed our personal biases to bar a better solution from consideration. When a study is a poor one it is rarely because the computer was not powerful enough or because the methods of optimization were not sufficiently sophisticated, but because it had the wrong objective or poor criteria. There are some characteristics of a study, however, that seem to be associated with good analysis. Let me identify some of these.

Principles of Good Analysis

1. It is all important to tackle the "right" problem. A large part of the investigators' efforts must be invested in thinking about the problem, exploring its proper breadth, and trying to discover the appropriate objectives and to search out good criteria for choice. If we have not chosen the best set of alternatives to compare we will not discover the best solution. But if we have chosen the wrong objective then we might find a solution to the wrong problem. Getting an accurate answer to the wrong question is likely to be far less helpful than an incomplete answer to the right question.

2. The analysis must be systems oriented. Rather than isolating a part of the problem by neglecting its interactions with other parts, an effort should be made to extend the boundaries of the inquiry as far as required for the problem at hand, to find what interdependencies are important, and to study the entire complex system. This should be done even if it requires the use of purely intuitive judgment.

An interdisciplinary team of persons having a variety of knowledge and skills is helpful here. This is not so merely because a complex problem is likely to involve many diverse factors that cannot be handled by a single discipline. More importantly, a problem looks different to an economist, an engineer, a political scientist, or a professional bureaucrat, and their different approaches may contribute to finding a solution.

3. The presence of uncertainty should be recognized, and an attempt made to take it into account. Most important decisions are fraught with uncertainty. In planning urban redevelopment we are uncertain about city growth patterns, about the extent to which freeways or rapid transit systems will be used, about costs, about tax revenues, about the demand for services. For many of these things, there is no way to say with confidence that a given estimate is correct. The analyst attempts to identify these uncertainties and evaluate their impact. Often he can say the value of a parameter will be more than A but less than B. Sometimes it is possible to indicate how the uncertainty can be reduced by further testing and how long that will take. Most important, the analysis should determine the effect of uncertainty on the answers. This is done by a sensitivity analysis that shows the answers change in response to changes in assumptions and estimates.[6]

The study report should include the presentation of a contingency table showing the effectiveness and cost associated with each significant alternative for various future environments and for each set of assumptions about the uncertainties.

4. The analysis attempts to discover new alternatives as well as to improve the obvious ones. The invention of new alternatives can be much more valuable than an exhaustive comparison of given alternatives, none of which may be very satisfactory.

5. While in problems of public policy or national security the scientific method of controlled repeated experiment cannot be used, the analysis should strive to attain the standards traditional to science. These are (1) intersubjectivity: results obtained by processes that can be duplicated by others to attain the same results; (2) explicitness: use of calculations, assumptions, data, and judgments that are subject to checking, criticism, and disagreement; and (3) objectivity: conclusions do not depend on personalities, reputations, or vested interests; where possible these conclusions should be in quantitative and experimental terms.

THE MODELS

As mentioned earlier, systems analysis is flexible in the models it uses. Indeed, it has to be. Mathematics and computing machines, while extremely useful, are limited in the aid they can give in broad policy questions. If the important aspects of the problem can be completely formulated mathematically or represented numerically, techniques such as dynamic programming, game theory, queuing theory, or computer simulation may be the means of providing the best solution. But in most policy analyses, computations and computers are often more valuable for the aid they provide to intuition and understanding, rather than for the results they supply.

While a computer can solve only the problems that the analyst knows conceptually how to solve himself, it can help with many others. The objection that one cannot use results which depend on many uncertain parameters represents a lack of understanding of how systems analysis can help a decision-maker. For a study to be useful it must indicate the *relative* merit of the various alternatives and identify the critical parameters. The great advantage of a computerized model is that it gives the analyst the capability to do numerous excursions, parametric investigations, and sensitivity analyses and thus to investigate the ranking of alternatives under a host of assumptions. This may be of more practical value to the decision-maker than the ability to say with high confidence that a given alternative will have such and such a rank in a very narrowly defined situation.

The type of model appropriate to a problem depends on the problem and what we know or think we know about it.

For example, suppose we are concerned with long-range economic forecasting or decisions about the development of a national economy. The type of model to use will depend on the particular economy and on the kind of questions that must be answered. If the questions were about the United States, the model might be mathematical and possibly programmed for a computer because of its size and complexity. (By a mathematical model I mean one in which the relationships between the variables and parameters are represented by mathematical equations.) In the case of the United States, because of the vast amount of data available in the form of economic and demographic time series regarding just about every conceivable aspect of economic life, numerous mathematical and computer models have been formulated and used with more or less success.

If we are not able to abstract the situation to a series of equations or a mathematical model, some other way to represent the consequences that follow from particular choices must be found. Simulation may work. Here, instead of describing the situation directly, each element making up the real situation may be simulated by a physical object or, most often, by a digital computer using sets of random numbers, and its behavior analyzed by operating with the representation. For example, we might use computer simulation to study the economy of some Latin American country. The distinction between a computer simulation and the use of a computer to analyze a mathematical model is often a fuzzy one, but the fundamental difference is that in simulation the overall behavior of the model is studied through a case-by-case approach.

For studying the economy of a newly emerging nation such as is found in Africa, where the situation is even more poorly structured and where we have little firm knowledge of existing facts and relationships, a possible approach would be through the direct involvement of experts who have knowledge of the problem.

Ordinarily, we would like to have the judgment of more than

one expert, even though their advice usually differs. There are several ways to try for a consensus; the traditional way has been to assemble the experts in one place, to let them discuss the problem freely, and to require that they arrive at a joint answer. They could also be put to work individually, letting others seek methods for the best combined use of their findings. Or they could be asked to work in a group exercise—ranging from a simple structured discussion to a sophisticated simulation or an "operational game"—to obtain judgments from the group as a whole.

This latter approach is a laboratory simulation involving role-playing by human subjects who simulate real-world decision-makers. To study the economy of an underdeveloped country the various sectors of the economy might be simulated by specialized experts.[7] They would be expected, in acting out their roles, not so much to play a competitive game against one another, but to use their intuition as experts to simulate as best they could the attitudes and consequent decisions of their real-life counterparts. For instance, a player simulating a goods-producing sector of the economy might, within constraints, shut down or expand manufacturing facilities, modernize, change raw material and labor inputs, vary prices and so on. There would also need to be government players who could introduce new fiscal or monetary policies and regulations (taxes, subsidies, tariffs, price ceilings, etc.) as well as social and political innovations with only indirect economic implications (social security, education, appeals to patriotism, universal military service, etc.). In laying down the rules governing the players' options and constraints and the actions taken within these rules, expert judgment is essential. It is also clear that for this problem political and sociological experts will be needed, as well as economists.

There is, of course, no guarantee that the projections obtained from such a model would be reliable. But the participating experts might gain a great deal of insight. Here the game structure—again a model—furnishes the participants with an artificial, simulated environment within which they can jointly and simultaneously experiment, acquiring through feedback the insights necessary to make successful predictions within the gaming context and thus indirectly about the real world.

Another useful technique is one that military systems analysts call "scenario writing." This is an effort to show how, starting with the present, a future state might evolve out of the present one.

The idea is to show how this might happen plausibly by exhibiting a reasonable chain of events. A scenario is thus a primitive model. A collection of scenarios provides an insight on how future trends can depend on factors under our control and suggests policy options to us.

Another type of group action, somewhat less structured than the operational game, attempts to improve the panel or committee approach by subjecting the views of individual experts to each other's criticism without actual confrontation and its possible psychological shortcomings. In this approach, called the Delphi method, direct debate is replaced by the interchange of information and opinion through a carefully designed sequence of questionnaires. At each successive interrogation, the participants are given new refined information, and opinion feedback is derived by computing consensus from the earlier part of the program. The process continues until either a consensus is reached, or the conflicting views are documented fully.[8]

It should be emphasized that in many important problems it is not possible to build really quantitative models. The primary function of a model is "explanatory," to organize our thinking. As I have already stated, the essence of systems analysis is not mathematical techniques or procedures, and its recommendations need not follow from computation. What counts is the effort to compare alternatives systematically, in quantitative terms when possible, using a logical sequence of steps that can be retraced and verified by others.

The Virtues

In spite of many limitations, the decision-makers who have made use of systems analysis find it extremely useful. In fact, for some questions of national defense, analysis is essential. Without calculation there is no way to discover how many missiles may be needed to destroy a target system, or how arms control may affect security. It may be essential in other areas also; one cannot experiment radically with the national economy or even change the traffic patterns in a large city without running the risk of chaos. Analysis offers an alternative to "muddling through" or to settling national problems by yielding to the strongest pressure group. It forces the devotees of a program to make explicit their lines of argument, to calculate the resources their programs will require as well as the advantages they might produce.

It is easy, unfortunately, to exaggerate the degree of assistance that systems analysis can offer the policy-maker. At most, it can help him understand the relevant alternatives and the key interactions by providing an estimate of the costs, risks, payoffs and the time span associated with each course of action. It may lead him to consider new and better alternatives. It may sharpen the decision-maker's intuition and will certainly broaden his basis for judgment, thus helping him make a better decision. But value judgments, imprecise knowledge, intuitive estimates, and uncertainties about nature and the actions of others mean that a study can do little more than assess some of the implications of choosing one alternative over another. In practically no case, therefore, should the decision-maker expect the analysis to demonstrate that, beyond all reasonable doubt, a particular course of action is best.

The Limitations

Every systems analysis has defects. Some of these are limitations inherent in all analysis of choice. Others are a consequence of the difficulties and complexities of the question. Still others are blunders or errors in thinking, which hopefully will disappear as we learn to do better and more complete analyses.

The alternatives to analysis also have their defects. One alternative is pure intuition. This is in no sense analytic, since no effort is made to structure the problem or to establish cause-and-effect relationships and operate on them to arrive at a solution. The intuitive process is to learn everything possible about the problem, to "live with it," and to let the subconscious provide the solution.

Between pure intuition, on one hand, and systems analysis, on the other, other sources of advice can, in a sense, be considered to employ analysis, although ordinarily of a less systematic, explicit, and quantitative kind. One can turn to an expert. His opinion may, in fact, be very helpful if it results from a reasonable and impartial examination of the facts, with due allowance for uncertainty, and if his assumptions and chain of logic are made *explicit*. Only then can others use his information to form their own considered opinions. But an expert, particularly an unbiased expert, may be hard to find.

Another way to handle a problem is to turn it over to a committee. Committees, however, are much less likely than experts to make their reasoning explicit, since their findings are usually obtained by bargaining. This is not to imply that a look by a "blue ribbon" committee into such problems as poverty or the allocation of funds for foreign aid might not be useful, but a committee's greatest usefulness is likely to be in the critique of analysis done by others.

However, no matter whether the advice is supplied by an expert, a committee, or a formal study group, the analysis of a problem of choice involves the same five elements and basic structure we discussed earlier.

It is important to remember that all policy analysis falls short of being scientific research. No matter how we strive to maintain standards of scientific inquiry or how closely we attempt to follow scientific methods, we cannot turn systems analysis into science. Such analysis is designed primarily to recommend—or at least to suggest—a course of action, rather than merely to understand and predict. Like engineering, the aim is to use the results of science to do things well and cheaply. Yet, when applied to national problems, the difference from ordinary engineering is apparent in the enormous responsibility involved in the unusual difficulty of appraising—or even discovering—a value system applicable to the problems, and in the absence of ways to test the validity of the analysis.

Except for this inability to verify, systems analysis may still look like a purely rational approach to decision-making, a coldly objective, scientific method free from preconceived ideas, partisan bias, judgment and intuition.

It really is not. Judgment and intuition are used in designing the models; in deciding what alternatives to consider, what factors are relevant, what the interrelations between these factors are, and what criteria to choose; and in interpreting the results of the analysis. This fact—that judgment and intuition permeate all analysis—should be remembered when we examine the apparently precise results that seem to come with such high-precision analysis.

Many flaws are the results of pitfalls faced by the analyst. It is all too easy for him to begin to believe his own assumptions and to attach undue significance to his calculations, especially if they involve bitter arguments and extended computations. The most dangerous pitfall or source of defects is an unconscious adherence to a "party line." This is frequently caused by a cherished belief or an *attention bias*. All organizations foster one to some extent; Rand, the military services, and the civilian agencies of the government are no exception. The party line is "the most important single reason for the tremendous miscalculations that are made in foreseeing and preparing for technical advances or changes in the strategic situation."[9] Examples are plentiful: the political adviser whose aim is so fixed on maintaining peace that he completely disregards what might happen should deterrence fail; the weaponeer who is so fascinated by the startling new weapons that he has invented that he assumes the politician will allow them to be used; the union leader whose attention is so fixed on current employment that he rejects an automatic device that can spread his craft into scores of new areas. In fact, this failure to realize the vital interdependence of political purpose, diplomacy, military posture, economics, and technical feasibility is the typical flaw in most practitioners' approach to national security analysis.

There are also pitfalls for the bureaucrat who commissions a study or gives inputs to it. For instance, he may specify assumptions and limit the problem arbitrarily. When a problem is first observed in one part of an organization, there is a tendency to seek a solution completely contained in that part. An administrator is thus likely to pose his problems in such a way as to bar from consideration alternatives or criteria that do not fit into his idea of the way things should be done; for example, he may not think of using ships for some tasks now being done by aircraft. Also, to act wisely on the basis of someone else's analysis one should, at the very least, understand the important and fundamental principles involved. One danger associated with analysis is that it may be employed by an administrator who is unaware of or unwilling to accept its limitations.

Pitfalls are one thing, but the inherent limitations of analysis itself are another. These limitations confine analysis to an advisory role. Three are commented on here: analysis is necessarily incomplete; measures of effectiveness are inevitably approximate; and ways to predict the future are lacking.

Analysis is Necessarily Incomplete

Time and money costs obviously place sharp limits on how far any inquiry can be carried. The very fact that time moves on means that a correct choice at a given time may soon be outdated by events and that goals set down at the start may not be final. The need for reporting almost always forces a cutoff. Time considerations are particularly important in military analysis, for the decision-maker can wait only so long for an answer. Other costs are important here, too. For instance, we would like to find out what the Chinese Communists would do if we put an end to all military aid of Southeast Asia. One way to get this information would be to stop such aid. But while this would clearly be cheap in immediate dollar costs, the likelihood of other later costs precludes this type of investigation.

Still more important, however, is the general fact that, even with no limitations of time and money, analysis can never treat all the considerations that may be relevant. Some are too intangible—for example, how some unilateral United States action will affect NATO solidarity, or whether Congress will accept economies that disrupt cherished institutions such as the National Guard or radically change the pattern of domestic military spending. Considerations of this type should play as important a role in the recommendation of alternative policies as any idealized cost-effectiveness calculations. But ways to measure these considerations even approximately do not exist today, and they must be handled intuitively. Other immeasurable considerations involve moral judgments —for example, whether national security is better served by an increase in the budget for defense or for welfare, or under what circumstances the preservation of an immediate advantage is worth the compromise of fundamental principles. The analyst can apply his and others' judgment and intuition to these considerations, thus making them part of the study; but *bringing them to the attention of the decision-maker,* the man with the responsibility, is extremely important.

Measures of Effectiveness are Approximate

In military comparisons, measures of effectiveness are at best reasonably satisfactory approximations for indicating the attainment of such vaguely defined objectives as deterrence or victory. Sometimes the best that can be done is to find measures that point in the right direction. Consider deterrence, for instance. It exists only in the mind—and in the enemy's mind at that. We cannot, therefore, measure the effectiveness of alternatives we hope will lead to deterrence by some scale of deterrence, but must use instead such approximations as to the potential mortalities that we might inflict or the roof cover we might destroy. Consequently, even if a comparison of two systems indicated that one could inflict 50 percent more casualties on the enemy than the other, we could not conclude that this means the system supplies 50 percent more deterrence. In fact, since in some circumstances it may be important *not* to look too dangerous, we encounter arguments that the system threatening the greatest number of casualties may provide the *least* deterrence!

Similarly, consider the objective of United States government expenditures for health. A usual measure of effectiveness is the dollar value of increased labor force participation. But, this is clearly inadequate; medical services are more often in demand because of a desire to reduce the everyday aches and pains of life. Moreover, we cannot be very confident about the accuracy of our estimates. For example, one recent and authoritative source estimates the yearly cost of cancer to the United States at $11 billion, while another equally authoritative source estimates $2.6 billion.[10]

No Satisfactory Way to Predict the Future Exists

While it is possible to forecast events in the sense of mapping out possible futures, there is no satisfactory way to predict a single future for which we can work out the best system or determine an optimum policy. Consequently, we must consider a range of possible futures or contingencies. In any one of these we may be able to designate a preferred course of action, but we have no way to determine such action for the entire range of possibilities. We can design a force structure for a particular war in a particular place, but we have no way to work out a structure that is good for the entire spectrum of future wars in all the places they may occur.

Consequently, defense planning is rich in the kind of analysis that tells what damage could be done to the United States given a particular enemy force structure; but it is poor in the kinds of analysis that evaluate how we will actually stand in relation to the Soviets in years to come.

In spite of these limitations, it is not sensible to formulate policy or action without careful consideration of whatever relevant numbers can be discovered. In current Department of Defense practice, quantitative estimates of various kinds are used extensively. Many people, however, are vaguely uneasy about the particular way these estimates are made and their increasingly important role not only in military planning but elsewhere throughout the government.

Some skepticism may be justified, for the analytical work may not always be done competently or used with its limitations in mind. There may indeed be some dangers in relying on systems analysis, or on any similar approach to broad decisions. For one thing, since many factors fundamental to problems of federal policy are not readily amenable to quantitative treatment, they may possibly be neglected, or deliberately set aside for later consideration and then forgotten, or improperly weighed in the analysis itself, or in the decision based on such analysis. For another, a study may, on the surface, appear so scientific and quantitative that it may be assigned a validity not justified by the many subjective judgments involved. In other words, we may be so mesmerized by the beauty and precision of the numbers that we overlook the simplifications made to achieve this precision, neglect analysis of the qualitative factors, and overemphasize the importance of idealized calculations in the decision process. But without analysis we face even greater dangers in neglect of considerations and in the assignment of improper weights!

THE FUTURE

And finally, what of the future? Resistance by the military to the use of systems analysis in broad problems of strategy has gradually broken down. Both government and military planning and strategy have always involved more art than science; what is happening is that the art form is changing from an ad hoc, seat-of-the-pants approach based on intuition to one based on analysis *supported by* intuition and experience. This change may come more slowly in the nonmilitary aspects of government. For one thing, the civilian employees of the government are not so closely controlled "from the top" as those in the military; also the goals in these areas are just as vague and even more likely to be conflicting.[11] The requirements of the integrated Planning—Programming—Budgeting System will do much to speed the acceptance of analysis for other tasks, however.

With the acceptance of analysis, the computer is becoming increasingly significant—as an automaton, a process-controller, an information processor, and a decision aid. Its usefulness in serving these ends can be expected to grow. But at the same time, it is important to note that even the best computer is no more than a tool to expedite analysis. Even in the narrowest decisions, considerations not subject to any sort of quantitative analysis can always be present. Big decisions, therefore, cannot be the *automatic* consequence of a computer program or of any application of mathematical models.

For broad studies, intuitive, subjective, even *ad hoc* study schemes must continue to be used—but supplemented to an increasing extent by systems analysis. The ingredients of this analysis must include not only an increasing use of computer-based models for those problems where they are appropriate, but for treatment of the non-quantifiable aspects, a greater use of techniques for better employment of judgment, intuition, and experience. These techniques—operational gaming, "scenario" writing, and the systematic interrogation of experts—are on the way to becoming an integral part of systems analysis.

CONCLUDING REMARKS

And now to review. A systems analysis is an analytic study designed to help a decision-maker identify a preferred choice among possible alternatives. It is characterized by a systematic and rational approach, with assumptions made explicit, objectives and criteria clearly defined, and alternative courses of action compared in the light of their possible consequences. An effort is made to use quantitative methods, but computers are not essential. What is essential is a model that enables expert intuition and judgment to be applied efficiently. The method provides its answer by processes that are accessible to critical examination, capable of duplication by others, and, more or less, readily modified as new information becomes available. And, in contrast to other aids to decision-making, which share the same limitations, it extracts everything possible from scientific methods, and therefore its virtues are the virtues of those methods. At its narrowest, systems analysis has offered a way to choose the numerical quantities related to a weapon system so that they are logically consistent with each other, with an assumed objective, and with the calculator's expectation of the future. At its broadest, through providing the analytic backup for the plans, programs, and budgets of the various executive departments and establishments of the federal government, it can help guide national policy. But, even within the Department of Defense, its capabilities have yet to be fully exploited.

NOTES

1. O. Helmer, *Social Technology*, P-3063 (The Rand Corporation, February, 1965); presented at the Futuribles Conference in Paris, April, 1965.

2. For a further discussion of this distinction, see J. R. Schlesinger, "Quantitative Analysis and National Security," *World Politics* 15, no. 2 (January, 1963): 295–315.

3. Or, alternatively, cost-utility and cost-benefit analysis.

4. C. J. Hitch in E. S. Quade (ed.), *Analysis for Military Decisions* (Chicago: Rand McNally, 1964), p. 23, states: "Systems analyses should be looked upon not as the antithesis of judgment but as a framework which permits the judgment of experts in numerous subfields to be utilized —to yield results which transcend any individual judgment. This is its aim and opportunity."

5. Olaf Helmer, op. cit., p. 7, puts it this way: "The advantage of employing a model lies in forcing the analyst to make explicit what elements of a situation he is taking into consideration and in imposing upon him the discipline of clarifying the concepts he is using. The model thus serves the important purpose of establishing unambiguous intersubjective communication about the subject matter at hand. Whatever intrinsic uncertainties may becloud the area of investigation, they are thus less likely to be further compounded by uncertainties due to disparate subjective interpretations."

6. See, for example, Donald M. Fort, *Systems Analysis as an Aid in Air Transportation Planning*, P-3293 (Santa Monica, Calif.: The Rand Corporation, January, 1966), pp. 12–14.

7. O. Helmer and E. S. Quade, "An Approach to the Study of a Developing Economy by Operational Gaming," in *Recherche Operationnelle et Problemes du Tiers-Monde*, Colloquium organized by the French Society of Operational Research, with the participation of the Institute of Management Sciences, Operations Research Society of America (Paris: Dunod, 1964), pp. 43–54.

8. O. Helmer and Norman C. Dalkey, "An Experimental Application of the Delphi Method to the Use of Experts," *Management Sciences* 9, no. 3 (April, 1963): 458–67; and O. Helmer and Nicholas Rescher, "On the

Epistemology of the Inexact Sciences," *Management Sciences* 6, no. 1 (October, 1959): 25–52.

9. Ibid.

10. H. Kahn and I. Mann, *Ten Common Pitfalls*, RM-1937 (Santa Monica, Calif.: The Rand Corporation, July 17, 1957).

11. James R. Schlesinger, op. cit., has a slightly different view: "Thus the mere uncovering of ways to increase efficiency is not sufficient. Even where a decision is clear to the disinterested observer, it is difficult to persuade committed men that their programs or activities should be reduced or abandoned. The price of enthusiasm is that those who have commitment will be "sold" on their specialty and are incapable of viewing it in cold analytic terms. This may be especially true of the military establishment, where the concepts of duty, honor, and country *when particularized* lead to a certain inflexibility in adjusting to technological change and the new claims of efficiency. But it is also true in the civilian world: for conservationists, foresters, water resource specialists, businessmen, union leaders, or agrarians, some aspects of their value-systems run directly counter to the claims of efficiency. The economic view strikes them all as immoral as well as misleading. (After all, is it not a value judgment on the part of economists that efficiency calculations are important?)

"Even in the case of fairly low-level decisions, if they are political, systematic quantitative analysis does not necessarily solve problems. It will not convince ardent supporters that their program is submarginal. Nevertheless, quantitative analysis remains most useful. For certain operational decisions, it either provides the decision-maker with the justification he may desire for cutting off a project or forces him to come up with a nonnumerical rationalization. It eliminates the purely subjective approach on the part of devotees of a program and forces them to change their lines of argument. They must talk about reality rather than morality. Operational research creates a bridge to budgetary problems over which planners, who previously could assume resources were free, are forced, willingly or unwillingly, to walk."

REFERENCES

Dorfman, Robert (ed.), *Measuring Benefits of Government Investments* (Washington, D.C.: The Brookings Institution, 1965).

Ellis, J. W., Jr., and T. E. Greene, "The Contextual Study: A Structured Approach to the Study of Limited War," *Operations Research* 8, no. 5 (September–October, 1960): 639–51.

Fisher, G. H., *The World of Program Budgeting*, P-3361 (Santa Monica, Calif.: The Rand Corporation, May 1966).

Hitch, C. J., and R. N. McKean, *The Economics of Defense in the Nuclear Age* (Cambridge, Mass.: Harvard University Press, 1960).

McKean, R. N., *Efficiency in Government Through Systems Analysis* (New York: Wiley, 1958).

Marshall, A. W., *Cost/Benefit Analysis in Health*, P-3274 (Santa Monica, Calif.: The Rand Corporation, December, 1965).

Mood, Alex M., "Diversification of Operations Research," *Operations Research* 13, no. 2 (March-April, 1965): 169–78.

Novick, D. (ed.), *Program Budgeting: Program Analysis and the Federal Budget* (Washington, D.C.: Government Printing Office, 1965; Cambridge, Mass.: Harvard University Press, 1965).

Peck, M. J., and F. M. Scherer, *The Weapons Acquisition Process: An Economic Analysis* (Cambridge, Mass.: Harvard University Press, 1962).

the future: integrating rationality, humanism, and politics

The earlier readings have argued that a theoretical basis for change does exist. Organizations probably can adapt to changes in the environment through restructuring of the work itself and by applying techniques of socioeconomic analysis to attempt to deal with the future rather than merely respond to it. The two final selections deal with some key problems of public bureaucracies of the future. The specific issues considered are (1) what organizational forms are going to be most able to cope with changes that the future may bring and (2) unmasking the ideological components of those organizational forms and processes.

Warren Bennis has been one of the outspoken critics of bureaucracy:

It does not take a great critical imagination to detect the flaws and problems in the bureaucratic model. We have all *experienced* them: bosses with less technical competence than their underlings: arbitrary and zany rules; and informal organization which subverts or replaces the formal apparatus; confusion and conflict among roles; and cruel treatment of subordinates based not on rational grounds but on quasi-legal, or worse, inhumane grounds.[1]

To avoid some of these negative features of bureaucracy, Bennis advocates greater participative management, which he thinks can be brought about by organization development (OD).

Organization development is an effort to increase organizational effectiveness through planned interventions in the organization's "processes." Among the processes that concern OD consultants are the following: communication, member roles and functions in groups, group problem-solving and decision-making, group norms and group growth, leadership and authority, and intergroup cooperation and competition.[2] These planned efforts at change are generally managed from the top and use behavioral science knowledge and techniques. Bennis refers to organization development as *"an educational strategy adopted to bring about a planned organizational change."*[3] The aim of the strategy is to enable the organization to cope more effectively with changes in the organization's environment.

An organization development effort involves altering organizational values to include more democratic-oriented values in addition to the values that tend to predominate in hierarchical organizations. To this end, organization development uses such behavioral science training techniques as T-groups, confrontation sessions, and role playing, and it generally operates over a long time period. The use of such methods and goal development procedures in public bureaucracies, however, has been limited.

At one time, Bennis held that *"democracy becomes a functional necessity whenever a social system is competing for survival under conditions of chronic change."*[4] His change in roles from behavioral science consultant to public administrator at a university has caused him to reassess his earlier position that foresaw an "end of bureaucracy."[5] Why did Bennis think bureaucracy would change drastically? In what ways was he right? In what ways was he wrong? What are the reasons for periodic crises of legitimacy? What roles might these crises have in stimulating change? Who is responsible for change in Bennis's organizations of the future? Can a pragmatic bureaucratic ideology coexist with a democratic, consensus-oriented ideology? In what ways is a public university similar to other public agencies? Are there differences that might affect leadership and decision-making?

But ideological conflicts are not limited to humanistic versus pragmatic perspectives in public bureaucracy. As Fred Kramer points out, different ways of seeing the world lead to different conclusions about how to cope with change. In a world that idolizes science and technology, information methods that are clothed in the mantle of science may have a better reception in decision-making circles than more traditional methods. In a democratic political society, where the career public administrators are several steps removed from the people but supposedly still accountable to them, possible misuses of science can have serious consequences.

In the early 1970s many observers looked to refined information systems and analytic practices to increase public administrators' ability to support change in favor of groups traditionally left out of the group power struggle.[6] Many of these groups are the same ones that Bennis had problems with as an administrator—the blacks, students, gays, etc. When data was churned through the analytic mills, however, often the "objective" results told of the futility of helping these very groups. It was not cost-effective, it turned out, to operate a War on Poverty. But can we be sure? Were the analytical models flawed? Certainly there is political impact from analysis that is used to justify curtailment of programs designed to enhance social equity, unless some other programs are offered in their place.

Analysis does have an impact on public decisions today. It will probably have a greater impact in the future. Is policy analysis ideological? Should not administrators always seek to be rational? Is Kramer antianalysis? What alternate ways are there to gather and treat information? How might these alternative decision-making modes affect the scope and speed of policy changes?

NOTES

1. Warren G. Bennis, "Organizational Developments and the Fate of Bureaucracy," *Industrial Management Review* 7 (1966): 42.

2. Edgar Schein, *Process Consultation: Its Role in Organization Development* (Reading, Mass.: Addison-Wesley, 1969), p. 13.

3. Warren G. Bennis, *Organization Development: Its Nature, Origins, and Prospects* (Reading, Mass.: Addison-Wesley, 1969), p. 10. Emphasis in the original.

4. Warren G. Bennis and Philip E. Slater, *The Temporary Society* (New York: Harper & Row, 1968), p. 4. Emphasis in the original.

5. Bennis, "Organizational Developments," loc. cit., p. 41.

6. See H. George Frederickson, "Toward a New Public Administration," in Frank Marini (ed.), *Toward a New Public Administration* (San Francisco: Chandler Publishing Company, 1971), pp. 316–31.

a funny thing
happened on the
way to the future

warren g. bennis

Analysis of the "future," or, more precisely, inventing relevant futures, has become in recent years as respectable for the scientist as the shaman. Inspired by Bertrand de Jouvenal, Daniel Bell, Olaf Helmer, and others, there seems to be growing evidence and recognition for the need of a legitimate base of operations for the "futurologist." . . .

However difficult it may be to identify a truly scientific study of the future, most scholars would agree that it should include a number of objectives:

1.   It should provide a survey of possible futures in terms of a spectrum of major potential alternatives.

2.   It should ascribe to the occurrence of these alternatives some estimates of relative a priori probabilities.

3.   It should, for given basic policies, identify preferred alternatives.

4.   It should identify those decisions which are subject to control, as well as those developments which are not, whose occurrence would be likely to have a major effect on the probabilities of these alternatives [Helmer, 1969].

From American Psychologist 25 (*July, 1970*): 595–608. *Copyright 1970 by the American Psychological Association. Footnotes deleted. Reprinted by permission.*

With these objectives only dimly in mind, I wrote a paper on the future of organizations . . . which was called "Organizational Developments and the Fate of Bureaucracy" (Bennis, 1964). Essentially, it was based on an evolutionary hypothesis which asserted that every age develops a form of organization most appropriate to its genius. I then went on to forecast certain changes in a "post-bureaucratic world" and how these changes would affect the structure and environment of human organizations, their leadership and motivational patterns, and their cultural and ecological values. A number of things have occurred since that first excursion into the future in September 1964 which . . . have served to reorient and revise substantially some of the earlier forecasts. . . .

In his *Report to Greco*, Nikos Kazantzakis tells us of an ancient Chinese imprecation: "I curse you; may you live in an important age." Thus, we are all damned, encumbered, and burdened, as well as charmed, exhilarated, and fascinated by this curse. . . .

Reactions to our spastic times vary. There are at least seven definable types:

1. First and most serious of all are the *militants*, composed for the most part of impotent and dependent populations who have been victimized and infantilized, and who see no way out but to mutilate and destroy the system which has decimated its group identity and pride. Excluded populations rarely define their price for belated inclusion in intellectual terms, which confuses and terrifies the incumbents who take participation for granted.

2. The *apocalyptics*, who with verbal ferocity burn everything in sight. So, in *Supergrow*, Benjamin DeMott (1969) assumes the persona of a future historian and casts a saddened eye on everyone from the Beatles to James Baldwin, from the *Berkeley Barb* to Alfred Kazin, while contemplating the age of megaweapons. DeMott writes:

By the end of the sixties the entire articulate Anglo-American community . . . was transformed into a monster-chorus of damnation dealers, its single voice pitched ever at hysterical level, its prime aim to transform every form of discourse into a blast.

These voices are hot as flamethrowers, searing all that get in their way and usually fired from a vantage point several terrain features away.

3. The *regressors,* who see their world disintegrating and engage in fruitless exercises in nostalgia, keening the present and weeping for a past: orderly, humane, free, civilized, and nonexistent. Someone recently recommended that the university insulate itself from outside pollutants—I suppose he meant students and the community —and set up, medieval Oxford style, a chantry for scholars which he warmly referred to as a "speculatorium."

4. There are the *retreaters,* apathetic, withdrawn, inwardly emigrating and outwardly drugged, avoiding all environments except, at most, a communal "roll your own" or a weekend bash at Esalen, longing for a "peak experience," instant nirvana, hoping to beat out reality and consequence.

5. The *historians,* who are always capable of lulling us to sleep by returning to a virtuous past, demonstrating that the "good old days" were either far better or worse. "The good old days, the good old days," said a Negro comedienne of the 30s, "I was there; where were they?" I learned recently, for example, that the university, as a quiet place devoted to the pursuit of learning and unaffected by the turbulence of the outside world, is of comparatively recent date, that the experience of the medieval university made the turbulence of recent years seem like a spring zephyr. It was pointed out that a student at the University of Prague cut the throat of a Friar Bishop and was merely expelled, an expedient that may have had something to do with the fact that in dealing with student morals, university officials were constrained to write in Latin.

6. The *technocrats,* who plow heroically ahead, embracing the future and in the process usually forgetting to turn around to see if anybody is following or listening, cutting through waves of ideology like agile surfers.

7. And, finally, the rest of us, "we happy few," the *liberal-democratic reformers,* optimists believing in the perfectibility of man and his institutions, waiting for a solid scientific victory over ideology and irrationality, accepting the inevitability of technology and humanism without thoroughly examining *that* relationship as we do all others, and reckoning that the only way to preserve a democratic and scientific humanism is through inspiriting our institutions with continuous, incremental reform.

The 1964 paper I mentioned earlier was written within the liberal-democratic framework, and it contained many of the inherent problems and advantages of that perspective. The main strategy of this paper and its focus of convenience are to review briefly the main points of that paper, to indicate its shortcomings and lacunae in light of five years' experience (not the least of which has been serving as an administrator in a large, complex public bureaucracy), and then proceed to develop some new perspectives relevant to the future of public bureaucracies. I might add, parenthetically, that I feel far less certainty and closure at this time than I did five years ago. The importance of inventing relevant futures and directions is never more crucial than in a revolutionary period, exactly and paradoxically at the point in time when the radical transition blurs the shape and direction of the present. This is the dilemma of our time and most certainly the dilemma of this paper.

THE FUTURE: 1964 VERSION

Bureaucracy, I argued, was an elegant social invention, ingeniously capable of organizing and coordinating the productive processes of the Industrial Revolution, but hopelessly out-of-joint with contemporary realities. There would be new shapes, patterns, and models emerging which promised drastic changes in the conduct of the organization and of managerial practices in general. In the next 25–50 years, I argued, we should witness and participate in the end of bureaucracy as we know it and the rise of the new social systems better suited to twentieth-century demands of industrialization.

This argument was based on a number of factors:

1. The exponential growth of science, the growth of intellectual technology, and the growth of research and development activities.

2. The growing confluence between men of knowledge and men of power or, as I put it then, "a growing affinity between those who make history and those who write it [Bennis, 1964].

3. A fundamental change in the basic philosophy which underlies managerial behavior, reflected most of all in the following three areas: (a) a new concept of man, based on increased knowledge of his complex and shifting needs, which replaces the oversimplified, innocent push-button concept of man; (b) a new concept of power, based on collaboration and reason, which replaces a model of power based on coercion and fear; and (c) a new concept of organizational values, based on humanistic-democratic ideals, which replaces the depersonalized mechanistic value system of bureaucracy.

4. A turbulent environment which would hold relative uncertainty due to the increase of research and development activities. The environment would become increasingly differentiated, interdependent, and more salient to the organization. There would be greater interpenetration of the legal policy and economic features of an oligopolistic and government-business-controlled economy. Three main features of the environment would be interdependence rather than competition, turbulence rather than a steady, predictable state, and large rather than small enterprises.

5. A population characterized by a younger, more mobile, and better educated work force.

These conditions, I believed, would lead to some significant changes:

The increased level of education and rate of mobility would bring about certain changes in values held toward work. People would tend to (a) be more rational, be intellectually committed, and rely more heavily on forms of social influence which correspond to their value system: (b) be more "other-directed" and rely on their temporary neighbors and workmates for companionships, in other words, have relationships, not relatives; and (c) require more involvement, participation, and autonomy in their work.

As far as organizational structure goes, given the population characteristics and features of environmental turbulence, the social structure in organizations of the future would take on some unique characteristics. I will quote from the original paper.

First of all, the key word will be temporary: Organizations will become adaptive, rapidly changing temporary systems. Second, they will be organized around problems-to-be-solved. Third, these problems will be solved by relative groups of strangers who represent a diverse set of professional skills. Fourth, given the requirements of coordinating the various projects, articulating points or "linking pin" personnel will be necessary who can speak the diverse languages of research and who can relay and mediate between various project groups. Fifth, the groups will be conducted on organic rather than on mechanical lines; they will emerge and adapt to the problems, and leadership and influence will fall to those who seem most able to solve the problems rather than to programmed role expectations. People will be differentiated, not according to rank or roles, but according to skills and training.

Adaptive, temporary systems of diverse specialists solving problems, coordinated organically via articulating points, will gradually replace the theory and practice of bureaucracy. Though no catchy phrase comes to mind, it might be called an organic-adaptive structure.

(As an aside: what will happen to the rest of society, to the manual laborers, to the poorly educated, to those who desire to work in conditions of dependency, and so forth? Many such jobs will disappear; automatic jobs will be automated. However, there will be a corresponding growth in the service-type of occupation, such as organizations like the Peace Corps and AID. There will also be jobs, now being seeded, to aid in the enormous challenge of coordinating activities between groups and organizations. For certainly, consortia of various kinds are growing in number and scope and they will require careful attention. In times of change, where there is a wide discrepancy between cultures and generations, an increase in industrialization, and especially urbanization, society becomes the client for skills in human resources. Let us hypothesize that approximately 40% of the population would be involved in jobs of this nature, 40% in technological jobs, making an organic-adaptive majority with, say, a 20% bureaucratic minority) [Bennis, 1964].

Toward the end of the paper, I wrote that

The need for instinctual renunciation decreases as man achieves rational mastery over nature. In short, organizations of the future will require fewer restrictions and repressive techniques because of the legitimization of play and fantasy, accelerated through the rise of science and intellectual achievements [Bennis, 1964].

To summarize the changes in emphasis of social patterns in the "postbureaucratic world" I was then describing (using Trist's, 1968, framework), the following paradigm may be useful:

From   *Toward*

Cultural Values

Achievement	Self-actualization
Self-control	Self-expression
Independence	Interdependence
Endurance of stress	Capacity for joy
Full employment	Full lives

Organizational Values

Mechanistic forms	Organic forms
Competitive relations	Collaborative relations
Separate objectives	Linked objectives
Own resources regarded as owned absolutely	Own resources regarded also as society's resources

. . . New experiences and other emergent factors all help to provide a new perspective which casts some doubt on a number of assumptions, only half implied in the earlier statement. For example:

1. The organizations I had in mind then were of a single class: instrumental, large-scale, science-based, international bureaucracies, operating under rapid growth conditions. Service industries and public bureaucracies, as well as nonsalaried employees, were excluded from analysis.

2. Practically no attention was paid to the boundary transactions of the firm or to interinstitutional linkages.

3. The management of conflict was emphasized, while the strategy of conflict was ignored.

4. Power of all types was underplayed, while the role of the leader as facilitator—"linking pin"— using an "agricultural model" of nurturance and climate building was stressed. Put in Gamson's (1968) terms, I utilized a domesticated version of power, emphasizing the process by which the authorities attempt to achieve collective goals and to maintain legitimacy and compliance with their decisions, rather than the perspective of "potential partisans," which involves diversity of interest groups attempting to influence the choices of authorities.

5. A theory of change was implied, based on gentle nudges from the environment coupled with a truth-love strategy; that is, with sufficient trust and collaboration along with valid data, organizations would progress monotonically along a democratic continuum.

In short, the organizations of the future I envisaged would most certainly be, along with a Bach Chorale and Chartres Cathedral, the epiphany to Western civilization.

The striking thing about truth and love is that whereas I once held them up as the answer to our institution's predicaments, they have now become the problem. And, to make matters worse, the world I envisaged as emergent in 1964 becomes, not necessarily inaccurate, but overwhelmingly problematical. It might be useful to review some of the main organizational dilemmas before going any further, both as a check on the previous forecast, as well as a preface to some new and tentative ideas about contemporary human organizations.

SOME NEW DILEMMAS

The Problem of Legitimacy

The key difference between the Berkeley riots of 1964 and the Columbia crisis of May 1969 is that in the pre-Columbian case the major impetus for unrest stemmed from the perceived abuse or misuse of authority ("Do not bend, fold, or mutilate"), whereas the later protest denied the legitimacy of authority. The breakdown of legitimacy in our country has many reasons and explanations, not the least of which is the increasing difficulty of converting political questions into technical-managerial ones. Or, put differently, questions of legitimacy arise whenever "expert power" becomes ineffective. Thus, black militants, drug users, draft resisters, student protestors, and liberated women all deny the legitimacy of those authorities who are not black, drug experienced, pacifists, students, or women.

The university is in an excruciating predicament with respect to the breakdown of legitimacy. Questions about admissions, grades, curriculum, and police involvement—even questions concerning rejection of journal articles—stand the chance of being converted into political-legal issues. This jeopardizes the use of universalistic-achievement criteria, upon which the very moral imperatives of our institutions are based. The problem is related, of course, to the inclusion of those minority groups in our society which have been excluded from participation in American life and tend to define their goals in particularistic and political terms.

Kelman (1969) cites three major reasons for the crisis in legitimacy: (a) serious failings of the system in living up to its basic values and in maintaining a proper relationship between means and ends, (b) decreasing trust in leadership, and (c) dispositions of our current youth. On this last point, Flacks (1969)

suggests the existence of an increasingly distinct "humanist" subculture in the middle class, consisting primarily of highly educated and urbanized families, based in professional occupations, who encourage humanist orientations in their offspring as well as questioning attitudes to traditional middle class values and to arbitrary authority and conventional politics. . . . Although this humanist subculture represents a small minority of the population, many of its attributes are more widely distributed, and the great increase in the number of college graduates suggests that the ranks of this subculture will rapidly grow.

In short, as the gap between shared and new moralities and authoritative norms (i.e., the law) widens, questions of legitimacy inevitably arise.

Populist versus Elite Functions?

Can American institutions continue to fulfill the possibly incompatible goals of their elitist and populist functions? Again, the American university is an example of this dilemma, for the same institution tries to balance both its autonomous-elite function of disinterested inquiry and criticism and an increasingly service-populist-oriented function. This has been accomplished by insulating the elite (autonomous) functions of liberal education, basic research, and scholarship from the direct impact of the larger society, whose demands for vocational training, certification, service, and the like are reflected and met in the popular functions of the university. As Trow (1969) puts it:

These insulations take various forms of a division of labor within the university. There is a division of labor between departments, as for example, between a department of English or Classics, and a department of Education. There is a division of labor in the relatively unselective universities between the undergraduate and graduate schools, the former given over largely to mass higher education in the service of social mobility and occupational placement, entertainment, and custodial care, while the graduate departments in the same institutions are often able to maintain a climate in which scholarship and scientific research can be done to the highest standards. There is a familiar division of labor, though far from clear-cut, between graduate departments and professional schools. Among the faculty there is a division of labor, within many departments, between scientists and consultants, scholars and journalists, teachers and entertainers. More dangerously, there is a division of labor between regular faculty and a variety of fringe or marginal teachers—teaching assistants, visitors and lecturers—who in some schools carry a disproportionate load of the mass teaching. Within the administration there is a division of labor between the Dean of Faculty and Graduate Dean, and the Dean of Students. And among students there is a marked separation between the "collegiate" and "vocational" subcultures, on the one hand, and academically or intellectually oriented subcultures on the other [p. 2].

To a certain extent, the genius of American higher education is that it *has* fulfilled both of these functions, to the wonder of all, and especially to observers from European universities. But with the enormous expansion of American universities, proportional strains are being placed on their insulating mechanisms.

Interdependence or Complicity in the Environment

The environment I talked about in 1964, its interdependence and turbulence, is flourishing today. But my optimism must now be tempered, for what appeared then to be a "correlation of fates" turns out to have blocked the view of some serious problems. The university is a good example of this tension.

The relationship between the university and its environment has never been defined in more than an overly abstract way. For some, the university is a citadel, aloof, occasionally lobbing in on society the shells of social criticism. Both the radical left and the conservative right seem to agree on this model, maintaining that to yield to the claims of society will fragment and ultimately destroy the university. Others, for different reasons, prefer a somewhat similar model, that of the "speculatorium," where scholars, protected by garden walls, meditate away from society's pollutants. Still others envisage the university as an "agent of change," a catalytic institution capable of revolutionizing the nation's organizations and professions. In fact, a recent sociological study listed almost 50 viable goals for the university (Gross, 1968) (a reflection of our ambivalence and confusions as much as anything), and university catalogs usually list them all.

The role of the university in society might be easier to define if it were not for one unpalatable fact. Though it is not usually recognized, the truth is that the university is not self-supporting. The amount available for our educational expenditures (including funds necessary to support autonomous functions) relates directly to the valuation of the university by the general community. The extent to which the university's men, ideas, and research are valued is commensurate with the amount of economic support it receives (Parsons, 1968). This has always been true. During the Great Awakening, universities educated ministers; during the agricultural and industrial revolutions, the land-grant colleges and engineering schools flourished; during the rise of the service professions, the universities set up schools of social welfare, nursing, public health, and so on. And during the past 30 years or so, the universities have been increasingly geared to educate individuals to man the Galbraithean "technostructure."

Thus, the charge of "complicity" of the universities with the power structure is both valid and absurd; without this alleged complicity, there would be no universities, or only terribly poor ones. In the late 60s, the same attack comes from the New Left. The paradox can be blinding, and often leads to one of two pseudo-solutions, total involvement or total withdrawal—pseudosolutions familiar enough on other fronts, for example, in foreign policy.

If I am right that the university must be valued by society in order to be supported, the question is not should the university be involved with society, but what should be the *quality* of this involvement and *with whom?* For years, there has been tacit acceptance of the idea that the university must supply industry, the professions, defense, and the technostructure with the brains necessary to carry on their work. Now there are emerging constituencies, new dependent populations, new problems, many without technical solutions, that are demanding that attention of the university. We are being called upon to direct our limited and already scattered resources to newly defined areas of concern—the quality of life, the shape and nature of our human institutions, the staggering problems of the city, legislative processes, and the management of human resources. Will it be possible for the modern university to involve itself with these problems and at the same time avoid the politicization that will threaten its autonomous functions? One thing is clear, we will never find answers to these problems if we allow rational thought to be replaced by a search for villains. To blame the establishment, or Wall Street, or the New Left for our problems is lazy, thoughtless, and frivolous. It would be comforting if we *could* isolate and personalize the problems facing the university, but we cannot.

The last two dilemmas that I have just mentioned, elitist *versus* populist strains vying within a single institution and the shifting, uncertain symbiosis between university and society, contain many of the unclear problems we face today, and I suspect that they account for much of the existential groaning we hear in practically all of our institutions, not just the university.

The Search for the Correct Metaphor

Metaphors have tremendous power to establish new social realities, to give life and meaning to what was formerly perceived only dimly and imprecisely. . . .

Most of us have internalized a metaphor about organizational life, however crude that model or vivid that utopia is—or how conscious or unconscious—which governs our perceptions of our social systems. How these metaphors evolve is not clear, although I do not think Freud was far off the mark with his focus on the family, the military, and the church as the germinating institutions.

Reviewing organizational metaphors somewhat biographically, I find that my first collegiate experience, at Antioch College, emphasized a "community democracy" metaphor, obviously valid for a small, town-meeting type of political life. In strong contrast to this was the Massachusetts Institute of Technology, which employed the metaphor (not consciously, of course) of "The Club," controlled tacitly and quite democratically, but without the formal governing apparatus of political democracies, by an "old-boy network," composed of the senior tenured faculty and administration. The State University of New York at Buffalo comes close, in my view, to a "labor-relations" metaphor, where conflicts and decisions are negotiated through a series of interest groups bargaining as partisans. There are many other usable metaphors: Clark Kerr's "City," Mark Hopkins' "student and teacher on opposite ends of a log," "General Systems Analysis," "Therapeutic Community," "Scientific Management," and my own "temporary systems," and so on, that compete with the pure form of bureaucracy, but few of them seem singularly equipped to cope with the current problems facing large-scale institutions.

Macrosystems versus Microsystems

One of the crude discoveries painfully learned during the course of recent administrative experience in a large public bureaucracy turns on the discontinuities between microsystems and macrosystems. For quite a while, I have had more than a passing *theoretical* interest in this problem, which undoubtedly many of you share, but my interest now, due to a sometimes eroding despair, has gone well beyond the purely theoretical problems involved.

My own intellectual "upbringing," to use an old-fashioned term, was steeped in the Lewinian tradition of small-group behavior, processes of social influence, and "action-research." This is not terribly exceptional, I suppose, for a social psychologist. In fact, I suppose that the major methodological and theoretical influences in the social sciences for the last two decades have concentrated on more microscopic, "manageable" topics. Also, it is not easy to define precisely where a microsocial science begins or where a macrosocial science ends. Formally, I suppose, microsystems consist of roles and actors, while macrosystems have as their constituent parts other subsystems, subcultures, and parts of society. In any case, my intellectual heritage has resulted in an erratic batting average in transferring concepts from microsystems into the macrosystem of a university. . . .

The theory of consensus falters under those conditions where competing groups bring to the conference table vested interests based on group membership, what Mannhein referred to as "perspectivistic orientation." Where goals are competitive and group (or subsystem) oriented, despite the fact that a consensus might rationally create a new situation where all parties may benefit—that is, move closer to the Paretian optimal frontier—a negotiated position may be the only practical solution. There was a time when I believed that consensus was a valid operating procedure. I no longer think this is realistic, given the scale and diversity of organizations. In fact, I have come to think that the quest for consensus, except for some microsystems where it may be feasible, is a misplaced nostalgia for a folk society as chimerical, incidentally, as the American search for "identity."

The collaborative relationship between superiors and subordinates falters as well under those conditions where "subordinates" —if that word is appropriate—are *delegates* of certain subsystems. Under this condition, collaboration may be perceived by constituents as a threat because of perceived cooption or encroachment on their formal legal rights.

Or, to take another example, in the area of leadership, my colleagues at the State University of New York at Buffalo, Hollander and Julian (1969), have written for *Psychological Bulletin* one of the most thoughtful and penetrating articles on the leadership process. In one of their own studies (Julian & Hollander, 1966), reported in this article, they found that aside from the significance of task competence, the "leader's interest in group members and interest in group activity" were significantly related to the group acceptance of the leader. Yet, in macropower situations, the leader is almost always involved in boundary exchanges with salient interorganizational activities which inescapably reduce, not necessarily interest in group members or activities, but the amount of interaction he can maintain with group members. This may have more the overtones of a rationalization than an explanation, but I know of few organizations where the top leadership's commitment to internal programs and needs fully meets constituent expectations.

In short, interorganizational role set of the leader, the scale, diversity, and formal relations that ensue in a pluralistic system place heavy burdens on those managers and leaders who expect an easy transferability between the cozy gemütlichkeit of a Theory Y orientation and the realities of macropower.

Current Sources for the Adoption or Rejection of Democratic Ideals

I wrote (Bennis, 1966b) . . . that

While more research will help us understand the conditions under which democratic and other forms of governance will be adopted, the issue will never be fully resolved. . . . I. A. Richards once said that "language has succeeded until recently in hiding from us almost all things we talk about." This is singularly true when men start to talk of complex and wondrous things like democracy and the like.[3] For these are issues anchored in an existential core of personality [p. 35].

Today I am even more confused about the presence or absence of conditions which could lead to more democratic functioning. Somedays I wake up feeling "nasty, brutish, and short," and, other times, feeling benign, generous, and short.* This may be true of the general population, for the national mood is erratic, labile, depending on repression or anarchy for the "short" solution to long problems.

Let us consider Lane's (1962) "democraticness scale," consisting of five items: (a) willingness or reluctance to deny the franchise to the "ignorant or careless"; (b) patience or impatience with the delays and confusions of democratic processes; (c) willingness or

*Editor's note: Bennis is well under six feet tall.

reluctance to give absolute authority to a single leader in times of threat; (d) where democratic forms are followed, degree of emphasis (and often disguised approval) of underlying oligarchical methods; (e) belief that the future of democracy in the United States is reasonably secure.

Unfortunately, there has been relatively little research on the "democratic personality," which makes it risky to forecast whether conditions today will facilitate or detract from its effective functioning. On the one hand, there is interesting evidence that would lead one to forecast an increased commitment to democratic ideals. Earlier I mentioned Flacks' (1969) work on the "transformation of the American middle-class family," which would involve increased equality between husband and wife, declining distinctiveness of sex roles in the family, increased opportunity for self-expression on the part of the children, fewer parental demands for self-discipline, and more parental support for autonomous behavior on the part of the children. In addition, the increase in educated persons, whose status is less dependent on property, will likely increase the investment of individuals in having autonomy and a voice in decision making.

On the other hand, it is not difficult to detect some formidable threats to the democratic process which make me extremely apprehensive about an optimistic prediction. Two are basically psychological, one derived from some previous assumptions about the environment, the other derived from some recent personal experience. The third is a venerable structural weakness which at this time takes on a new urgency.

1. Given the turbulent and dynamic texture of the environment, we can observe a growing uncertainty about the deepest human concerns: jobs, neighborhoods, regulation of social norms, life styles, child rearing, law and order; in short, the only basic questions, according to Tolstoi, that interest human beings are How to live? and What to live for? The ambiguities and changes in American life that occupy discussion in university seminars and annual meetings and policy debates in Washington, and that form the backbone of contemporary popular psychology and sociology, become increasingly the conditions of trauma and frustration in the lower middle class. Suddenly the rules are changing—all the rules.

A clashy dissensus of values is already clearly foreshadowed that will tax to the utmost two of the previously mentioned democraticness scale items: "impatience or patience with the delays and confusions of democratic processes" and the "belief that the future of democracy in the United States is reasonably secure."

The inability to tolerate ambiguity and the consequent frustration plus the mood of dissensus may lead to the emergence of a proliferation of "minisocieties" and relatively impermeable subcultures, from George Wallace's blue-collar strongholds to rigidly circumscribed communal ventures. Because of their rejection of incremental reform and the establishment, and their impatience with bureaucratic-pragmatic leadership, their movements and leadership will likely resemble a "revolutionary-charismatic" style (Kissinger, 1966).

2. The personal observation has to do with experience over the past two years as an academic administrator, experience obtained during a particularly spastic period for all of us in the academy. I can report that we, at Buffalo, have been trying to express our governance through a thorough and complete democratic process, with as much participation as anyone can bear. There are many difficulties in building this process, as all of you are undoubtedly aware: the tensions between collegiality and the bureaucratic-pragmatic style of administrators, the difficulty in arousing faculty and students to participate, etc. I might add, parenthetically, that Buffalo, as is true of many state universities, had long cherished a tradition of strong faculty autonomy and academic control. Our intention was to facilitate this direction, as well as encourage more student participation.

When trouble erupted last spring, I was disturbed to discover—to the surprise of many of my colleagues, particularly historians and political scientists—that the democratic process we were building seemed so fragile and certainly weakened in comparison to the aphrodisia of direct action, mass meetings, and frankly autocratic maneuverings. The quiet workings of the bureaucratic-democratic style seemed bland, too complex and prismatic for easy comprehension, and even banal, contrasted to the headlines of the disruptions. Even those of us who were attempting to infuse and reinforce democratic functioning found ourselves caught up in the excitement and chilling risks involved.

Erich Fromm (1941) said it all, I reflected later on, in his *Escape from Freedom,* but what was missing for me in his formulation was the psychic equivalent for democratic participants.

During this same period, I came across a paper by Argyris (1969) which reinforced my doubts about the psychological attractiveness of democracy. Using a 36-category group observational system on nearly 30 groups, in 400 separate meetings, amounting to almost 46,000 behavioral units, he found that only 6 of the 36 categories were used over 75% of the time, and these 6 were "task" items such as "gives information, asks for information," etc. Almost 60% of the groups showed no affect or interpersonal feelings at all, and 24% expressed only 1% affect or feelings. These groups represented a wide cross-section of bureaucratic organizations, research and development labs, universities, and service and business industries.

Argyris' data, along with my own personal experience, have made me wonder if democratic functioning can ever develop the deep emotional commitments and satisfactions that other forms of governance evoke, as for example, revolutionary-charismatic or ideological movements? The question which I leave with you at this time is not the one from the original paper ("Is democracy inevitable?"), but, "Is democracy sexy?"

3. The structural weakness in present-day democracy, using that term in the broadest possible political sense, is the 200-year-old idea first popularized by Adam Smith (1776) in *The Wealth of the Nations*. This was "the idea that an individual who intends only his own gain is led by an invisible hand to promote the public interest." The American Revolution brought about a deep concern for the constitutional guarantees of personal rights and a passionate interest in individuals' emotions and growth, but without a concomitant concern for the community.

In [an] issue of *Science*, Hardin (1968), the biologist, discusses this in an important article, "The Tragedy of the Commons." Herdsmen who keep their cattle on the commons ask themselves: "What is the utility to me of adding one more animal to my herd [p. 1244]?" Being rational, each herdsman seeks to maximize his gain. It becomes clear that by adding even one animal, as he receives all the proceeds from the sale of the additional increment, the positive utility is nearly +1, whereas the negative utility is only a fraction of −1 because the effects of overgrazing are shared by all herdsmen. Thus, "the rational herdsman concludes that the only sensible course for him to pursue is to add another animal to his herd. And another, and another . . . [p. 1244]," until

Each man is locked into a system that compels him to increase his herd without limit . . . Ruin is the destination toward which all men rush . . . Freedom in a commons brings ruin to all [p. 1244].

A recent, less elegant example along these lines occurred at my own campus where there is a rather strong commitment against institutional racism. A recent form this commitment has taken is the admission of at least double the number of black students ever before admitted. However, more disadvantaged students could have been accepted if the students had chosen to vote for "tripling" in the dormitories. It was voted down overwhelmingly, and it was interesting to observe the editor of the student newspaper supporting increased admission for black students and at the same time opposing tripling.

The democratic process as we know it, expressed through majority vote, contains many built-in guarantees for individual freedom without equivalent mechanisms for the "public interest," as Gans' (1969) . . . article in the Sunday Magazine section of *The New York Times* argues.

A character in Balchin's (1949) *A Sort of Traitors* expresses this structural problem with some force:

You think that people want democracy and justice and peace. You're right. They do. But what you forget is that they want them on their own terms. And their own terms don't add up. They want decency and justice without interference with their liberty to do as they like.

These are the dilemmas as I see them now: the threat to legitimacy of authority, the tensions between populist and elitist functions and interdependence and complicity in the environment, the need for fresh metaphors, the discontinuities between microsystems and macrosystems, and the baffling competition between forces that support and those that suppress the adoption of democratic ideology. All together, they curb my optimism and blur the vision, but most certainly force a new perspective upon us.

A NEW PERSPECTIVE

These profound changes lead me to suggest that any forecast one makes about trends in human institutions must take into account the following:

- The need for fundamental reform in the purpose and organization of our institutions to enable them to adapt responsively in an exponentially changing social, cultural, political, and economic environment.
- The need to develop such institutions on a human scale which permit the individual to retain his identity and integrity in a society increasingly characterized by massive, urban, highly centralized governmental, business, educational, mass media, and other institutions.
- The significant movement of young persons who are posing basic challenges to existing values and institutions and who are attempting to create radical new life styles in an attempt to preserve individual identity or to opt out of society.
- The increasing demands placed upon all American institutions to participate more actively in social, cultural, and political programs designed to improve the quality of American life.
- The accelerating technical changes which require the development of a scientific humanism: a world view of the social and humanistic implications of such changes.
- The necessity of a world movement to bring man in better harmony with his physical environment.
- The need for change toward a sensitive and flexible planning capability on the part of the management of major institutions.
- The rising demand for social and political justice and freedom, particularly from the American black community and other deprived sectors of society.
- The compelling need for world order which gives greater attention to the maintenance of peace without violence between nations, groups, or individuals.

A NEW FORECAST FOR PUBLIC BUREAUCRACY

The imponderables are youth, and tradition, and change. Where these predicaments, dilemmas, and second thoughts take us, I am not exactly sure. However, by way of a summary and conclusion— and at the risk of another five-year backlash, there are a number of trends and emphases worth considering.

The Organization's Response to the Environment Will Continue to Be the Crucial Determinant for Its Effectiveness

Economists and political scientists have been telling us this for years, but only recently have sociologists and social psychologists, like Terreberry (1968), Emery and Trist (1965), Levine and White (1961), Litwak and Hylton (1962), and Evan (1966), done so. . . .

Three derivatives of this protean environment can be anticipated: First, we will witness new ecological strategies that are capable of anticipating crisis instead of responding to crisis, that require participation instead of consent, that confront conflict instead of dampening conflict, that include comprehensive measures instead of specific measures, and that include a long planning horizon instead of a short planning horizon.

Second, we will identify new roles for linking and correlating interorganizational transactions—"interstitial men."

Third, and most problematical, I anticipate an erratic environment where various organizations coexist at different stages of evolution. Rather than neat, linear, and uniform evolutionary developments, I expect that we will see both more centralization (in large-scale instrumental bureaucracies) and more decentralization (in delivery of health, education, and welfare services); both the increase of bureaucratic-pragmatic and of revolutionary-charismatic leadership; both the increase in size and centralization of many municipal and governmental units and the proliferation of self-contained minisocieties, from the "status-spheres" that Tom Wolfe writes about like Ken Kesey's "electric kool-aid acid-heads" and the pump-house gang of La Jolla surfers to various citizen groups. Ethnic groups organize to "get theirs," and so do the police, firemen, small property owners, and "mothers fighting sex education and bussing," and so on.

Large-Scale Public and Private Bureaucracies Will Become More Vulnerable Than Ever Before to the Infusion of Legislative and Juridical Organs

These probably will become formalized, much like the Inspector General's office in the Army. In one day's issue of a recent *New York Times*, three front-page stories featured: (*a*) the "young Turks" within the State Department who are planning to ask the Department to recognize the Foreign Service Association as the exclusive agent with which the Department would bargain on a wide scale of personnel matters, (*b*) antipoverty lawyers within the Office of Equal Opportunity who have organized for a greater voice in setting policy, and (*c*) the informal caucus of civil rights lawyers in the Justice Department to draft a protest against what they consider a recent softening of enforcement of the civil rights laws.

I have always been fascinated by Harold Lasswell's famous analogy between the Freudian trinity of personality and the tripartite division of the federal government. Most bureaucracies today contain only one formal mechanism, that is, the executive or ego functions. The legislative (id) and the judicial (superego) have long been underrepresented; this will likely change.

There Will Be More Legitimization for "Leave-Taking" and Shorter Tenure at the Highest Levels of Leadership

One aspect of "temporary systems" that was underplayed in my 1964 paper was the human cost of task efficiency. Recently, James Reston observed that the reason it is difficult to find good men for the most responsible jobs in government is that the good men have burnt out, or as my old infantry company commander once said, "In this company, the good guys get killed." Perhaps this creates the appearance of the Peter Principle, that is, that people advance to the level of their greatest incompetence. What is more likely is that people get burnt out, psychologically killed. Many industries are now experimenting with variations on sabbaticals for their executives, and I think it is about time that universities woke up to the fact that a seven-year period, for a legalized moratorium, is simply out of joint with the recurring need for self- and professional renewal.

It may also be that leaders with shorter time horizons will be more effective in the same way that interregnum Popes have proven to be the most competent.

New Organizational Roles Will Develop Emphasizing Different Loci and Commitments of Colleagueiality

Aside from consultants and external advisory groups, organizations tend to arrogate the full working time and commitments of their memberships. One works for Ford, or the Department of Health, Education and Welfare, or Macy's, or Yale. Moonlighting is permitted, sometimes reluctantly, but there is usually no doubt about the primary organization or where there might be a possible "conflict of interest." This idea of the mono-organizational commitment will likely erode in the future where more and more people will create pluralistic commitments to a number of organizations.

To use my own university as an example once again, we have set up one new experimental department which includes three different kinds of professors, different in terms of their relatedness and loci to the department. There is a core group of faculty with full-time membership in the department. There is an associated faculty with part-time commitments to the department, but whose appointment is in another department. And finally, there is a "network faculty," who spend varying periods of time in the department, but whose principal affiliation is with another university or organization. Similar plans are now being drawn up for students.

Similarly, a number of people have talked about "invisible colleges" of true colleagues, located throughout the world, who convene on special occasions, but who communicate mainly by telephone, the mail, and during hasty meetings at airports. I would wager that these "floating crap-games" will increase, and that we will see at least three distinct sets of roles emerge within organizations: those that are *pivotal* and more or less permanent; those that are *relevant*, but not necessarily permanent; and those that are *peripheral*. A person who is pivotal and permanent to one organization may have a variety of relevant and peripheral roles in others.

There are many reasons for this development. First and most obvious is the fact that we live in a jet age where air travel is cheap and very accessible. . . . Second, the scarcity of talent and the number of institutions "on the make" will very likely lead more of the top talent to start dividing their time among a number of institutions. Third, the genuine motivational satisfaction gained from working within a variety of comparable institutions seems to be important not for all, but among an increasingly growing fraction of the general population.

We must educate our leaders in at least two competencies: (*a*) to cope efficiently, imaginatively, and perceptively with information overload. Marxist power was property. Today, power is based on control of relevant information. (*b*) As Michael (1968) says in his *The Unprepared Society:*

We must educate for empathy, compassion, trust, nonexploitiveness, nonmanipulativeness, for self-growth and self-esteem, for tolerance of ambiguity, for acknowledgement of error, for patience, for suffering.

Without affective competence, and the strength that comes with it, it is difficult to see how the leader can confront the important ethical and political decisions without succumbing to compromise or to "petite Eichmannism."

We will observe in America a society which has experienced the consequences of unpreparedness and which has become more sanguine about the effects of planning—more planning not to restrict choice or prohibit serendipity, but to structure possibilities and practical visions.

Whether or not these forecasts are desirable, assuming their validity for the moment, really depends on one's status, values, and normative biases. One man's agony is another's ecstasy. It does appear as if we will have to reckon with a number of contradictory and confusing tendencies, however, which can quickly be summarized:

1. More self- and social consciousness with respect to the governance of public bureaucracies.

2. More participation in this governance by the clients who are served, as well as those doing the service, including lower levels of the hierarchy.

3. More formal, quasi-legal processes of conflict resolution.

4. More direct confrontations when negotiation and bargaining processes fail.

5. More attention to moral-ethical issues relative to technical efficiency imperatives.

6. More rapid turnover and varying relationships within institutions.

I think it would be appropriate if I concluded this paper with a quote from the earlier 1964 paper which still seems valid and especially pertinent in light of the new perspectives gained over the past five years. I was writing about the educational requirements necessary for coping with a turbulent environment (Bennis, 1964):

Our educational system should (1) help us to identify with the adaptive process without fear of losing our identity, (2) increase tolerance of ambiguity without fear of losing intellectual mastery, (3) increase our ability to collaborate without fear of losing our individuality, and (4) develop a willingness to participate in social evolution while recognizing implacable forces. In short, we need an educational system that can help make a virtue out of contingency rather than one which induces hesitancy or its reckless companion, expedience.

REFERENCES

Argyris, C., "The Incompleteness of Social-Psychological Theory: Examples from Small Group, Cognitive Consistency, and Attribution Research," *American Psychologist* 24 (1969): 893–908.

Balchin, N., *A Sort of Traitors* (New York: Collins, 1949).

Bennis, W. G., "Organizational Developments and the Fate of Bureaucracy." Paper presented at the annual meeting of the American Psychological Association, Los Angeles, September 4, 1964.

———, "Organizational Developments and the Fate of Bureaucracy," *Industrial Management Review* 7 (1966): 41–55. (a)

———, "When Democracy Works," *Trans-action* 3 (1966): 35. (b)

———, "Future of the Social Sciences," *Antioch Review* 28 (1968): 227.

DeMott, B., *Supergrow* (New York: Dutton, 1969).

Duhl, L., "Letter to the Editor," *Journal of Applied Behavioral Science* 5 (1969): 279–80.

Emery, F. E., and E. L. Trist, "The Causal Texture of Organizational Environments," *Human Relations* 18 (1965): 1–10.

Evan, W. M., "The Organization-Set: Toward a Theory of Interorganizational Relationships," in J. D. Thompson (ed.), *Approaches to Organizational Design* (Pittsburgh: University of Pittsburgh Press, 1966).

Flacks, R., "Protest or Conform: Some Social Psychological Perspectives on Legitimacy," *Journal of Applied Behavioral Science* 5 (1969): 127–50.

Fromm, E., *Escape from Freedom* (New York: Farrar & Rinehart, 1941).

Gamson, W. A., *Power and Discontent* (Homewood, Ill.: Dorsey Press, 1968).

Gans, H. J., "We Won't End the Urban Crisis until We End Majority Rule," *New York Times Magazine* 119 (August 3, 1969): Sect. 6.

Greer, S., *The Logic of Social Inquiry* (Chicago: Aldine, 1969).

Gross, E., "Universities as Organizations: A Research Approach," *American Sociological Review* 33 (1968): 518–44.

Hardin, G., "The Tragedy of the Commons," *Science* 162 (1968): 1243–48.

Helmer, O., "Political Analysis of the Future." Paper presented at the annual meeting of the American Political Science Association, New York, September 4, 1969.

Hollander, E. P., and J. W. Julian, "Contemporary Trends in the Analysis of Leadership Processes," *Psychological Bulletin* 71 (1969): 387–97.

Julian, J. W., and E. P. Hollander, "A Study of Some Role Dimensions of Leader-Follower Relations." (Tech. Rep. No. 3, Office of Naval Research Contract No. 4679) State University of New York at Buffalo, Department of Psychology, April 1966.

Kelman, H. C., "In Search of New Bases for Legitimacy: Some Social

Psychological Dimensions of the Black Power and Student Movements." Paper presented at the Richard M. Elliott Lecture, University of Michigan, April 21, 1969.

Kissinger, H. A., "Domestic Structures and Foreign Policy," *Daedalus* 96 (1966): 503–29.

Lane, R. E., *Political Ideology* (New York: Free Press, 1962).

Levine, S., and P. E. White, "Exchange as a Conceptual Framework for the Study of Interorganizational Relationships," *Administrative Science Quarterly* 6 (1961): 583–601.

Litwak, E., and L. Hylton, "Interorganizational Analysis: A Hypothesis on Coordinating Agencies," *Administrative Science Quarterly* 6 (1962): 395–420.

Michael, D., *The Unprepared Society* (New York: Basic Books, 1968).

Parsons, T., "The Academic System: A Sociologist's View," *The Public Interest* 13 (1968): 179–97.

Sartori, G., "Democracy," in E. R. A. Seligman (ed.), *Encyclopedia of Social Sciences* (New York: Macmillan, 1957).

Terreberry, S., "The Evolution of Organizational Environments," *Administrative Science Quarterly* 12 (1968): 590–613.

Trist, E., *The Relation of Welfare and Development in the Transition to Post-Industrialism* (Los Angeles: Western Management Science Institute, University of California, 1968).

Trow, M., "Urban Problems and University Problems." Paper presented at the 24th All-University Conference, University of California at Riverside, March 23–25, 1969.

policy analysis
as ideology

fred a. kramer

The battle between alternative decision-making theories in the public policy sphere has changed little since Charles Lindblom's seminal article, "The Science of 'Muddling Through.'"[1] The basic elements of the polar positions presented in that article—rational/comprehensive analysis versus incremental decision-making derived through the pluralistic bargaining process—have not changed in theory, but, in practice, a *modus vivendi* has been achieved. Although truly rational/comprehensive analysis is impossible on most great questions of public policy, public policy analysis of acceptable quality has been done on some suboptimal level operations. In some cases, analytic work has altered the styles at the bargaining table just as William Capron and Henry Rowen suggested it would.[2] But whether analysis—primarily economic analysis—has changed the outcomes of social public policy decisions is subject to dispute. Apparently, analysis is used primarily to justify actions that are based on political predilections.[3]

Although public policy analysis is only partial, not comprehensive, analysis, the techniques used and the emphasis on quantification give the results of analysis a "scientific" appearance—an appearance of value-free rationality at work. Nonanalysts, whether

This is a slightly modified version of "Policy Analysis as Ideology" which appeared in the Public Administration Review 35, no. 5 (September–October, 1975): 509–17. Used with permission.

administrative generalists, congressmen, or ordinary citizens, disregard these scientific results of analysis at their peril. How can people in this "post-industrial age"[4] disregard science? If they do, they must be acting on ideological, not scientific, grounds. Nonanalysts who wish to set aside a given piece of analytic work must be able to raise the questions that are, of necessity, left out of partial analysis. To avoid the castigations of the analyst, who has staked out the claim to science, the nonanalyst decision-maker must be able to see that the scientific results of analysis are in fact the result of an ideology. This ideology leads the analyst to direct his or her inquiry to certain sources and ignore others or to alter the weights of various factors according to perceptions of reality reflected in his or her models.

I can hear the analysts protesting: "What do you mean by ideology? Microeconomics is not ideological! It is as close to natural science as anything in the social sciences. Ideological, indeed!" If the protester will bear with me for awhile, however, I hope he or she will see analytic work through another perspective.

WHAT IS AN IDEOLOGY?

Many of us feel that we can easily recognize an ideology when we see one. In the sixties, when "Yippie" leader Jerry Rubin pranced around in a revolutionary war costume and cataloged the deficiencies of "Amerika," we had no difficulty classifying his comments as part of some ideology. The term "ideology" often carries a pejorative connotation. The person one disagrees with often is assumed to be a victim of some kind of ideology that clouds his perspective and makes him somewhat less than rational. His irrational ideological bias keeps him from seeing the truth of one's own argument.

In this paper, ideology will be treated in the manner suggested by L. T. Sargent:

An ideology is a value or belief system that is accepted as fact or truth by some group. It is composed of sets of attitudes toward the various institutions and processes of society. It provides the believer with a picture of the world both as it is and as it should be, and, in so doing, it organizes the tremendous complexity of the world into something fairly simple and understandable.[5]

Sargent goes on to suggest that an ideology may be distinguished from a person's simple belief in something. To Sargent, "an ideology must be a more or less interrelated collection of beliefs that provide the believer with a fairly thorough picture of the entire world."[6]

If we look at ideology in this way, we recognize that ideology is not simply a failure of rational processes on the part of our opponent in an argument, but a different world view. We probably look at problems from perspectives that differ from those of people with different ideologies. We would probably look to different sources for facts. We might see the same set of facts as meaning one thing; others might see the same facts and arrive at a different interpretation. Alternative ideologies lead to alternative conclusions. Generally this is the case because the "facts" themselves are rarely so complete that they permit conclusions to be drawn without reference to some outside perspective.

In the natural sciences, the perspective that permits an observer to put together any given set of facts and draw conclusions is called a "paradigm."[7] If one accepts the analogy that rational processes in the social sciences are similar to rational processes in the natural sciences, then social science also deals in paradigms. In the public policy arena, however, these paradigms have exactly the same effect as ideology in Sargent's terms. Therefore, the perspectives of analysts themselves, as far as those perspectives are conditioned by the prevailing paradigms of social science, are ideological.[8]

This is *not* to say that *every* disagreement on policy is a disagreement based on differing ideologies. When people look for different facts using different methodologies, however, I would suspect that these differences are inherently ideological. They stem from the acceptance of varying world views. They stem from the acceptance of different paradigms.[9]

AWARENESS OF IDEOLOGICAL BIAS

We are often not aware of the ideological blinders that we wear because of our presence in a particular culture at a particular time and the particular training and experiences we have had. One observer, Daniel Bell, who prematurely noted the end of ideology in 1960, now sees America entering a "post-industrial society," which will be the triumph of rationality à la Max Weber's forecast.[10] Since we live in an increasingly specialized and professional-ized society, Bell sees the techniques of specialists—one is tempted to say the scientifically proven techniques of specialists—to be value neutral. Bell is thrilled with the prospects of value-free social science:

With the growing sophistication of simulation procedures through the use of computers—simulations of economic systems, of social behavior, of decision problems—we have the possibility, for the first time, of large-scale "controlled experiments" in the social sciences. These, in turn, will allow us to plot alternative futures in different courses thus greatly increasing the extent to which we can choose and control matters that affect our lives.[11]

Who will do this choosing? To Bell, the problems of the "post-industrial society" are not technical, but political. Even though "social engineering is involved, the essential questions are those of values."[12] Value decisions are rightly a matter of power. Apparently, politicians will make the choices from among alternatives devel-oped by analysts. Implicit in this argument is the notion that there are technical solutions available in areas in which there is basic agreement on values.

Bell looks at national defense as an area in which there is agree-ment over values. If one can accept the dubious proposition that "society, by and large, is agreed on the importance—and priority—of these [defense] efforts,"[13] then the way to have an efficient and effective defense policy is to rely on the analysis presented by the rational technocrats in the Department of Defense. But is the analysis of the potential performance of weapons systems compre-hensive enough to make us comfortable with the decisions that we as nonanalysts have to make?

Two main questions arise. First, can we *trust* the analysis, or was it doctored in response to real or perceived demands from higher in the hierarchy? The Pentagon Papers and David Halber-stam's account of the Vietnam involvement have corroborated John Kenneth Galbraith's notion of "bureaucratic truth" in the defense establishment.[14] The organizational humanists, who have noted the problems of the hierarchy in inhibiting truth, stress the obstacles to the kind of analysis that would be politically neutral in its inception.[15]

The second question is more important for us. Are analysts bound by their own methods and disciplines to emphasize certain aspects of a problem while ignoring other aspects of a particular system? Could these analysts, who really want to be honest, assign incorrect weights to various events because their perspectives lead them toward certain emphases?

With unabashed approval, Daniel Bell has spelled out the main characteristics of the "technocratic mind-view":

In its emphasis on the logical, practical, problem-solving, instrumental, orderly, and disciplined approach to objectives, in its reliance on a calculus, on precision and measurement and a concept of a system, it is a world view quite opposed to the traditional and customary religious, esthetic, and intuitive modes. It draws deeply from the Newtonian world-view, . . .[16]

By "Newtonian world-view," I take it Bell is referring to a search for a rational ordering of phenomena.

I am not against a rational ordering of phenomena, but I want to have some guidance as to *whose* rational ordering of phenomena I am to believe. In science, the issue is clear, Thomas Kuhn points out. Rational orderings of phenomena have changed over time. Newtonian physics has given way to relativity physics which gives a vastly different perspective on the problems in physics than did the earlier view.[17] Similarly, systems analysis of social programs, which depends on a welfare economics rationale of the Pareto criterion or the Kaldor-Hicks criteria, probably would lend a different perspective to analysis than, say, the criterion proposed by I. M. D. Little, a critic of welfare economics.[18] Who is to say which perspective is the "true" one? If natural science can be taken as a guide, the accepted perspectives of one age may be the object of ridicule in a succeeding era.

Indeed, in the past ten or fifteen years, we have seen accepted perspectives that guided analytic work in the past change drastically. Today we look back at the work of transportation analysts who undervalued the sense of community in an ethnic neighborhood that happened to be in the way of a new highway. Today, a good analyst would deal with the problem from a different perspective. But the perspective which was favored a few years back did affect policy decisions. It affected policy decisions in a predictable way. It affected these decisions in a way that systematically downplayed some political interests as opposed to others. Although the rationale for taking action was clothed in the value-neutral terms of analysis, the analysis reflected a particular world view of what is the common good or the public interest. It did, I would maintain, reflect an ideology.

SO WHAT?

If analysis resembles an ideology in some respects—that is, it provides a way of simplifying complex reality—what are the implications for public policy decision-making? Should analysis be ignored even more than it is today? Probably not, because most administrators feel more comfortable with order rather than chaos. Analysis—primarily economic analysis—of social programs gives us a feeling of orderliness and rationality that is valued. Many of us might agree with Robert McNamara's observation that good management is necessary for freedom in a democracy. As he wrote in *The Essence of Security:*

To undermanage reality is not to keep free. It is simply to let some force other than reason shape reality. That force may be unbridled emotion; it may be greed; it may be aggressiveness; it may be hatred; it may be ignorance; it may be inertia; it may be anything other than reason. But whatever it is, if it is not reason that rules man, then man falls short of his potential.

. . . rational decision-making depends on having a full range of rational options from which to choose, and successful management organizes the enterprise so that men can most efficiently exercise their reason, initiative, creativity and personal responsibility.[19]

Based on McNamara's management style at the Department of Defense from 1961 through 1967, he may be considered a true believer in the efficacy of analysis. Yet even a far more skeptical observer of analysis, Aaron Wildavsky, has made a similar plea:

Everyone knows that the nation needs better policy analysis. Each area one investigates shows how little is known compared to what is necessary in order to devise adequate policies. In some organizations there are no ways at all of determining the effectiveness of existing programs; organizational survival must be the sole criterion of merit. . . . If there is a demand for information the cry goes out that what the organization does cannot be measured. Should anyone attempt to tie the organization to any measure of productivity, the claim is made that there is no truth in numbers. . . . Anyone who has weathered this routine comes to value policy analysis.[20]

It is clear that most people in decision-making positions in this society want to apply more reason to problem solving. Even if rational analysis is only partial analysis, it is a source of information that is useful to decision makers. Even if it reflects an ideology, it may be only one of many positions reflecting various ideologies. In the satisficing world of decision makers, some information is usually valued over no information, even if that "some information" turns out to be false.

The question of the hidden ideological component in analysis raises two problems that administrators should consider before they completely rely on analytic output for decision-making. First, policy analysis, with its emphasis on quantification and its claim to be value-free, might dominate other means of looking at policy without such claims to scientific orderliness. Bertram Gross has noted a kind of Gresham's law of analysis whereby "hard" data drives out the "soft."[21] Perhaps this "soft" qualitative data is critically important to decision-making. The "seductive potential of the new system concepts,"[22] which often glorifies the quantitative over the qualitative, does represent a problem for decision makers.

The second aspect of the problem relates to the social science theories behind analysis. Daniel P. Moynihan, a strong advocate of analysis and evaluation of governmental programs, has raised this problem. One of the themes of his *Maximum Feasible Misunderstanding* is that the use of inadequate social science theory can lead to unanticipated and unwanted consequences. It is not surprising that analysis based on inadequate social science theory failed to bring to light the problems that later plagued the short-lived war on poverty.[23] How can we *know* when the social and economic theories inherent in our attempts at policy analysis are correct? We cannot.

MUST ANALYSIS BE BIASED?

So far I have referred to analysis—primarily economic analysis of social programs—as if there is only one accepted way to do analytic work. There are many accepted techniques that may be applicable in some situations but not others. In general, however, analysis, as Chester Wright and Michael Tate have pointed out, is developed through several conceptual stages:

It includes a stage where we set *objectives*, a stage where we explore *alternatives*, a stage where we examine *cost*, a stage where we construct a *model*, a stage where we compare the results obtained with the model to a *criterion*. In addition to these stages, systems analysis is characterized by a number of other factors. It is an *iterative* process, that is, several cycles of the analysis will probably be necessary, since (for example) the cost of an alternative may cause us to redefine that alternative. For example, we must always make *assumptions* about the world; we must always operate under certain *constraints*; the world is full of *uncertainty*. We must, therefore, try to account for the assumptions and the constraints, and allow for the uncertainty of the world.[24]

It would be a gross oversimplification to maintain that all analysts would advance through these stages and deal with the same problem in exactly the same way. Despite its pretensions as policy *science*, analysis is still an art or a craft. The way practitioners practice their craft is necessarily varied. In analysis, as in any field, there are highly skilled, creative people, and there are the journeymen who do a reasonably competent job. It is the cookbook analysis by journeymen that often fails to reflect reality to the extent that really good analysis might. In the absence of critiques of their work by respected, highly skilled analysts, these journeymen may be certain that they have the monopoly on truth. They are the ones who feel their analysis is ignored because the decision maker has some ideological bent that precludes his or her seeing the innate truth of the analyst's objective product.

Rather than denigrating the decision maker's dismissal of the analytic work as merely "politics," analysts should engage in some self-analysis. Why wasn't the analysis used by the decision maker? "Politics" is the easy answer. But perhaps the analysis did not meet the needs of the decision maker. Perhaps the analysis was faulty in some respect with which the decision maker was familiar. Perhaps the analysts did not spell out adequately the implicit assumptions in the analysis. More likely, the analysts probably did not spell out the weaknesses in their work because *their perspective— their implicit ideology—made it impossible for them to see the weaknesses.* The journeymen analysts may be so tied to their methodological perspective that they may be incapable of seeing the limitations of the analytic work in question.

The crux of the problem which I have been calling ideology is often reflected in the criteria chosen to evaluate programs. Often we see certain criteria chosen because they are implied by the methodology used in the evaluation or because information relating to a particular criterion is readily available. In the last days of the Planning Programming Budgeting Systems (PPBS) in the federal government, good analysts sought to get beyond administrative convenience by postulating a difference between readily available output measures (e.g., number of registered nurses graduated as a result of a certain program) and accomplishment or impact measures (e.g., effect of a particular program on infant mortality rates, or incidence of types of infectious diseases). If one chooses the simple output measure and then relates program costs to that figure, one may be giving a false picture of agency effectiveness in relation to the agency's mission. We must remember that an agency's mission is not to produce X number of nurses, but to accomplish a public health goal. Naturally the latter criterion demands a great deal more sophistication to develop. In some cases, it may even be impossible to do so.

In recent years it appears that attempts to search for meaningful accomplishment measures in social policy areas have been sidetracked in favor of reliance on output measures. The goals of program budgeting as conceived by people like David Novick have been radically altered by journeymen analysts. In much of what is called program budgeting, measures of agency mission have been reduced to mere output measures. As Novick has noted, "Obviously, the word program is available for anyone to use in any manner he sees fit."[25] Much program budgeting today is "program" in little more than name. Most "program" budgeting is not as goal-oriented as the salesmen for systems analysis and "rational" budget systems have told us it should be. Instead, the practical need for output measures has reflected Lindblom's view that means and ends are inseparable at the margin.[26]

WHAT CAN BE DONE?

In good analytic work, this criteria problem can be minimized by reasonable people—both generalists and analysts—working together. Often the problem of unused and unusable analysis is simply a lack of communication between the analyst and the non-analyst decision maker. C. W. Churchman and A. H. Schainblatt have noted "that the politician manager and the systems analyst have qualitatively different approaches for solving problems." However, "these differences in style need not imply a contest in which one is the winner, the other the loser."[27] Churchman and Schainblatt call for a recognition of the symbiotic relationship that must exist between various functional elements in any effective organization. The first step toward forming this new relationship, Churchman and Schainblatt suggest, should be humility. "Each must recognize that he does not have solid answers to the questions, or even solid ways of getting the answers."[28] Once they come to this realization, the analyst and the decision maker can work out a meaningful synthesis through a formalized debate technique. Through this, they confront each other with counter-proposals based on their varying perceptions of the same set of facts. This debate should occur at all stages of the analytic process. Churchman and Schainblatt decry the practice of managers giving problems to analysts; analysts giving reports back at the specified time; and the managers ignoring the results of the work.

An example of another technique for institutionalizing a kind of intellectual pluralism needed to broaden the perspectives of an analytic operation comes from the U.S. Forest Service. Jeanne Nienaber and Aaron Wildavsky reported that the service formally considered early budgetary estimates, which reflected policy choices or suggestions, from three institutional sources. The operating divisions came up with a budget, the PPB staff came up with one, and a third group—Forests and Related Resources (FARR), an in-house study group—came up with yet another. The three estimates were incorporated into a working paper in the format presented in figure 1.[29]

The formalized debate technique and the Forest Service approach may be fruitful in cases where there is a clash of values between the decision maker and the systems analyst. Perhaps some synthesis that approaches the truth can come out of such debates. But what safeguards the truth from excessively narrow analysis if both the manager and the analyst have the same perspective or the same policy goals? If an analyst presents work that supports the political predilections of the manager, even an avowed "seat

FIGURE 1

Presentation of Alternative Estimates in the Forest Service
(From Nienaber and Wildavsky, op. cit., p. 91)

	DIVISION	FARR	PPB	REMARKS (Justification)
Budget item	Estimate	Estimate	Estimate	

of the pants" manager might very well accept and use that analysis
regardless of its quality. In another case, the manager and the
analyst might share methodological perspectives on the same problem. They might agree to accept the results of honest analytical
work that is limited by narrow methodological perspectives. Advocates of this limited—indeed, poor analysis—might claim that
the policy preferences supported by the analysis are scientifically
valid.

To be more specific, what happens when Robert McNamara fights
a war through systems analysis? What happens when the decision
maker and the analyst really believe their models of reality and
accept the same constraints? It appears that McNamara and his
analysts plugged data into systems that were programmed to respond to the constraint that Lyndon Baines Johnson would not be
the first United States president to lose a war.

If the Vietnam experience can be used as a guide, the unified
perspective of managers and analysts can have disastrous results
on public policy. Of course, it is difficult to ascertain whether it
was the political will of Johnson, the managerial arrogance of
McNamara, or the apathy of the American people that most contributed to the inability of the antiwar forces to demonstrate convincingly the real problems of the war in human and economic
terms. In part, however, the arguments used by the Administration
to convince the American people that a particular course of policy
was correct were based on the "scientific," value-neutral stance that

objective measures showed that we were winning the war. These measures and the models that spawned them proved to be invalid when held up to the light of the real world. The analysis was inadequate.

TOWARD THEORETICAL SELF-CONSCIOUSNESS

There is no way to expunge what I have called ideology from policy analysis, but we must take off the mantle of objectivity that often masks analytic work.[30] The people best able to do this are the analysts themselves.

The hope for meaningful contributions from policy analysis in a democracy comes from what the political philosopher William E. Connolly has called "theoretical self-consciousness." Drawing on the work of various philosophers of science, principally Thomas Kuhn and Stephen Toulmin, Connolly draws parallels between paradigms in natural sciences and what he calls "perspectives" in the social sciences. Although Connolly does not call these perspectives ideological, *per se*, he argues convincingly that two broad perspectives of dealing with society—conflict versus consensus—lead people to vastly different conclusions about what should be done to solve a society's problems. Indeed, these perspectives are what determine problem identification in the first place.[31]

Connolly sees that these different perspectives work against the development of political and social theories that are useful for understanding society. He clearly states his objective and suggests some ways of reaching the objective:

A theory is responsibly formulated and advanced when its proponents make a serious effort to elaborate and defend publicly all the factors which sustain the theory. Such an enterprise involves, first, an effort to clarify for self and others the basic presumptions and conceptual organization of the perspective brought to inquiry; second, an assessment of the extent to which the available evidence supports or contravenes the perspective; third, a full statement of the normative import of the theory adopted; finally, an assessment of the extent to which available evidence and other explicit considerations justify acting in support of those normative conclusions.[32]

Since the types of analysis that we have been talking about here are really applied social science, Connolly's arguments and prescriptions are germane.

Clarification of the perspectives underlying the kinds of analysis of social programs might be accomplished "by exploring sympathetically alternative ways to comprehend[33] the problems that analysts face. Perhaps this can take place, in Stuart Hampshire's phrase, "by communication with minds that are outside the circle of convention and custom within which [the analyst] is confined.[34] The problems between evidence and theoretical perspectives are probably impossible to resolve in the social policy sphere because, as Connolly points out, "the evidence used to test social science theories" is "constituted in some problematic degree by the theories we . . . adopt.[35] Analysts must also develop the ability or the will to point out the normative implications of their recommendations and provide arguments to justify recommendations that point to certain favored normative conclusions.

Since analytic work generally takes place under time and resource constraints, the chances of analysts developing broadened perspectives while on the job are minimal. For the sake of more useful and usable analysis, analysts might be able to broaden their theoretical perspectives through liberal sabbatical-leave policies. Technical training in some particular analytic technique might be useful, but the long-range payoff probably would be greater if analysts studied in a different academic field. The purpose of these leaves would be to encourage analysts to appreciate more fully the limitations of social science models. Hopefully, such recognition would not stymie their analytic efforts but encourage them to discard the mask of value-free objectivity behind which many professional analysts hide.[36] Such a leave policy goes against the typical training orientation of extended leave policies in the past. There is, however, some evidence that the Civil Service Commission through its Executive Manpower Development Programs, notably the Individual Development Planning (IDP) approach, might be ready to move in this direction.

SUMMARY AND CONCLUSIONS

Perhaps calling the perspectives of run-of-the-mill analytic work ideological is a bit strong. Yet analysts often do not see the full political weight of what they are doing and the possible political bias of their limited tools. This bias is tied to the perspectives and assumptions that underlie economic analysis of social policy. It is necessary to keep emphasizing this for reasons raised by Nienaber and Wildavsky:

Time and again program analysts refused to acknowledge that what they did had a political side to it. Program analysis appeared to them as free from bias and therefore as purely objective analysis. Case in point: regarding the expenditures of the Land and Water Conservation Fund, "politics" comes in only when Congress (or the department, responding to outside pressure) starts wanting to have a say in where LWCF funds will be spent. Program analysis, however, which unearthed the urban recreation deficiency and which provides both the Agriculture and Interior Departments with supportive data on this deficiency, is not seen as "political."[37]

This paper has argued that analysis is not purely objective and the claims to objectivity, if honored, can have potentially dangerous impact. Orion White and Bruce Gates have argued that Bayesian statistical theory,

By elevating the role of subjectivity in analysis, ... socializes the decision maker to the important idea that human intuition is an important part of human rationality, whereas in the classical view such "soft," intuitive knowledge is suppressed.[38]

But there is the danger that Bayesian techniques, despite their innate and obvious subjectivity, can be used as "scientific" cover for a weak argument. Subjective probability, when applied to quantitative data, presents results that are often passed off as "objective." What I have been stressing here is that there is no pure objectivity. Analysis that adopts the appearance of objectivity is misleading.

Many analysts and teachers of analysts are probably saying, "So what else is new?" Every basic book in systems analysis presents a list of caveats similar to that found in Wright and Tate:

- Analysis is always incomplete.
- We always operate under constraints.
- The future is always uncertain.
- No one has yet found a satisfactory way to predict the future.
- Many significant aspects of many problems cannot be satisfactorily quantified.

● There is a danger that analysts and or customers of analysts will rely too heavily on quantification.

● Political considerations are sometimes paramount.

● Not everyone at every time has to ration his resources.

● One can always use more time to do more analysis.

● One never has enough facts.[39]

And I might add another caveat: Make all assumptions explicit.

A way these caveats can have an impact on the role of analysis in the policy-making process may be through the application of greater theoretical self-consciousness on the part of analysts themselves.

NOTES

1. Lindblom, "The Science of 'Muddling Through,'" *Public Administration Review* (hereafter abbreviated as *PAR*) 19 (Spring, 1959): 79–88.

2. William M. Capron, "The Impact of Analysis on Bargaining in Government." Paper delivered before the American Political Science Association Annual Meeting, New York City, September, 1966. Reprinted in Louis C. Gawthrop, *The Administrative Process and Democratic Theory* (Boston: Houghton-Mifflin, 1970), pp. 354–71. Also Henry Rowen, "Objectives, Alternatives, Costs and Effectiveness," in H. H. Hinrichs and Graeme M. Taylor (eds.), *Program Budgeting and Benefit-Cost Analysis* (Pacific Palasades, Calif.: Goodyear, 1969) pp. 83–93.

3. If not, why is analysis used so selectively? Analysis has been used as the rationale to kill unpopular Office of Economic Opportunity (OEO) programs but not defense programs, which did not meet their specifications, but which were able to attract political support. Also analytic documentation through federal PPB was primarily of the advocacy or justification type.

In an excellent article, Ida R. Hoos has suggested that analytic studies are generally "shrouded from critical review . . . cited when they bolster a particular ideological position, sealed when they are likely to embarrass persons in power." See her "Systems Techniques for Managing Society: A Critique," *PAR* 33, no. 2 (1973): 157–64, 158.

4. Daniel Bell has coined the term "post-industrial society." See his *The Coming of Post-Industrial Society* (New York: Basic Books, 1973). He certainly does not share this author's view that analysis reflects an ideology. See below.

5. Lyman Tower Sargent, *Contemporary Political Ideologies* (Homewood, Illinois: The Dorsey Press, 1972), p. 1.

6. Ibid., p. 2.

7. Thomas Kuhn, *The Structure of Scientific Revolutions,* 2nd ed. (Chicago: University of Chicago Press, 1970). The paradigm notion has been accepted by many social scientists who may harbor some reservations as to Kuhn's notions of how paradigms change. For a treatment of paradigms in political science, see Thomas L. Thorson, *Biopolitics* (New York: Holt, Rinehart and Winston, 1970).

8. Of course, this is a bare bones argument. For an extended treatment of the ideology of analysis see Lawrence H. Tribe, "Policy Science: Analysis or Ideology?" *Journal of Philosophy and Public Affairs* (January, 1972), pp. 66–110.

9. It could be argued that all policy disagreements are based on differences in values and should be considered ideological. Ideology is used here to describe various world views, not value differences at the margin.

10. The 1960 reference is to Bell's *The End of Ideology* (New York: The Free Press, 1960). Other references in the paper will be to *The Coming of Post-Industrial Society,* op. cit.

11. Bell, *Post-Industrial*, p. 344.

12. Ibid., p. 337.

13. Ibid., p. 358.

14. *Pentagon Papers* (New York: Bantam, 1972); David Halberstam, *The Best and Brightest* (New York: Random House, 1972); and J. K. Galbraith, *How to Control the Military* (New York: Signet Books, 1969), p. 17.

15. Among the people identified as organizational humanists are Chris Argyris, Robert Blake, Warren Bennis, Rensis Likert, Jane Mouton, and Douglas McGregor. See Fred A. Kramer (ed.), *Perspectives on Public Bureaucracy* (Cambridge, Mass.: Winthrop Publishers, 1973), pp. 93–96.

16. Bell, op. cit., p. 349.

17. Kuhn, op. cit.

18. For an excellent discussion of these criteria, see Leonard Merewitz and Stephen H. Sosnick, *The Budget's New Clothes* (Chicago: Markham Publishing Company, 1971), pp. 78–85. Just briefly, the Pareto criterion holds that change is desirable if it makes some people better off but no one worse off. Kaldor-Hicks accepts the Pareto criterion but adds that people who gain in a change must compensate those who lost. Little also accepts the Pareto criterion if people accept the redistribution of wealth so effected and also if the "potential losers could not profitably bribe the

potential gainers to oppose it." [I. M. D. Little, *A Critique of Welfare Economics*, 2nd ed. (Oxford: Clarendon Press, 1957), p. 109, quoted in Merewitz and Sosnick, p. 82.]

19. Robert S. McNamara, *The Essence of Security* (New York: Harper and Row, 1968), pp. 109–110.

20. Aaron Wildavsky, "Rescuing Policy Analysis from PPBS," *PAR* 29, no. 2 (March/April 1969): 189.

21. Gross made the Gresham's law comment at a panel session during the 1968 American Political Science Association annual meeting in Washington, D.C.

22. Anatol Rappoport, "Foreword," in Walter Buckley (ed.), *Modern Systems Research for the Behavioral Scientist* (Chicago: Aldine, 1968), pp. xxi–xxii. Cited in Bertram M. Gross, "The New Systems Budgeting," *PAR* 29, no. 2 (March/April 1969): 130.

23. For his advocacy of analysis, see Daniel P. Moynihan, *Coping* (New York: Random House, 1973). For the critique of inadequate social science theory, see his *Maximum Feasible Misunderstanding* (New York: The Free Press, 1969).

24. Chester Wright and Michael Tate, *Economics & Systems Analysis: Introduction for Public Managers* (Reading, Mass.: Addison-Wesley, 1973), p. 140.

25. David Novick, *Current Practice in Program Budgeting (PPBS): Analysis and Case Studies Covering Government and Business* (New York: Crane, Russak and Company, 1973), p. 15.

26. See Lindblom, op. cit. For a full treatment see his *Intelligence of Democracy* (New York: The Free Press, 1965).

27. C. W. Churchman and A. H. Schainblatt, "PPB: How Can It Be Implemented?" *PAR* 29, no. 2 (March/April 1969): 178.

28. Ibid., p. 187.

29. Jeanne Nienaber and Aaron Wildavsky, *The Budgeting and Evaluation of Federal Recreation Programs* (New York: Basic Books, 1973), pp. 91 and 163.

30. This is Lawrence Tribe's main point, too. See Tribe, op. cit.

31. William E. Connolly, "Theoretical Self-Consciousness," *Polity* 6 no. 1 (Fall, 1973): 5–35. It is doubtful that Connolly, a political theorist, would agree with my use of the term *ideology*, but my use of that term is principally the same as his term *perspective*.

32. Ibid., p. 26.

33. Ibid., p. 27.

34. Quoted in ibid., p. 27.

35. Ibid., p. 30.

36. Liberal sabbatical leaves for program managers might be useful, too, but rarely do program managers claim scientific validity for their decisions. Sabbaticals for nonanalysts, worthwhile though they may be, are not the main concern before us now.

37. Nienaber and Wildavsky, op. cit., p. 96.

38. Orion White, Jr., and Bruce L. Gates, "Statistical Theory and Equity in the Delivery of Social Services," *PAR* 34, no. 1 (January/February, 1974): 50.

39. Wright and Tate, op. cit., p. 157.